The Encyclopaedia of the Loch Ness Monster

Paul Harrison has studied and actively researched the phenomenon of the Loch Ness Monster for over ten years, during which time he has made many private expeditions to the loch. He owns a huge collection of books, newspaper cuttings and other ephemera relating to the enigma. His work as President of the Loch Ness Monster Society has taken him all over the world discussing the subject of Nessie and other phenomena. He has appeared on television and radio. A full-time writer and journalist, he is the author of many other books including *Jack the Ripper: The Mystery Solved*. Paul Harrison is married with two children and lives in Market Harborough, Leicestershire.

By the same author

Jack the Ripper: The Mystery Solved

The
Encyclopaedia
of the
Loch Ness Monster

PAUL HARRISON

ROBERT HALE · LONDON

ISBN 0 7090 6795 X

Robert Hale Limited
Clerkenwell House
Clerkenwell Green
London EC1R 0HT

2 4 6 8 10 9 7 5 3 1

Typeset in 10/13 Classical Garamond
by
Derek Doyle & Associates, Mold, Flintshire.
Printed in Great Britain by
St Edmundsbury Press Limited, Bury St Edmunds, Suffolk.
Bound by WBC Book Manufacturers Limited, Bridgend.

Acknowledgements

No book of this kind could be accomplished without the generous assistance of others. First among them stands Elaina Harrison, who supported my countless years of postulations and research, during which time she became herself something of a 'Nessie addict'. My two children, Paula Jayne and Mark Daniel Harrison, both spent hundreds of hours scouring the Loch in the hope of catching a glimpse – sadly, to date, their efforts have been in vain.

I am grateful to John and Sheila Carter for their enthusiasm in completing the task and for their kind and professional observations; to Stein Murray, for his tales of the Loch; and to Billy and Joan Main of Dingwall, who provided much data on local phenomenon and sightings. My thanks to Alison J. Lindsay for her lengthy and efficient searches into official archives in the West Search Room of the Scottish Records Office; to Emily Naish, Archivist at the British Medical Association, London, for her efforts in the Dr Farquhar MacRae research; and to Dr Mike Dash whose outstanding delving into the mystery of the Farquhar MacRae film greatly aided my own research. I am indebted to the staff of the public libraries of Edinburgh, Inverness, Glasgow, Leeds, Leicester, and in particular to Jackie Knight of Market Harborough library for looking out those difficult items; and to the staff of the British and Scottish Natural History Museums; the British Newspaper library, Colindale; the Public Record office, Kew; the Society for Psychical Research; the International Cryptozoological Society and the Scottish Records Office. I have had great help from the *Inverness Courier*, the *Daily Mail*, *The Times*, the *Scottish Daily Record*, the *Sunday Post*, the *Daily Express*, the *Daily Mirror* and the *Scots Magazine*, as well as from the Official Loch Ness Monster Fan Club, The Highlands Tourist Board, The Home Office (Scotland), The Official Loch Ness Monster Research Society and the Original Loch Ness Monster Exhibition. Sincere appreciation goes to Gary

Campbell, for the countless hours spent on the telephone discussing the case, and to Calum MacLeod of the *Inverness Courier*, Rip Hepple of the Ness Information Service, Paul Alexander, Alastair Dallas junior, Gerry Bream, Stan Thompson, Oliver McIntyre, M't Mannetje, Nicholas Witchell, Brenda McGrattan, Neville Smyth, Terry Downs, Ian McGill, Elspeth McFadzean, Isla Brown, Duncan Smith (librarian for the *Aberdeen Press and Journal*), Fiona McGeorge, Wendy Ferguson, and John at Kettering Bookshop.

My thanks, also, to all the previous authors and commentators upon the 'Nessie' phenomenon, without whom my addiction to the case study would never have taken root; each and every one has added something to the study, not least the late Tim Dinsdale, whose work at the Loch laid the foundation for further scientific research and who made the fairy tale a reality.

Finally, my sincere appreciation goes to John Wheelwright, my copy-editor, for his examination and crafting of the completed typescript.

Every effort has been made to authenticate and research the data within this book. However, mistakes do occur. I would welcome any corrections, advice on omissions, or new information.

Contents

Introduction

By and large, writers, researchers, and the media in general would have us believe that the Loch Ness Monster is nothing more than an exaggerated myth. According to some, the legend was created and subsequently maintained in an attempt to ensure a healthy tourist trade for the Scottish Highlands district. The mere mention of 'Nessie' in public forum will always raise a bemused smile, and the general consensus of public opinion is that the monster is nothing but a fairy tale, a giant hoax, since the evidence for an unknown 'something' in the Loch is beyond the realms of sensible understanding. Many people remain impartial, preferring to ignore the phenomenon in public, although privately, and perhaps subconsciously, they hope that one day the mystery will eventually be solved.

There can be no denying that 'Nessie' is one of the world's greatest tourist attractions, and her legend (unlike so much which has been written about her activities) is very real. It is impertinent of those who deny her existence to claim that she exists only in the minds of those who want to see her. It is downright foolish to claim that she does not, or could not, exist.

The fact that 'Nessie' is real struck home to me in July 1995. There was no sighting of her, no suspicious wake or water disturbance – in fact I was some forty-odd miles away from Loch Ness. Fishermen returning from a trip off the west coast of Scotland told me of an incident which adequately depicts how Nessie is viewed by those who know the area. Late one pitch-black night the fishing boat on which these men had travelled arrived at the western end of the Caledonian Canal. Their load was over the quota prescribed by the Fishery Board. Realizing the punishment for such an act, the captain of the vessel told his crew that he was going to cut through the canal, so as to get to their destination during the hours of darkness and

9

make a 'black landing'. This is when all lights on the vessel are extinguished and silence is maintained, in order to avoid detection by Fishery Board officials. Realizing that the short cut would take them through Loch Ness, in the dark and without lights, the crew unanimously outvoted the captain, and told him that they would get off the boat before it passed through the Loch. The reason? Most of them were concerned that they might encounter the strange creature of Loch Ness, the monster.

I could hardly believe what I was hearing, here were hardened fishermen admitting to flouting the law, and yet confessing to a fear of crossing a stretch of water at night because tales of a mysterious monster had been prevalent for many decades. One of the crew – a 52-year-old fisherman who had worked on the water since the age of fourteen – told me how he had seen 'the monster' move across a Lochside road in front of his car in 1994:

> I saw what I saw. It was the monster of the Loch all right – big, black and with a powerful tail. It moved with a lurching motion. I could not see any legs or any other features; I was too shocked and couldn't believe what I was seeing. I know dozens of fishermen who have seen the thing. The scientists at the Loch have got it all wrong, I'm telling you. There is no way that I would cross that Loch after darkness – something peculiar is in there. People around here don't openly discuss what they have seen on the Loch with strangers. Whatever it is, it's large and not of the twentieth century. We should leave it be.

Others on board the same fishing vessel had at one time or another witnessed the odd 'queer' incident on the Loch, and none, including the captain, dismissed the belief that a 'monster' existed in there.

Many reading this work will claim that these fishermen were simply providing me with typical tourist tales. I can categorically deny this, for some were members of my family, along with their close friends. None of these people would or ever have uttered in public the private tales that they passed on to me. These people are private, and trust is a great thing among their sort.

The legend that a mysterious animal lurks within the depths of Loch Ness has been with us since AD 565, when it is said that St Columba cast away an evil carnivorous creature in the River Ness with a holy blessing. Since then, it has been claimed that there have been some three thousand further sightings of an anonymous creature in the immediate area of the Loch, yet still no one has obtained positive, definitive evidence of its existence. Countless books and articles have been published on the subject, and many of them are subjective case studies, their conclusions depending upon whether the authors are believers or non-believers. In essence, any student researching the Loch Ness phenomenon will find that literature relating to the subject is a virtual minefield: thousands of pages of personal opinions from self-proclaimed experts. This book has been compiled to ease the passage of those interested in the phenomenon.

I confess to having spent countless weeks at the Loch in the vain hope of taking that definitive photograph, or perhaps getting that all-important conclusive sighting which would ease my own mind on the question of the animal's existence. I make no spurious claims as to whether it exists or not, but prefer to leave that to the reader.

No matter how you feel about the idea of a real-life 'monster' existing in the twentieth century, there is much to be said of the feasibility of such a creature living in Loch Ness today. Previous commentators upon the case have stated that a high percentage of eye-witness accounts are self-induced, derived from perception becoming intertwined with imagination, conjuring up confusing illusions created by a desire to see something – anything. This is an inappropriate assumption: an easy solution which makes it virtually impossible to believe the 'unbelievable'.

Sceptics will remind us of the hoax sightings, doctored photographs and practical jokes. Even so, far too many people have witnessed something in the Loch, and their reports of its physical appearance and actions are all too incredibly similar to be so cavalierly dismissed.

Even if the self-proclaimed experts can justify their dismissive claims (which, to their dismay, they are unable to do), what of the sightings made by persons who know the Loch better than they do, or those whose public standing might suffer from an open confession to seeing a 'monster'? The truth is that no witness testimony can be ignored. Nothing relating to this phenomenon should be brusquely cast aside simply on the basis of a prior assumption.

The majority of sightings are not accompanied by photographic evidence. Instead they are straightforward statements of incidents which seem to defy all previously recorded logic. The public embarrassment that follows the statement, 'I have seen the Loch Ness Monster', is in itself enough to make most people shy away from such an admission. So why, then, if the witnesses have made it all up, do they draw upon themselves such a barrage of criticism and sceptical abuse? Many people reading this book would not publicly admit to seeing something which defies all human logic, and many more would think that anyone who claimed to have seen the 'monster' must either have a drink problem or have suffered some form of temporary insanity. The Loch Ness Monster is a real-life fairy tale. Indeed, one wonders whether it should be classified as a monster at all. We know that whatever it is that lurks in the Loch seems to shun public attention and is easily scared by sound. Moreover, it has not as yet done anyone any physical harm. And yet we humans hunt it down, like a predator stalking its prey.

If the Monster does exist, then my only hope is that it is never truly discovered. Mankind is destructive, and there is no doubt that someone, somewhere, would feel the desire to interfere with it, thus possibly causing it some harm. If there is a creature in the Loch, then it may well have survived for tens of thousands of years, without any assistance from the human race or from science. For this reason alone it should perhaps remain an enigma; it should remain a real-life fairy tale. Long may she escape detection, and maintain her dignified liberty.

A

Abriachan Situated on the north-west side of the Loch (virtually opposite Dores), with an old pier, Abriachan is the scene of many sightings: 12 August 1933, (**Patrick Grant**); 17 June 1934, (**Col. E.G. Henderson**); 5 January 1934, (**Mr Arthur Grant**); 1966, (**Mrs Margaret Edwards**); 13 June 1967, (**Dick Raynor**), 21 July 1987 (**Barbara Grant**).

On 7 August 1996 the staff of the Clansman Hotel reported several black humps which appeared in the middle of the Loch close to Abriachan. The most recent sighting in this area took place on 17 March 1997, when a local (anonymous) Glen Urquhart man, well used to Loch conditions and wave formations, saw two humps travelling through the water near to Abriachan.

See also **Edwards, Margaret; Grant, Arthur; Grant, Barbara; Grant, Patrick; Hay, H.F.; Henderson, Col. E.G.; MacKenzie, D.; Miller, William; Raynor, Dick.**

Academy of Applied Science A private organization initially formed in 1963 and based at Belmont, Massachusetts, USA. Its goal is to investigate unexplored areas of science, such as unidentified phenomena. In 1970, it arrived at the Loch and assisted the **Loch Ness Investigation Bureau** with a surface watch. The President of the Academy, **Dr Robert H. Rines**, had found his interest aroused by tales of Loch Ness when he attended a lecture on the subject by **Prof. Roy Mackal** in 1969. He immediately offered to assist the bureau in its endeavours.

In 1971 the Academy team brought underwater electronic stroboscopic cameras to the Loch, in the hope that this equipment would locate the unknown creature. Sadly, these efforts failed to detect any unidentified or other direct evidence. Undeterred, the team returned in August 1972, better equipped and more knowledgeable about the geographical environment of the Loch. On this occasion they were armed not only with stroboscopic cameras but also with Raytheon sonar equipment, which Rines felt would vastly increase the team's chances of tracing something.

A strobe camera was lowered into the waters from a surface cruising boat to a depth of 45 feet and a sonar transducer was lowered to a level of about 35 feet in the hope of detecting a large trace. At about 1.45 a.m. on 8 August 1972, near **Temple Pier** the equipment picked up a strange object, causing the underwater camera to snap into action. The results were, to say the least, spectacular. The sonar echo trace picked up an inordinately large object which in size did not resemble any known species of fish and one particular photograph shows what appears to be a flipper-like appendage adjoined to a rough-textured body.

The photographs were developed by Eastman Kodak and computer-enhanced by NASA experts. Every individual who handled the photographs or negatives had to sign an official declaration certifying that they had not been altered or added to in any way. This did not, however, exclude the possibility of the negatives or future prints undergoing deliberate 'touching up' after being publicly released.

Further photographic evidence was taken by Rines in 1975, when underwater shots provided images of what appeared to be a hideous 'gargoyle'-type head. Another frame shows what was claimed to be a complete view of the underside of a creature that looks like an archetypal form of something similar to a plesiosaur.

Unfortunately for the Academy, the authenticity of these same illustrations has since been questioned. Despite the efforts of some top photographic/computer experts, the **'flipper' photograph** cannot be computer-enhanced from its original format to give the clear image that is popularly known. Experts have failed to enhance the form into a definable flipper shape – indeed, some claim that it is virtually impossible to recreate this image without some 'additional' work. Furthermore, the image has been questioned by developers in the USA, who now claim that the infamous 'flipper' photograph is not the one which their laboratory submitted to Rines. Some authorities have subsequently rubbished the Academy's 'flipper' photograph, declaring:

> too many questions remain unanswered. Without positive first-hand knowledge, science cannot accept this photograph as being

what it is portrayed to be. It could be a fin or some appendage, but it could also belong to a commonly known species, and may have been exaggerated.

The **'gargoyle' head** has similarly been deemed to be nothing more than a view of a weather-beaten log at the bottom of the Loch. Similarly, the 'underside' view, when scrutinized, has been categorized as an obscure view of part of some debris on the Loch's rocky bottom.

The sonar readings do, however, seem to indicate the possible presence of two large creatures in the area being investigated by the Academy.

There are those who believe that Dr Rines' enthusiasm for the task in hand clouded his vision of what the Academy team had photographed. Nonetheless, his work aroused major interest in the scientific work being carried out at Loch Ness, and the publicity it created ultimately aided the commercial funding of future expeditions.

See also **dolphins**; **'flipper' photograph**; **'gargoyle' head**; **Mackal, Prof. Roy**; *Nan*; *Nessiteras rhombopteryx*; **Rines, Dr Robert**; **Temple Pier**; **Wiseman, David**.

Achnahannet   Located on the north-west shore of the Loch, south of Drumnadrochit, Achnahannet is the scene of numerous sightings. Most notably on 10 July 1960 (**Bruce Ing**); 21 May 1964 (**Peter Hodge**); April 1967 (**Dorothy Fraser**). It was here also that **John Cobb** died in 1952, whilst attempting to break the world water speed record; his boat crashed, and he was recovered from the wreckage to die on the nearby hillside.

See also **Cobb, John**.

Adamnan, St (625-704)   Born and educated in Donegal, he became Abbot of Iona in 679, and was described by the Venerable Bede as 'a good and wise man, and very well instructed in the lore of the scriptures'. Adamnan's biography of **St Columba**, *Vita Sancti Columbae*, (vol. 6, bk II, chap. 27) tells of the 'driving away of a certain monster by virtue of the prayer of a holy man'.

Many writers on the monster have failed to research Adamnan's work in any depth: the incident involving St Columba to which he refers occurred on the River Ness and not in Loch Ness. Moreover,

Adamnan wrote his book almost a century after St Columba's death, and thus, having no direct first-hand knowledge of incidents relating to Columba, was forced to rely upon tales passed down in the passage of time.

One of two original surviving copies of *Vita Sancti Columbae* is preserved in the library of Schaffhausen, Switzerland. Editions have been published by W. Reeves (1857), J.T. Fowler (1894, 1920) and A.O. and M.O. Anderson (1961).

See also **Columba, St.**

Adams, F.C. After an alleged sighting of an anonymous creature in the Loch on 24 August 1934, a photo was published in the *Daily Mail* on 25 August of the same year. The photograph, taken from Urquhart Castle, seems to show some kind of dark shape rising out of the water amidst a large disturbance. However, the photograph is so unclear that it is virtually impossible to identify any distinctive form. It has subsequently been suggested that what Adams photographed could be nothing more than a fallen tree branch floating in the water. Most researchers dismiss the photograph as a misinterpretation of a natural phenomenon, so it has never been taken seriously.

advertising The mystery of the Loch Ness Monster has been utilized by a number of well-known companies to promote their products. The most notable recent examples of such advertisements have been from the Ford Motor Company and the National Lottery, to name but two. One of the most curious advertisements was that run by Smirnoff vodka. This portrayed a female water-skier being towed along the Loch by the monster, accompanied by the legend 'At Loch Ness things are never what they seem'. For this advertisement they weren't; it transpired that the female skier had been born a male!

Aldourie Located on the south-east shore of the Loch at virtually its most northerly point and identifiable by its old castle, Aldourie is the scene of notable sightings; *see also* **Lowie, R.H.**; **MacLeod, Torquil and Elizabeth.** The most recent sighting in this area occurred on 21 March 1997, when a South African couple holidaying in the region apparently told staff at the Drumnadrochit Hotel that they saw 'two humps sticking out of the water' opposite Aldourie Castle.

Alexander, Paul   A store manager from Inverness, Paul Alexander witnessed something in the Loch on 25 August 1996. At about 3.45 p.m., whilst in a boat moored beneath **Urquhart Castle**, he saw wakes of water steadily build up on the Loch about three-quarters of a mile away, south-south-east of the castle. After about 30-40 seconds the wake began to break at certain points, apparently as a large submerged object broke the surface. Although he never physically saw what it was that created the wake, he felt that it must have been some considerable size to cause such a movement of water. The *Aberdeen Press and Journal* of 11 September 1996 incorrectly reported that Alexander saw something 'solid, black and alive' during the sighting.

Alltsaigh   Referred to in numerous other works as Altsigh, Alltsigh, Alltsaich, Aultsaigh, Aultsigh, this lies on the north-west shore of the Loch, just north of Invermoriston on the north-west side of the Loch. From here **Miss Janet Fraser, Mrs G. Fraser** and **Miss Howden** had a surface sighting of a mysterious creature in the Loch on 22 September 1933 as did **Henry Henderson** and **George MacKenzie** in October 1931, and **Count Bentinck** in August 1934. Before World War II there was a tearoom (the Halfway House) located here, but this later became a youth hostel.

Amery, Mike, B.Sc.   Crew member on the motor yacht *Pharma*, which, according to **Nicholas Witchell** (*The Loch Ness Story*) was a British Medical Association vessel. On 22 August 1966, Amery, along with others, witnessed and tracked a moving object on the Loch surface for a period of about half an hour. On the on-board radar screen Amery and the others detected an object which he estimated to be approximately 30 feet long – this being the part of the creature visible above water. It was described as having the appearance of the 'belly of a horse', and at least one other witness claimed to see five humps at a distance of three-quarters of a mile astern.
   See also **Pharma**.

amphibian   *See under* identity.

Anderson, David   Member of the British Broadcasting Corporation team that visited the Loch in 1958 to carry out their own investigation. A Marconi echo-sounder was used aboard the

Clyde puffer *Kaffir*. Anderson, who operated the equipment, noted an object some 70 yards north-east of Urquhart Castle. This appeared on the sonar screen as a black heavy mark, corresponding to an object thought to be about 20 feet long. The object dived from a depth of 12 feet to 60 feet before it was lost. None of the Marconi technicians could identify what the mark may have represented.

Anderson, Peter   Crew member on board the Peterhead drifter *Rival III*, which used sonar equipment to search the Loch on 2 December 1954. At 11.30 a.m. Anderson saw the echo-sounder chart recording agitated movements as the vessel approached Urquhart Castle. The chart mirrored the shape of the object, which, it was claimed, was no shoal of fish, but rather a solid mass with some kind of extended body (presumably an extended neck). As the boat passed through the locks leading to the west coast Anderson showed the chart to the excited lock staff. By the time *Rival III* had reached Oban, local journalists had been alerted to the occurrence and were waiting for her; the chart was subsequently sold to the highest bidder – the *Daily Herald*. A reading of the calibrated scale of the chart revealed that the object was 480 feet down and 120 feet above the Loch bed, and that its length was about 50 feet.

See also **Rival III.**

anonymous sightings   It is impossible to verify every alleged sighting of some unidentified creature in Loch Ness, and the majority of witnesses, understandably, prefer to remain anonymous. A degree of stigma attaches itself to anyone making a claim about something that is beyond the reasonable realms of human understanding – even though most people fail to appreciate the fact that human knowledge is decidedly limited.

It has been suggested that all scientific methods used to trace an unidentified creature in Loch Ness have failed to provide positive proof of its existence. In the past, some scientists have indeed dismissed the Loch Ness enigma as nothing more than a legend which has survived the passage of time. Because of the association of science with such claims, the public in general automatically believes that this must be 'expert analysis', and therefore classifies all claims about sightings in the 'unbelievable' category.

Science is not always correct (mistakes are made, since its practitioners are, after all, only human). But, since it virtually (and, in the light of its own limitations, correctly) discredits the theory that a large unidentified creature may reside within the Loch's murky waters, society in general tends to take the same view. Consequently, the rationality of anyone making a claim to the contrary is questioned. It is clear, therefore, why so many people wish to maintain anonymity about what they may or may not have seen – particularly those with social standing in the community. They face ridicule, and as a result may find their professional position and judgement placed in jeopardy.

I have personally interview judges, magistrates, company directors, senior officers of HM Forces and the emergency services, all of whom claim to have seen something peculiar in the waters of the Loch and who as a result are deeply fascinated by the mystery.

Many sightings therefore remain unreported, although some occasionally make their way into the pages of the press, without the witnesses names being reported. On 15 May 1971, someone described as a 'very trustworthy man' had an encounter at the Loch side at 5.30 a.m., whilst travelling in his car towards Foyers. Apparently, a large grey animal appeared from the woods to his left. It was lizard-like and dragged itself over the road and down into the water. In its mouth were parts of an animal, possibly a cow. The creature was estimated as being around thirty feet long and approximately six feet tall with a sheen on its skin which looked oily.

On 9 August 1997, a camper at the Loch Ness Caravan Park at Invermoriston heard strange noises coming from the Loch at around 3.00 a.m. The female camper was initially alerted by the increased agitation of a flock of resident ducks, this was followed by the loud humming noise which again seemed to emanate from the Loch. The noise was not mechanical, thus the woman elected to remain within the sanctuary of her tent. Further research indicated that no known vessels or plant machinery were in operation within the locality at the time in question.

Appleby, Mrs Mary *See under Grant, Barbara.*

Arrow The *Arrow* was a steam tug making its maiden voyage from Leith to Manchester, on 30 August 1938. The ship was about two-and-a-half miles west of **Urquhart Castle,** and the Loch itself was calm, when two of its crew sighted a large, dark object in the water. The Master, **Captain William Brodie**, made an entry into the ship's log:

> August 30th 1938. Saw wake of a large animal to south-west while close inshore, two and a half miles from Castle Urquhart. In sight again for half a minute 4.50 p.m. Seen by all crew on deck.

The crew members who witnessed this sighting were: Captain William Brodie, A. Rich, Chief Engineer Sprout, Donald Campbell, William Lamb and P. Byrne.

See also **Brodie, Capt. William.**

Atkin, Miss C.W. Sighting at 9.40 p.m. on 22 May 1967. On a flat calm Loch, a black object, estimated as being around 40 feet in length, was seen at a distance of approximately 35 yards, cruising just below the surface. It travelled for about 100 yards before submerging. Atkin and others watched its course and movements for around five minutes but were unable to determine exactly what it was. None of the witnesses had 'seen anything quite like it before'.

autogiro In 1970 the Loch Ness Investigation Bureau co-opted the services of **Wing Commander Ken Wallis** and his autogiro Wallis 117. The Bureau's initial intention had been that Wallis should drop biopsy darts from the autogiro into specific sonar tracing areas. These would sink to the bottom of the Loch allowing a greater, more concise trace to be made. In the event of darts striking a living creature on their way down, they were equipped to scrape a sample from it and to expel gas, propelling them to the surface. What the Bureau were not aware of was that it is illegal to drop anything from the air over the British Isles. Wallis therefore had to refuse to co-operate in this scheme. He did, however, complete one month's flying over the Loch, but failed to locate anything suspicious. He also carried out one week's flying over **Loch Morar**, where a similar monster is said to reside.

See also **Wallis, Wg.-Comdr K.**

B

Baillie, Lady Maud, CBE   Surface sighting on the afternoon of 19 April 1950. Whilst she was driving along the Dores to Foyers road and pointing out Urquhart Castle to the rest of the party in her car (which included her grandsons **Angus and Jonathan Warr** and **Lady Spring-Rice,** accompanied by her grandchildren) one of the children suddenly asked about what appeared to be a rock, which was one third of the way across the Loch. Lady Maud stopped the car to get a better look at the object, and the occupants of the vehicle quickly realized that it would be impossible for a rock to project above the surface so far from the shore. Without warning the object moved off at a rapid pace towards Lochend. The entire party got out of the car and clambered down to the water's edge. Looking towards the point where they had seen the object they also saw a V-shaped wash, along with a white foaming wake similar to that created by a moving motor boat. As they continued to watch the object one large, dark hump could be seen, with foam breaking around it. Within a few minutes it had submerged, creating a great swirl of water as it did so.

Bain, Raymond   A resident of Fort Augustus who had a sighting some time in December 1957. Bain was about three miles south of Urquhart Castle, driving north along the Loch, when he saw a large animal swimming about 150 yards from the shore. A head and a long neck of swan-like appearance were clearly visible. Behind this was a 30-foot-long body. Bain tracked the creature as he drove, and estimated it to be travelling in excess of 35 m.p.h. It eventually disappeared near Urquhart Castle.

Baker, Gerry   Gerry Baker and **Ian Shield** were both active members of the **Loch Ness Investigation Bureau.** While the two men were carrying out a surface watch of the Loch on 16 September 1969, they

21

saw mysterious 'wakes' moving through the Loch. There was nothing to be seen in the area which could account for the creation of these disturbances, which were captured on film.

The experts who examined the footage later believed that the wakes had been caused by wildlife – possibly birds swimming – although this could not be confirmed.

See also **Shield, Ian; film footage**

Baker, Dr Peter Leader of an Oxford and Cambridge University expedition to the Loch in July 1962, working alongside Mark Westwood. The team carried out a surface watch of the area for a total of 480 hours, using cine cameras positioned along the Loch shore to record any sightings, and sounding equipment to track any possible movements.

Although three unidentified sightings were claimed by the surface watchers, no one film of any of these events was recorded. The sonar search detected three contacts, one of which was preceded by a surface sighting, but overall the team's results were inconclusive.

Ballantyne, James M. Ballantyne and his sister-in-law Miss E.M. Keith sighted an unidentified creature on the evening of 30 March 1965. He later described what they saw as follows:

a head and neck rose and stood about four to six feet out of the water. The head [was] similar to that of a python and was held at a right angle to neck, which was elongated and slim, thickening at a point about one foot above the water.

No body was physically sighted, although the speed with which the animal travelled through the water gave him the impression that it must have had a large body which was muscularly propelled.

See also **Keith, Miss E.M.**

Banjer, Nikhl *See under* **Demaio, Emalio.**

Barron, Dr Evan Editor of the *Inverness Courier*, who, it is claimed, initially categorized the Loch Ness creature a 'monster'. It was so christened after one of the paper's correspondents, **Alex Campbell**, reported a sighting that was published in the 2 May 1933 edition of the *Courier*. The article that Campbell submitted to

Barron indicated that an animal of some phenomenal size had been seen in the Loch. According to the Loch Ness legend, Barron is reported to have said: 'Well, if it is as big as Campbell says it is we can't just call it a creature, it must be a real monster.'

Barsky, Harvey   At 2.00 p.m., on 27 May 1969, Harvey Barsky and a troop of boy scouts were out beside the Loch, opposite Temple Pier. It was a clear, warm day and the water was calm. Barsky, armed with cine camera, noticed something moving in the Loch and began to film. The object maintained a low position in the water, hardly breaking the surface. It seemed to move in a slow but somewhat erratic manner, changing direction frequently. When viewed, the film footage could add little more to this description, and no material evidence could be gained from the film.
   See also **Film Footage**.

basking shark   The idea that the Loch Ness monster might be a basking shark first came to notice in a 1942 edition of America's *Time* magazine. A report contained therein stated that a 240-foot-long basking shark had been found, dead, and washed up on the shore of Loch Ness. So far as can be ascertained there is no evidence to substantiate this bizarre piece of journalism. The article failed to suggest how the shark initially entered the Loch, which would have been virtually impossible had it attempted to travel along the River Ness.

bathymetrical survey   The first recorded bathymetrical survey of the Loch was carried out in the early twentieth century by Sir John Murray KCB, FRS, and Laurence Pullar FRSE. Its results were reported in *Bathymetrical Survey of the Fresh Water Lochs of Scotland* in 1911.
   Loch Ness is described as a long V-shaped rock basin, ponded at its northern end by glacial and fluvioglacial and raised-beach deposits. The bottom is described as being as flat as a bowling green and the depth estimated at 750 feet. In all, some 1,700 measurements were recorded by Murray and Pullar, using what was then state-of-the-art equipment, a Wire Sounding Device – which more modern comparisons have shown to have been remarkably accurate.
   The most recent bathymetrical survey is being carried out in

conjunction with **Adrian Shine**, who intends to examine the Loch, layer by layer, until its contents and ecological history are thoroughly detailed. This time the survey measurements will be made by computer-aided Marconi sound equipment.

See also **Project Rosetta; Project Urquhart.**

Baynard, Richard Francis   Looking at the Loch through binoculars at 6.45 p.m. on the evening of 29 August 1967, Baynard saw a dark grey multi-humped object at a distance of about a quarter of a mile. This surfaced and submerged on three occasions. The object caused a great deal of turbulence in the water and appeared to be 20-30 feet long.

BBC   The British Broadcasting Corporation (BBC) carried out a rather subjective investigation into the existence of the Loch Ness Monster, the results of which were transmitted in the form of a 1½-hour television programme broadcast on 26 September 1951. Titled *Loch Ness Monster Enquiry* the setting was a mock courtroom, in which various witnesses were called to give evidence for and against the animal's existence. At the end of a poorly researched and presented programme, the court's final verdict was 'Not Proven'. Afterwards the BBC was heavily criticized for lack of objectivity in discussing the case.

Further coverage of the Loch Ness mystery was broadcast by *Panorama* on 13 June 1960, when presented Hugh Burnett interviewed eye-witnesses. The cine film taken by **Tim Dinsdale** was shown and discussed, and this time a great deal more credit was given to the possibility of an unknown species living in the Loch.

Beckjord, John Erik   Beckjord, an American wildlife photographer who was representing the National Cryptozoological Society, allegedly filmed a sighting on 6 August 1983. Two video cameras were used during his observations, one installed at the Clansman Hotel, the other in the old croft buildings at St Ninians, overlooking the western corner of **Urquhart Bay**. It was from the latter location that Beckjord claimed to have filmed something in the Loch. His film shows some kind of object moving in a 100-metre area of water in Urquhart Bay. Several wakes can be seen, and there are two large splashes which form a V shape; one leg of the splash is estimated as being 21 metres long. Three large, dark objects are seen to move off in the direction of Urquhart Castle, and these, claims Beckjord, are three independent monsters.

It should be noted that other persons watching the same area of bay at the same time as the Beckjord film was shot could not claim to have seen anything other than wildfowl in the area.

In July 1991, Beckjord announced one of the must curious proposals about the identity of the Loch Ness creature, published in the *Daily Express* on 15 July 1991. It reported that a *'Nessletter'*, produced by the Ness Information Service, contained an article by Beckjord suggesting that 'Space travellers could have come to earth and lost some of their pets. This pet could have been Nessie – which has grown through the ages.'

beluga whale   Explanation for sightings provided to the press by **Mr P.C. Grimshaw** of the Royal Scottish Museum in 1933.

Bentinck, Count A.   This famous Dutch naturalist sighted a beast from Halfway House, **Alltsaigh**, in August 1934. Bentinck claimed to have first noticed the top of the animal's head protruding above the water, before it rose upwards, providing an ideal view. From its mouth, he said, 'a kind of steam came forth, but was blown back by a slight cold breeze'. So far as records can be traced, this is the only sighting of the animal actually breathing. Bentinck, who had previously been to the Loch on just three occasions (each visit lasting a fortnight), was a correspondent of **Mrs Constance Whyte**. He claimed to have made a total of seven separate sightings of the monster and stated with some authority in the Dutch scientific journal, *Levende Natuur* (10 August 1934):

> My observations were sufficient to satisfy me that the animal is a mammal. It is one of the family of pinnipedia described by A.C. Oudemans in his book, *The Great Sea Serpent*.

betting   People will place bets on any subject, and the Loch Ness Monster is no exception. The odds on the existence of the monster have in general remained fairly static, at around 500-1. However between 1992 and 1997 the odds were reduced, this was due to more detailed sightings, and the production of video film footage. In February 1997, the bookmakers Ladbrokes lowered the betting to just 100-1 with the revelation that giant underwater caverns had been discovered in the Loch, large enough to support a family of creatures and more. It is unlikely that the odds will be further reduced without even more substantial evidence.

Bibby, Sir Derek   The *Sunday Express* of 11 August 1991 carried a book review of *Glimpses* by Sir Derek Bibby. In this work the author wrote of his belief that the invention of the Loch Ness monster was down to the advertising resources of Lord Royden, who created the whole thing in order to attract tourists to the area and fill his hotels, which were situated around the Loch.

birds   Many sightings have been attributed to birds on the water. Binns (*Loch Ness Mystery Solved*, 1983, pp. 196-7) examines the appearance of Red Breasted Mergansers, Grebes, and the Goosander as examples of possible head and neck sightings when swimming on the Loch surface.

Birmingham, University of   The University of Birmingham (England) carried out expeditions to the Loch in 1961, 1968 (April, August), 1969 (September), and 1970, the last three of which used new digital sonar equipment. All were headed by sonar experts **Professor Denys G. Tucker**, and later also by **Dr Hugh Braithwaite**. The University expeditions to the Loch have always maintained an air of level-headedness and remained objective. Despite the use of what was then 'modern sonar equipment' the University's findings were on the whole disappointing. A solitary 13-minute spell in August 1968 revealed a number of uncommon sonar readings, but these were later dispelled as possible misinterpretations of natural events.

Black and White Scotch expedition   Carried out in 1972, this US expedition was led by **Prof. James Ullrich** and Robert Lewis in collaboration with the **Loch Ness Investigation Bureau**. The team carried out a surface watch, concentrating on the animal's possible nocturnal activities. Infra-red night cameras were strategically positioned around the Loch, but they failed to detect anything worth serious consideration. A reward of £1 million for the capture of the monster, alive and unharmed, was offered by the whisky firm until May 1972, but it was never claimed.

Bland, Dennis   On 20 September 1967 Bland claimed to have sighted 'a nine foot by three foot hump' on the surface of the water whilst scanning the Loch area through binoculars. The hump appeared dark grey to black in colour and had a rough texture. As it moved through the water it created a small wave and left a wake behind it before submerging.

boat wakes   Due to the presence of numerous sailing vessels on the Loch, wakes created by their movement have been attributed as a possible explanation for sightings of the monster. This is the most popular explanation provided by the sceptics for sightings.

Boece, Hector   Sixteenth-century author of *Scotorum historia* ('History of the Scots'). Boece is said to have described, in one passage of this work, how 'a terrible beast came out of the Loch early one morning, about mid-summer, demolishing trees and killing three men.' Previous commentators have accepted this tale as being factual, but the incident related to is said to have occurred at 'Garloll, ane Loch of Argyle', and there is no mention of Loch Ness. **Tim Dinsdale** appears to have been the first author to misinterpret the tale and it has been incorrectly reported ever since, except in **Binns**, *The Loch Ness Mystery Solved*.

Borlum Bay   This is situated at the Loch's most southerly tip.
   See also **Campbell, Alex; Munro, Miss Margaret**.

Boulenger, E.G.   Boulenger, the director of the Aquarium at London Zoo, wrote in the *Observer* newspaper of 29 October 1933, 'The case of the Monster of Loch Ness is worthy of our consideration if only because it presents a striking example of mass hallucination.' He believed that the initial frenzy caused by the 1933 sightings led to natural events on the Loch being perceived as self-induced images of the monster.

Boyd, Alastair and Sue   The Boyds, who were teachers of art, claimed to have sighted an animal unknown to them in the Loch at around 4.15 p.m. on 30 July 1979. Both witnesses saw a small dark shape appear on the surface and disappear three times in quick succession. The object was moving into **Urquhart Bay** about 150 metres from shore and was visible for about 5 seconds only. Alastair

Boyd believed that the shape was in fact a hump and estimated it as being around 6 metres long. He stated that it moved forward in a rolling motion rather like a whale.

See also **Surgeon's Photograph.**

Brachla Situated four miles south of Lochend on the Loch's north-west side, this was the location of sightings by **Robin MacEwan** in the late 1930s, **Dale Bussell OBE** and **S. Hunter Gordon** in June 1939, and **Hamish Mackintosh** on 2 February 1959.

Braithwaite, Dr Hugh A member of the **Birmingham University** expeditions of 1968, 1969 and 1970, Braithwaite was an expert in the field of sonar. The August 1968 expedition led to a 13-minute sonar trace and reading of a large object which rose from the Loch floor at the rate of about 100 feet per minute. The object then descended to the floor before rising again. Simultaneously, a second object appeared on the reading apparently travelling at a speed of about 15 knots. This second object had a rate of dive of approximately 450 feet per minute.

Braithwaite and his colleague **Prof. D.G. Tucker** published their results in the *New Scientist* of 19 December 1968, which was reviewed with mixed opinions. Many scientists felt that Braithwaite and Tucker had jumped to conclusions, since sonar readings over such a large area can be distorted by natural events.

In 1970 Professor Tucker wrote in a report that 'the interpretation of the August 1968 expedition results may have been erroneous.' He further commented that one of the sonar readings may well have been caused by 'Gas bubbles released when the object being tracked disturbed the bottom'.

See also **Birmingham, University of, Tucker, Prof D.G.**

Breaks, Michael One of four people who, at 8.30 p.m. on the evening of 4 April 1967, sighted a single dark hump cruising through the water, from slightly different locations around Foyers Bay. The hump, thought to be about ten feet long, was seen at a distance of about 300-400 yards until it sank from view. Breaks could provide no further descriptive detail.

See also **Cary, Mrs E.W. and Heather; Morgan, Mary.**

Bright, Eric H. According to most previous authors, it was many years after it had occurred that Bright reported a sighting which took place whilst he was out walking on the Loch side near **Drumnadrochit**, sometime in 1880. Bright is supposed to have seen a large, dark grey animal emerge from a wooded area and plunge into the Loch. The creature was described as having a 'long neck and small head . . . it waddled down the hillside on four short legs from an area of woodland'. As it entered the water and moved off, it created a large wash behind it.

British Museum of Natural History The museum is often asked what research it has carried out into the Loch Ness phenomenon. The answer, quite simply, is none. Any physical expedition to the Loch, mounted by the museum in search of an unknown species, would create so much publicity that it would be used and abused by the media. It would cause a belief that the museum does concede that the creature exists. The problem is that it cannot do so until conclusive evidence is acquired.

In the past the museum has suffered much criticism for its apparent lack of interest in the Loch Ness phenomenon. Such criticism can be laid to rest. In the 1930s, when there was much publicity surrounding sightings, the trustees of the museum elected to dismiss such controversy as 'mythical', or mass hysteria. Members of staff received a memorandum dictating that no one, including those on annual holiday, was to have any connection with any matter relating to the so-called 'Loch Ness Monster'; anyone found with such connections would be disciplined. It is now known that **Dr Denys Tucker** was dismissed from his position at the museum in 1960 for participating in such physical research.

That, of course, was forty years ago, and opinions have changed since then – although it would still be difficult to get anyone at the museum to agree that a prehistoric creature, or something similar, lives in Loch Ness. There is now a sensible interest in the research which takes place at the Loch. The museum's zoological library holds books published upon the phenomenon, and I was fortunate enough to gain official access to files held in the archives relating solely to the Loch Ness Monster. There is nothing suspicious in the documents file, which contains internal memoranda, letters and official responses to some of the enquiries received over the years. There is also a file containing a wealth of newspaper and magazine cuttings dating back to 1933, indicating that someone in the organization felt it necessary to maintain a discreet but healthy interest in the Loch Ness saga.

Over the years there have been a few personal 'quotes' from staff of the museum, though these were not 'official' statements from the museum itself, but the personal opinions of individual staff members. The poor reporting of such quotes is one reason why official organizations like the museum prefer to remain aloof from amateur speculation.

The museum staff I have interviewed during my research have proved most helpful, and many maintain an 'open mind' on whether some unidentified species of creature lives in the Loch. There can be no doubt that, if and when the Loch Ness creature is discovered, there is no establishment in the world better equipped to identify and correctly categorize it than the British Museum of Natural History.

See also **Calman, Dr William Thomas; Charig, Dr Alan; Sheals, Dr John; Tucker, Dr Denys.**

Brodie, Captain William Captain William Brodie, from Leith, Scotland, was the captain of the steam tug *Arrow* on 30 August 1938, when it was making its maiden voyage from Leith to Manchester, via the **Caledonian Canal**. Captain Brodie's account of what was encountered that day was recorded in the *Scotsman* of 31 August 1938:

> When passing up Loch Ness, two-and-a-half miles west of Urquhart Castle, the mate (A. Rich) and myself noticed a huge black-coloured animal rather like a hump-backed whale emerge on the Loch surface and keep pace with the ship at some distance. We at once realised it was the monster. We were honestly astounded at seeing such a huge creature in an inland loch, but believe me, this was no whale, because, just beyond the foremost hump was another, and no whale on earth ever had two distinct humps.

Hearing the cries of their colleagues, several other crew members raced to the deck to witness a huge creature diving from view beneath the surface of the Loch. A few moments later it reappeared, this time showing seven distinct humps or coils. The creature tore past the tug at a terrific speed, just showing on the surface.

Another crew member recalled how the coils reminded him of a giant sea serpent glistening brightly in the sunshine. Captain Brodie, who made a record of the sighting in the ship's log, later estimated the size of the creature as being 'at least half the size of the tug, that is 30-40 feet long'.

Before the *Arrow*'s encounter, Captain Brodie had been very sceptical of the tales he had heard of the Loch Ness monster, but he told a further reporter:

> There is now no doubt in my mind that something very large and unusual resides within the Loch. I would never guess as to its origin. I have seen some very big fish in my time, but what I saw that day defied all logic; it is very much a monster.

See also **Arrow**.

Bronard, Miss   *See under* **Forbes, Mr and Mrs J.C.**

Brusey, Father Gregory   Sighted a monster on 14 October 1971 while walking by the Loch side with Roger Pugh. Both men were alarmed to see the creature's head and neck sticking some ten feet above the water. The animal appeared to swim towards them before diving below the surface, its head going down in a sideways movement.

Father Gregory had in fact made a previous sighting, on 3 May 1968, when he saw what appeared to be a creature, with a 'horse-like head and two large humps', dark in colour, which were similar in appearance to upturned boats. The animal moved at an estimated 40 m.p.h. across Fort Augustus bay.

Bull, Phillip   On 5 May 1968, at about 10.11 p.m., Bull and **Howard Pratt** saw a single hump protruding out of the water. This was estimated as being about 10-12 feet in size and was grey-brown in colour; it moved quickly through the water before submerging.

See also **Pratt, Howard**.

bull walrus   Explanation provided by **Mr H.F. Hay**, a Fellow of the Zoological Society of Scotland who investigated the **Grant** land sighting of 5 January 1934. From measurements and observations made at the scene by Hay, he was of the opinion that the creature sighted by Grant was probably a Bull walrus.

See also **Grant, Arthur; Hay, Mr H.F.**

Bureau for Investigating the Loch Ness Phenomena Limited *See under* **Loch Ness Investigation Bureau.**

Burnett, Jimmy On 7 March 1996 Burnett and a party of 15 schoolchildren were shocked to see a single 'large black hump' appear on the Loch surface, and travel across the Loch from **Dores** to **Abriachan**, where it disappeared from view. The object was not believed to be a mechanically propelled craft or a rowing boat.

Burr, Dr Malcolm Author of 'Sea Serpents and Monsters', an article published in *Nineteenth Century* in February 1934. Discussing the enigma of Loch Ness, he stated:

> I see no real reason why our sea-serpent should not be a hitherto unrecognised relative of the newts, adapted to life in the sea, developed to a relatively large size, timid and nocturnal in habit, and consequently little seen.

Burton, Dr Maurice In June 1960, Dr Burton led a team of five watchers on an eight-day surface watch expedition. During his stay, Burton interviewed a number of eye-witnesses and discussed the case in some depth with the local populace. On his return, he wrote his book *The Elusive Monster: An Analysis of the Evidence from Loch Ness* (Hart Davis, 1961), arguing that most of the sightings had been nothing more than rotting vegetable matter.

Before this visit to the Loch, Burton had stated his firm belief in the existence of the phenomenon and had written a number of articles about it (*Sunday Express*, 3 August 1959; *Illustrated London News*, 20 February 1960). In his *Illustrated London News* article he says of the 'surgeon's photograph': 'If this photograph is genuine, as I am now convinced beyond all doubt it is, then there is no argument about the reality of the Loch Ness monster.' In his book, however, he dismisses this same photograph as being nothing more than an otter's tail.

Burton was an experienced zoologist with the **British Museum of Natural History**, holding the position of Deputy Keeper. He wrote extensively on the case, most notably articles in the *Daily Express* (29 December 1933); the *Illustrated London News* (8 December 1951, 20 February 1960, 11 July 1960, 23 July 1960, 30 July 1960); the *New Scientist* (22 September 1960, 23 January 1969); *Animals* (30 July 1962). He died in 1992 at the age of 94.

See also **Elusive Monster, The.**

Bussell, Dale, OBE   Deputy director of Contracts for the Admiralty, who, some time in June 1939 was out in a car with S. **Hunter Gordon,** close to the shoreline at Brachla, when he saw, at a distance of about 200 yards, two distinct humps moving rapidly through the water. The humps rose some 4-5 feet above the surface.

See also **Hunter Gordon, S.**

Byrne, P   *See under Arrow.*

C

Caledonian Canal   The Caledonian Canal begins at the Beauly firth, close to Inverness, and debouches in Loch Linnhe, near Fort William. It links the three freshwater lochs in the Great Glen (Ness, Oich, and Lochy) to form a 60-mile waterway running from the North Sea to the Atlantic Ocean. The canal was surveyed by Scottish engineer Thomas Telford in 1801. Work began in 1804, and the canal opened in 1822 (although it was found unsatisfactory and was closed again from 1834 until its final completion in 1847. Its construction raised the water level of Loch Ness by about six feet. Only 22 miles of the waterway is built as a canal, the rest consisting of the three natural lochs. Its highest point is Loch Oich at some 106 feet above high water at Inverness.

On 1 March 1996 an anonymous report was received of the sighting of a cigar-shaped object in the water at the entrance to the Canal, close to **Fort Augustus.**

Call, Andy   One of two Inverness County Council employees (the other being Henry Wilson) working above **Urquhart Bay** who claimed to see what appeared to be 'a serpent with a horse's head' travelling through the water opposite **Urquhart Castle.** The creature, whatever it was, left a wake similar to that made by a submarine.

Calman, Dr William Thomas   Dr Calman was the Keeper of Zoology at the **British Museum of Natural History.** Born in Dundee in 1871, he became keeper of Zoology in 1921 and held the post until 1936. Along with **M.A.C. Hinton,** Deputy Keeper of Mammals at the Museum, he examined the cast of a footprint provided by **Marmaduke Wetherell** *see also* **hippopotamus hoax).** In his report Dr Calman stated 'We are unable to find any significant difference between these impressions and those made by the foot of a hippopotamus.'

Due to his official position Calman was often called to remark upon sightings at the Loch and was always very cautious, refusing to concede that something unknown might live in its waters. An insight into his, and apparently officialdom's, opinion of the mystery was published in the *Spectator* of 22 December 1933; in an article titled 'The Evidence for Monsters', Calman wrote:

> The man in the street is sometimes apt to be a little impatient or even slightly irritated by the scientific man's attitude in such cases. The evidence is abundant and the witnesses (or some of them) unimpeachable; what more do you want before giving a verdict? And yet the only scientific reply to the question is 'I do not know'.
>
> Perhaps only those who have worked in a great museum, where collections are constantly being received from the remotest corners of the earth and the depths of the seven seas, can realise just how seldom the unexpected comes to hand. That new and strange forms of animal life remain to be discovered we cannot doubt, and some of them may even be a great size. We know very little of the inhabitants of the deeper abysses of the ocean. **Dr Oudemans** and, more recently, **Commander Gould** have laboriously collated all the better-attested stories of the so-called 'sea serpent' and believe that they can discern in them some shadowy animal of monstrous size, of which not a bone, not a tooth, not a shred of skin, has ever come into the hands of a zoologist. It is possible that they are right, but it is only just possible.
>
> To suppose that anything of the sort is to be found in a freshwater lake in the British Islands is to pile improbability upon improbability. The freshwater fauna of Europe has been exhaustively studied, and it is as certain as anything of the sort can be that no species of much more than microscopic size remains to be added to the list.
>
> As to the evidence, Commander Gould has collected and proposes to publish the testimony of fifty-one witnesses. There is no need to doubt the good faith of any of these; there is no need to question that all of them saw something unusual in the familiar surroundings of the Loch; but there is a possibility that neither

they nor Commander Gould fully realise how easily and inevitably recollections of things seen become tinged and distorted by previous or even by subsequent impressions. The subject had been discussed in the popular press for many months; picture postcards, in which drawings of the monster (apparently studied from *Punch*) are superimposed on photographs of the Loch, have been widely sold; and the recurrent and meaningless adjective 'prehistoric' throws light on the nature and sources of some of the witnesses' preconceptions.

Nevertheless, if someone can find a scrap of concrete evidence, or even a convincing photograph, no one will be more pleased than the zoologist.

Calman wrote extensively upon zoology; his works include *Crustacea* (1909), *The Life of Crustacea* (1911), *The Classification of Animals: An Introduction to Zoological Taxonomy* (1949). He also wrote for the *Encyclopedia Britannica*. He died in September 1952.

Cambridge, University of   Carried out expeditions to the Loch in 1960 (June-July), 1961 (July-August) and 1962, accompanied by graduates from Oxford University. Initially they used a Marconi Marine Searchlight sonar (which had a range radius of 400 metres) on the 1960 expedition. They detected an object which moved from the surface to a depth of 47 metres at a speed of 1.8 metres per second. Almost immediately, the object climbed back up again, and contact was eventually lost. The team were unable to identify this object.

The 1961 visit provided very little new data with no reasonable sightings or readings being evident. The third expedition in 1962 swept the Loch from end to end, using boats fitted with echosounders. Despite a couple of strong contacts, the expedition leader, **Dr Peter Baker**, later stated that nothing was detected by any of the boats.

See also **Baker, Dr Peter**.

Cameron, B.M.   On 13 June 1966 Cameron, along with a friend, saw what appeared to be a disturbance in the water. At the front of this disturbance there seemed to be a small object (which Cameron presumed to be a head). Before it suddenly disappeared the object was moving at a speed of around 17 m.p.h. and left a wake behind as it did so.

Cameron, James   Sighting at about 4.00 p.m. on 7 February 1932, when he saw what appeared a large, dark, upturned boat out in the Loch. The object was stationary and suddenly submerged beneath the water. Cameron could not positively identify what the object was, although it was not like anything he had seen before.

Cameron, James   Cameron and **Dan McIntosh** were fishing in a small boat about 200 yards off Tor Point one July evening in 1963. It was about 10.00 p.m. when they felt the boat suddenly rocking on flat calm water. Without warning the head and neck of a monster reared 4-5 feet above the water about 20-30 yards away. A short distance behind the neck was a small hump. The creature immediately sank in a vertical motion. The area in which the men continued to fish had, since their attention had been drawn to the monster, suddenly become devoid of fish.

Cameron, John   Alleged sighting on 15 August 1933 at a distance of about 150-300 yards. Cameron initially thought the object, which was about 15 feet long and dark, was a floating telegraph pole. However, the object was moving very fast and created a V-shaped wake on the surface. Cameron believed he could see a long tail moving from side to side just beneath the surface.

Cameron, John   Cameron, a local farm worker, had an alleged sighting on 25 December 1933 of a solitary black hump moving slowly through the water, at a distance of about thirty yards, along with **A. Mack** and **D. McIntosh**. The hump progressed in what was believed to be a forward direction and gradually submerged.
    See also **Mack, A.; McIntosh, D.; Christmas Day.**

Cameron, John   A lock-keeper, employed on the Caledonian Canal at Fort Augustus, Cameron was salmon-fishing opposite Glendoe Pier on 17 March 1967. At about 3.00 p.m. a large 'upturned-boat'-type object appeared on the Loch surface and surged through the water against the waves and the wind, at a distance of about 35 yards from his position. Cameron thought that what he saw must have been about 15 feet in length, was dark brown in colour and had a 'crinkly' surface. The report was first recorded in the *Inverness Courier*.

Cameron, Margaret Incredible land sighting. Margaret Cameron claimed that, as a teenager playing on the beach at Inchnacardoch Bay in 1919, along with her two brothers and young sister, she saw something large coming from the trees behind them, edging its way back into the water. At the time, she estimated its size at about 20 feet. It had a huge body with two short round feet, and was, she felt, the typical colour of an elephant. It seemed to move like a caterpillar.

See also **Cameron, Mrs Peter**.

Cameron, Mrs Peter Along with her two brothers and older sister in September 1919, Mrs Cameron, then aged fifteen, claimed to have seen a large animal with the appearance of a 'camel' on land by the edge of the Loch in Inchnacardoch Bay. It was a sandy/gold colour and quite clearly had four limbs. The creature was described as having a long neck, a small head (like a camel's in shape), and a humped back. The creature appeared to move awkwardly, 'humping its great shoulders and twisting its head from side to side'; eventually it reached the water's edge and lurched in.

See also **Cameron, Margaret**.

Cameron, Simon Alleged sighting of the monster in 1926. Cameron, from Invergarry, watched the creature from **Cherry Island** at the **Fort Augustus** end of the Loch. He was watching two gulls skimming the surface of the Loch close to where he stood, when for no apparent reason, the birds suddenly rose up into the air 'screaming', as though startled. He then saw the creature, which he described as being similar to a large upturned boat, which sank as quickly as it rose. A report of this sighting was first published in the *Inverness Courier* on 6 November 1926.

Campbell, Alex Water bailiff and local correspondent for the *Inverness Courier*, he reported the sighting by **Mr and Mrs John Mackay** in the *Courier* of 2 May 1933. Curiously, at the time the article's authorship was left anonymous. It was later discovered that Campbell had in fact enhanced the story in order to influence the editor into publishing it; the MacKays basically claimed to have seen a violent commotion on the water, like two ducks fighting, but this was exaggerated into 'two blue/black humps' showing above the water.

Campbell also claims to have had a number of personal sightings of the creature. He caught his first glimpse of it in May 1934, when standing at the mouth of the River Oich on a beautiful sunny day. He was looking toward **Borlum Bay** when his attention was caught by something which seemed to 'shoot out of the calm waters' virtually opposite the Abbey boathouse. It had a 'swan-like' neck about 6 feet long and a darkish grey body, glistening with moisture, which was at least 30 feet long.

Campbell could see two herring drifters (trawlers) and the creature, on hearing their engine noise, seemed to turn its head from side to side before sinking. It was about four hundred yards from Campbell throughout the sighting.

Another sighting took place on 16 July 1958, when Campbell saw two animals near Borlum Bay: he initially saw one large black hump heading diagonally towards the far side of the Loch, churning the surface water around it, and then noticed a second black hump, similar in shape, lying quietly near St Benedict's Abbey. In addition to this, he claims to have had an experience sometime in 1955-6, whilst sailing on the Loch with his dog close to **Horseshoe Scree**. The boat suddenly began to heave beneath him, and the dog, frightened by the sudden movement, moved to lie shivering beneath Campbell's seat; he later said that it was 'as though the creature was directly beneath them'.

Much of what Campbell has written or said over the years has been filled with ambiguity, but there can be no doubting the sincerity of his belief in the creature's existence. However, perhaps through over-enthusiasm, he had a tendency to improve upon basic facts. Many researchers have discounted his claims and opinions as due to irresponsible reporting – and certainly, some of his methods would appear to have been unethical. He is said to have written a number of anonymous letters and sighting reports to the press, presumably in order to maintain an interest in the legend.

When confronted by expert opinion, Campbell was later forced to agree that some of his alleged sightings may have been misinterpretations of natural phenomena which occur on the Loch, such as freak waves and mirages.

See also **Point Clair.**

Campbell, D On 16 June 1957, while he was sitting reading on a hillside at the Loch's northern end, Campbell saw what appeared to be two rowing boats about half a mile west of **Dores** and a quarter of a mile from shore. They were some 150 yards apart and were travelling towards **Urquhart Castle**. Campbell estimated his position as being almost a mile from the objects.

Suddenly, the leftmost of the objects shot off at some speed, before stopping a short distance to the right of the other. Both objects then sank out of sight. Campbell later stated that he could not see any people or oars on the objects, and that there was no logical explanation for what he saw. Mr Campbell was headmaster of Aldourie Public School, a position he held for 32 years.

Campbell, Donald *See under Arrow.*

Campbell, William Mr Campbell claimed to have three separate sightings of the creature. The first occurred on 12 July 1934, when he was with **William McKay**; both men saw two humps surface on the Loch on no less than five separate occasions.

The second sighting took place on 25 July 1934 at midday, when Campbell saw, through a pair of binoculars, a 12-14 foot hump about one foot in diameter and dark brown to black in colour. At the uppermost tip of this appeared to be a head which gave the impression of being about one foot long and looking something like a hedgehog.

Campbell's third sighting came at 9.50 a.m. on 30 July 1934, when he saw what looked like a 4-foot neck on the Loch surface. This moved very slowly, at just about walking pace, for a distance of about 20 yards before submerging. Campbell believed that he had seen three 'egg-shaped' flippers on each side of this form.

capture In the mid-1930s there was a real belief that the animal could be caught alive. However, if successful, its captors would be left with the problem of containing the creature. All kinds of solutions were suggested, but it was the Steel Scaffolding Company Ltd of Regent Street, London, who captured the headlines. The company constructed a purpose-built cage in which the animal could be housed and in which it could be transported. However, it did not sell too many and none was ever used in earnest.

On 14 January 1992 *Weekly World News* featured a front-page headline which grabbed the attention of the world: 'Loch Ness Monster Captured'. The story, a hoax, was the invention of journalist Zack Hagar who claimed that scientists from seven countries had trapped the 70-foot-long creature, weighing 20 tons, in a steel net after luring it there with a bait of tuna fish on 22 December 1991. Photographs of the catch and the creature were published, and were clearly fake. Undeterred, the *Weekly World News* then reported in their edition of 14 April 1992, 'Loch Ness Monster Has a Baby'. Again the invention of Zack Hagar who claimed that the same scientists who had captured the creature in 1991 discovered that it was pregnant, and released it hours before it gave birth to a 2,000-pound baby monster on 21 March 1992. Once again faked photographs accompanied the article.

See also **Circus, Bertram Mills.**

Carruth, Father Aloysius   Author of the booklet *Loch Ness and Its Monster*, published by Fort Augustus Abbey in 1938. This popular booklet has since been reprinted on several occasions. Father Carruth is alleged to have sighted a strange creature in 1965, when he saw a large wake with a substantial object at its head moving up the centre of the Loch.

Carruth, Very Rev. Monsignor G.E.   Brother of Father Aloysius. Whilst walking by the Loch side in 1940 he is said to have seen the head, neck and humps of 'some very large animal' surface in the water close to Glendoe, and move away.

Carson, Howard   On the evening of 30 January 1934, Carson, an engineer, was out walking on the hills above Dores. He was about 300 feet above the Loch surface. At approximately 6.25 p.m., he saw what appeared to be 'two equally sized humps', each measuring approximately two feet by three feet, moving slowly in the Loch towards Tor Point. The humps were creating a great commotion in the water.

Closer inspection of the object revealed what appeared to Carson's eye to be a head and neck in front of the humps. The more slowly the creature moved forward, the closer the humps appeared to be. Watching its movements closely, Carson thought that it appeared to move through the water intermittently, with a 'paddle' motion on either side of the humps; there was further evidence of underwater disturbance, where he felt the tail might be. Carson estimated the total visible length of what he judged to be an animal as 13 feet.

Cary, Mrs E.W. and Heather   Surface sighting on 4 April 1967 at around 8.30 p.m. A dark-coloured hump which the witnesses believed was about 10 feet in length was seen on the Loch surface. It did not appear to be moving at any great speed and sank from view in what was described as 'perpendicular' motion.
See also **Breaks, Michael; Morgan, Mary.**

Cary, Wg.-Comdr and Mrs Basil   The Carys were residents of Strone, and were part of a group who witnessed a single dark-brown hump in **Urquhart Bay** on 18 July 1970. The hump glided through the water towards the far shore, where it disappeared after about 15-20 yards. Cary believed that the hump had been about 20 feet in length.
See also **Tyrrel, Mr and Mrs John.**

cave dwellers   One question, which remains the subject of much conjecture, is *where* any large animal may live in the Loch. Countless sonar searches have been made, covering virtually every possible area of the Loch, and yet few have resulted in positive sonar traces which could be deemed to be significant. Clearly, if a large creature was residing in the depths of the Loch, then one would expect these searches to identify any creature of such a size quite frequently.

It has been suggested that the reason not all sonar searches are successful may be due to the fact that the animal is in fact a cave-dweller and hides away in a cave when there is much activity on the Loch surface. There has, in fact, been a long-standing belief that deep in the Loch basin there are hidden caverns, too dark and treacherous to be explored by scientific means. It is here that many people believe the Loch Ness animal dwells. However no such location has yet been positively identified by any submersible vessel.
See also **Edwards Deep, Loch Lochy.**

Chambers, Maurice   *See under* **Wilson, Lt-Col R.K.**

Chapman, Andrew   Chapman and Gillian Christopher were both members of the **Loch Ness Investigation Bureau** team, carrying out a surface watch of the Loch with the instruction to film anything which seemed out of the ordinary. At 8.00 a.m. on 22 August 1967 the pair noticed a 'long, shiny object' that lay low in the water. They filmed this object, although this involved filming into the low sun, so it proved difficult to acquire a clear image.

The pair stopped filming, and continued to watch the object with the naked eye. After about 30 minutes, the sun had risen sufficiently for the camera rig to be used again, so further footage of the object was filmed. Unfortunately, when this was viewed later, it displayed a long dark thin area on the Loch surface. This was estimated as being about 90 feet in length, and appeared to be some kind of shadow; no solid object could be seen.

See also **film footage.**

Charig, Dr Alan   Curator of Fossil Reptiles at the **British Museum of Natural History.** Dr Charig appeared on a BBC television documentary discussing the Loch Ness phenomenon in 1976. His opinion was classed as being that of an expert. It came as some surprise when he told the viewers 'If I had to give a casting vote I would cast it in favour of the Loch Ness Monster.' This statement lent serious credibility to the belief in the existence of the creature.

See also **British Museum of Natural History.**

Cherry Island   Situated in Loch Ness close to **Fort Augustus,** it was once connected to the mainland by a rocky causeway which has long since disappeared. A notable sighting to occur here was that of **Simon Cameron (1926).**

Cheshire, Mrs   A tourist from Stafford, who in early August 1933 allegedly told the staff of a **Fort Augustus** shop that she had seen 'a big black object in the water, which looked like a piece of shining rock'. It is claimed that she was unaware of the tales of the 'great beast of the Loch' and was alarmed when she discovered what she must have seen. Certainly, Mrs Cheshire could provide no natural explanation for what she saw and left the district convinced that it was indeed the Loch Ness Monster.

Chisholm, Duncan   Correspondent for the *Inverness Courier* who in November 1962 stated that the reports of a beast living in Loch Ness dated back to the time of the Battle of Waterloo. Chisholm then recorded a tale of how his mother's great-aunt, Miss Bella MacGruer, who had lived at Markethill, **Fort Augustus**, would warn local youths not to bathe in the Loch, as she and others had frequently seen the '**water horse**'.

Chisholm, Hugh   Inverness lorry driver, who, along with his wife, Mhairi, and niece, Margaret Sutherland, had a strange sighting of an animal in the Loch on 7 August 1978. All three saw a head and hump rise out of the water, describing it as 'really huge'. He could not estimate how far offshore the creature was, nor could he estimate its size. Mrs Mhairi Chisholm later stated that her husband had claimed to have seen Nessie on a previous occasion, but then she had laughed at him.

Christmas Day sighting   The first reported sighting of anything unusual in the Loch on Christmas Day. **John Cameron, A. Mack**, and **D. McIntosh**, all saw a 10-foot-long black hump, motionless in the water, on 25 December 1933. When this moved off, closer scrutiny revealed that it appeared to have another object about 6 feet in front of it, which was deemed to be the creature's head. The animal seemed to move around slowly before submerging.
   See also **Cameron, John; Mack, A.; McIntosh, D.**

Christopher, Gillian   *See under* **Chapman, Andrew.**

Christopher, P.M.   *See under* **Pyman, Col. D.**

Circus, Bertram Mills   The circus, keen to find new and unique attractions, saw the Loch Ness monster as a most attractive proposition. In 1933, in an attempt to gain press publicity, it offered a reward of £20,000 for its capture. In order to protect this prize (displaying their genuine belief that the reward could be claimed) they took out insurance with Lloyds of London that cost them £80.

Clark, Muriel   Claimed to have made a sighting on 31 August 1979, along with **Isobel MacLeod**. They were driving past **Temple Pier** when they saw a man studying the Loch through a pair of binoculars. Looking out across the bay they saw a large water disturbance, with huge waves crashing towards the road. The two women stopped the car in which they were travelling and looked out over the Loch, where they saw a 'huge head' and what appeared to be a coil of a snake; below the surface there appeared to be a huge body. Both described the head as being flat and snake-like. Within a few seconds the creature submerged in a manner similar to that of a submarine.

See also **MacLeod, Isobel.**

Clayton, Mr and Mrs D. The couple made a sighting on 26 July 1969 at 3.30 p.m. from **Urquhart Bay.** A single, dark-coloured hump about 6 feet long and 3 feet high suddenly appeared on the water and moved (in what was felt to be a forward direction) at a speed estimated as 6-7 m.p.h. The Claytons were about 300-400 yards from the object, which was also independently sighted by **Mr and Mrs Maurice Smith** from a different location around the bay.

See also **Smith, Mr and Mrs Maurice.**

Cobb, John (1899-1952) A fur-broker by trade, John Cobb was obsessed by speed and breaking records. In 1938 he took the world land speed record to 350.2 m.p.h. The following year he increased it to 369.7 m.p.h., before finally reaching 403 m.p.h. in 1947. Satisfied with his records on land, Cobb turned his attention to the water, which brought him to Loch Ness. On the morning of 29 September 1952 Cobb broke the world water speed record in his 6,000-h.p. jet boat *Crusader*.

Having made a northerly run up the mirror-calm surface of the Loch he turned the boat around and commenced another record-breaking run which took him to 206 m.p.h., before the boat hit a patch of turbulence, shot into the air and disintegrated when it hit the water again. Cobb was dragged from the wreckage and died on a hillside at Achnahannet. The people of Glen Urquhart erected a memorial that now stands on the side of the road, to 'A Very Gallant Gentleman'.

It was later claimed that the boat crashed due to disturbance of the water caused by a wake created by the agitated monster; **Tim Dinsdale** studied camera footage of the event and believed that this was the cause of the crash. It is, however, now accepted that the water disturbance which caused the incident was the settling remnants of the wake created by Cobb's initial run.

Cockrell, H.L. A trout farmer, known locally as 'Gus', Cockrell carried out a one-man expedition in the autumn of 1958. He paddled about the Loch in a canoe, with a flash camera attached to his life-jacket, in the hope of catching a glimpse of the animal. On the final day of his outing he saw an unusual wake, about 50 yards away from his position, which appeared to be heading towards him at a steady pace. He turned his canoe towards the object and took a photograph; but when he reached the area where his sighting had been made all he found was a long stick about one inch thick.

Cockrell had his film developed and was surprised to see something completely different on the print. Whatever it was he had photographed gave the impression of a single large hump with what appeared to be a smaller object in front of it. The photograph was first reproduced in the *Weekly Scotsman* of 16 October 1958.

Cockrell remained uncertain of what he had seen, believing that the physical exhaustion of paddling over the Loch for the duration of his expedition might have induced a mental fatigue that caused him to believe that the small log or branch found at the scene of his photograph gave the appearance of a living creature. To this day it remains unclear just what Cockrell witnessed, and the common belief is that the object photographed was indeed little more than a floating log or tree branch.

coelacanth   Since 1933, when sightings of the Loch Ness phenomenon became more frequent, there has been a theory that the mysterious creature living in the Loch's depths may be a surviving prehistoric species. This, without doubt, is the most popular theory to date. It is an assumption which is instantly dismissed by the majority of the Western World, who cannot comprehend how such creatures could possibly survive, having been expertly proclaimed as extinct.

As with all things, mankind does not hold all the answers, for in 1938, a fishing boat off the coast of Africa caught alive a carnivorous fish known as a coelacanth. In 1952 a second specimen was found off Madagascar. Since then a number of others have been caught, some at depths of around 1,200 feet.

The coelacanth dates back to the Jurassic era, and the living specimens caught have hardly altered since the end of the Cretaceous period, some 70 million years ago. Believers in the Loch Ness monster often quote the existence of the coelacanth in the twentieth century as positive proof that such creatures can and still do exist.

Collins, Sir Godfrey   Secretary of State for Scotland in 1933. After much public hysteria about 'monster sightings', he wrote to the Chief Constable of Inverness inquiring whether any of the constables employed around the Loch had any knowledge of the said monster. At that point, no official reports had been received by the Chief Constable from any of his junior ranks, so Sir Godfrey could positively dispel all such suggestions that the Highlands of Scotland were in any danger from the presence of prehistoric creatures.

Collins, Norman   Deputy Chairman of Associated Television, who joined the **Loch Ness Investigation Bureau** as Chairman in 1964. Collins was an enthusiastic participant in much of what the Bureau attempted. He funded many of the Bureau's projects and also provided some excellent publicity for the efforts made to film the creature.

colour   Reports of sightings mention a number of different colours in connection with the alleged creature. The most popular and frequent descriptions indicate that dark brown or grey is the most likely skin coloration. There are, however, a number of differing opinions about the skin texture, with some witnesses claiming it to be 'oily', others 'scaly'.

Columba, Saint (521-597)   Irish missionary, born at Gartan (County Donegal) in Ireland in 521, and said to be of royal blood. It has been further claimed that Columba bore responsibility for the bloody battle of Culdremhne in 561, in which some 3,000 men were killed. Apparently, the wrath of families bereaved by the battle focused on Columba, so, for his own safety, he elected to leave his beloved Ireland. He came to the tiny island of Iona (then known as Icolmkill) off the west coast of Scotland, where he founded a monastery and became known for his missionary work in Scotland. According to his biographer, **Saint Adamnan**, in 565 Columba 'drove away a certain water monster'. Vol. 6, bk II, chap. 27 of his biography of St Columba contains the following description of events:

At another time again, when the blessed man was staying for some days in the province of the Picts, he found it necessary to cross the river Ness and when he came to the bank thereof he sees some of the inhabitants burying a poor unfortunate man, whom, as those who were burying him themselves reported, some water monster had a little while before snatched at as he was swimming, and bitten him with a most savage bite, and whose hapless corpse some men who came in a boat to give assistance, though too late, caught hold of by putting out hooks. The blessed man, however, on hearing this directs that one of his companions shall swim out and bring to him the boat that is on the other side, sailing it across.

On hearing the direction of the holy and famous man, Lugne Mocumin, obeying without delay, threw off all his clothes except his undergarments, and cast himself into the water. Now the monster, which was not so much satisfied as eager for prey, was lying hid at the bottom of the river, but perceiving that the water above was disturbed by him who was crossing, suddenly emerged, and swimming to the man who was crossing in the middle of the stream, rushed up with a great roar and open mouth.

Then the blessed man looked on, while all who were there, the heathen as well as the brethren, were stricken with very great terror, and with his holy hand raised high, he formed the sign of the cross in the empty air, invoked the Name of God, and commanded the fierce monster, saying, 'Think not to go further nor touch thou that man. Quick! Go Back!'

Then the beast, on hearing this voice of the saint, was terrified and fled backwards more rapidly than he came, as if dragged by cords, although it had come so near to Lugne as he swam, that there was not more than the length of a punt pole between the man and the beast. Then the brethren, seeing that the beast had gone away and that their comrade Lugne was returned to them safe and sound in the boat, glorified God in the blessed man greatly marvelling.

The above record is in fact the first recorded sighting of a monster in the region of Loch Ness, and it is perhaps feasible that this local legend survived for centuries afterwards, and thus underlies the modern legend. It is time to say, however, that the early biographers of holy persons usually tend to emphasize their over-coming of evil, or performance of miracles in some form or another, so it is reasonable to assume that the tale was elaborated during the years between Columba's death and Adamnan's biography on him.

There is also another tale involving St Columba and the monster of Loch Ness. Otta Swire, whose *The Highlands and their Legends* was published in 1963, relates an altogether separate legend involving Columba's visit to the Loch.

On arrival at Loch Ness, the saint was greeted by white-capped waves, which looked most uninviting. Suddenly, among the tossing white wave crests appeared a black head – it was the **water horse** of Loch Ness come to pay his duty to St Columba. The water horse, understanding that the party wanted to travel the length of the Loch in order to continue their journey, realized that the waters were far too rough for the party to row through. It took the form of an athletic young man, strung the boat tethers together, then resumed horse form and, taking the tethers between its teeth, it pulled the boats containing St Columba and his party down the Loch. The saint then blessed Each Uisge and gave him the freedom of Loch Ness forever.

According to a further legend, the Loch Ness water horse is believed at some stage to have made a pact with the devil. The water horse believed that as the River Ness ran through the Loch, and as it could not cross running water, it could never cross from one side of the Loch to the other. However, the devil promised the water horse, that if it agreed to give him one ride a year over any stretch of water he chose, then he would, in return, ensure that every drop of running water which entered the Loch would imme-diately flow back out. Unbeknown to the water horse, a similar pact had been made with the devil in olden times, preventing running water entering any of the Highland Lochs, in order that it should not trouble any of the Loch creatures.

A statue of Saint Columba can be found at Fort Augustus Abbey, and he is depicted in a stained-glass window in the Abbey chapel.

Considine, Anthony Alleged sighting in June 1937. Considine was out on the Loch in a boat with a fisherman friend, Andrew Smith, and the pair looked into the water from the stern of their craft. There they saw three separate creatures, dark grey in colour and about 3 feet long, with long necks; they looked distinctly similar to eels. The creatures, which were swimming away from the boat, appeared to have four limbs, which both witnesses likened to flippers; the rear two were held close to the body and were apparently used for pushing the animal forward.

Cottier, Kenneth On Good Friday, 4 April 1947, Cottier was in a car travelling with **Mr John MacKray, Mr J.W. McKillop CBE** and his son Norman. At a position about a mile from Drumnadrochit they sighted a creature in the water. Cottier reported that: 'I could see two shiny humps close together, of which the front one was the larger, travelling in a straight line up the Loch rather nearer to the opposite side. They then disappeared completely, leaving a considerable slipstream.' He dismissed suggestions that it was a motor boat, as the day was calm and clear, and mechanically created noise would have been clearly evident, yet no such noise was heard by any of the group.

See also **McKillop, J.W.**; **MacKay, John.**

Coulton, John Schoolboy who allegedly sighted something in the Loch on 22 August 1977. This was simultaneous with the sighting by **Gwen and Peter Smith** from the shore just north of **Urquhart Castle.** Coulton, who had been with **Christopher Idle**, later told author **Tim Dinsdale** that they were at the Loch carrying out a school project. This was not corroborated, because according to a school spokesperson, 'no such project was set to the pupils concerned'. As a result other researchers have questioned the authenticity of his story, casting doubt on whether the sighting was a genuine one or a hoax.

See also **Idle, Christopher.**

Cowan-Martin, Andy BBC reporter who allegedly sighted an animal in June 1939, while flying from Kirkwall to Inverness. The pilot of the aircraft had volunteered to take the plane over Loch Ness, so that the passengers might see the 'monster'. As the plane flew over the Loch, Cowan-Martin believed he had a clear sighting, lasting about half a minute, of an animal with two very prominent humps, and a head not dissimilar to that of a seal. No one else on board the aircraft saw anything which they could describe as unusual.

Cowan-Martin's belief that he had seen the infamous beast of Loch Ness never faltered; he could not conceive what else it could have been. He later said of his sighting, 'I cannot begin to believe what I saw. It was some form of aquatic creature the like of which I have never before seen.'

Craig, H.J.   Reported sighting in 1889. While Craig was out fishing with his brother in a small boat near **Urquhart Castle**, a great form suddenly reared out of the water and moved off at great speed. The boys returned home and described to their father what they had seen, presumably in the hope that he would be able to provide a reasonable explanation for the creature. However, when their father heard the tale, he told both boys that they should never repeat it again. The story was reproduced in the *Inverness Courier* on 27 September 1947.

Craven, Mr and Mrs Geoffrey   At 9.20 a.m. on 6 August 1969 the Cravens saw a two-humped object surface in the Loch, creating a disturbance in the water, and then submerged. The humps they described were estimated as being between 25-30 feet long, and projecting 3-4 feet out of the water. The Cravens thought they were about 60 yards from them.

crocodile claw   This was found at the side of the Loch close to **Urquhart Castle** in 1934. Well preserved, it had been placed there by an unknown prankster in an attempt to fool the media visiting the Loch searching for a story.

Cruickshank, Alfred   In April 1923 Cruickshank, from Buckie in Banffshire, made a land sighting of the monster. At about 5.00 a.m. he was driving his Model T Ford along the old road on the Loch's northern shore, about two miles north of **Invermoriston**. He crested a small hill, and his headlamps picked out a large object on the outside of a bend in the road about 50 yards ahead of him.

Cruickshank described the creature as having a large body and standing between 5 and 7 feet tall. It was a green-khaki colour, almost identical to a frog, with a lower belly that appeared to be cream in colour. The main bulk of the body was in a hump shape, its belly virtually trailing on the ground, and four thick legs were visible (he described them as being like an elephant's) with webbed feet. He estimated that the trailing tail was approximately 12 feet long. The creature moved with a waddling motion, and its head was described as big and pug nosed. As he passed the spot Cruickshank heard a grunting noise similar to the bark of a dog.

Cumming, Mrs Together with **D. McGillvray** reported sighting a 'hump' whilst looking at the Loch through a telescope at around 9.30 a.m. on 29 August 1923. A large dark-black hump 'the size of a horse's body' suddenly appeared on the Loch surface, and lay motionless before sinking with a splash.
See also **McGillvray, D.**

Currie, James Retired London bank manager who allegedly filmed a sighting whilst on holiday at the Loch in 1938. Currie, who was keen to film the creature, set up his hand-held cine camera on a tripod in order to maintain a watch on the Loch surface from the south shore opposite **Urquhart Bay**. On the eleventh day of his watch he is alleged to have sighted a long ripple moving at considerable speed about 300 yards from the shore. Three large humps then appeared, and finally a long neck and a small triangular-shaped head. The colour was described as grey-brown. The film of the creature is said to be stored in a London bank vault, where it has lain for some sixty years.

The story of the Currie film was brought to public attention by an article by a Charles Fraser in the *Aberdeen Evening Express* of 18 September 1973. This reported that a leading 'monster-hunter', Roland Brown, was attempting to meet with solicitors to have the film released. Brown was quoted as saying that James Currie, who placed the film in the bank vault, had died over twenty years earlier.

Efforts have been made to locate both Fraser and Brown. No one involved with the mystery in the 1970s seems to know of a Roland Brown, as might have been expected if he was a leading 'monster-hunter'. Attempts to trace Charles Fraser have also been unsuccessful. Staff reporters who have worked for the *Aberdeen Evening Express* since before the era of the report know of no one by that name, although he may have been a freelance reporter.

Searches with London banks, too, have provided a negative result, with none knowing of any approach from solicitors, or of any film. It was claimed that the film had been submitted to the

Kodak laboratories in London for examination, but again, a thorough search of records failed to trace any such incident.

The story of the Currie film bears a direct similarity to that of the film allegedly shot by **Dr Farquhar MacRae** in 1935. There is no evidence to indicate that it exists. (Tales of films of the Loch Ness Monster which are locked away in London bank vaults should be treated with extreme caution.)

D

Daily Mail Sponsored and mounted an expedition to Loch Ness in December 1933, employing self-proclaimed big-game hunter, **Marmaduke Wetherell**. Unfortunately, this expedition did more harm to serious research into the phenomenon than any other to date. Wetherell made wild and spurious claims to have located the animal's spoor within days of his arrival at the Loch, and these were published by the paper on 21 December 1933 under the headline: 'Monster of Loch Ness is Not A Legend But A Fact'.

The evidence Wetherell provided turned out to be the footprint of a hippopotamus, apparently planted as a hoax (*see* **Hippopotamus hoax**). Some claim that Marmaduke Wetherell was an accomplice to the hoax, others that he and the newspaper were totally innocent victims of it. Since then, the *Mail* has reported reasonably responsibly upon the case and has refrained from employing further self-proclaiming 'big-game' hunters to track down such phenomena.

Dallas, Alastair *See under* **MacRae, Dr Farquhar**

Davidson, Lorraine Eye-witness, interviewed by satellite television's Discovery Channel. Her home overlooks the Loch. Looking out across the water, she saw a large wake about half a mile long on the surface, with something protruding out of the water ahead of it. The sighting lasted for about 10-15 minutes. Lorraine Davidson claimed that she was used to seeing motor boats and other such explainable sightings, but on this occasion knew instinctively that what she was looking at was totally alien to everything she had previously observed.

Davidson, W.H. Eye-witness who had a fifteen-minute sighting at 9.30 a.m. in July 1954, along with his mother and sister, **Mrs Cary**.

A single hump appeared, measuring approximately 30 feet in length and 3 feet in height, and dark in colour. In front of this a 3-foot head and neck emerged from the water. The animal moved at about 5-6 m.p.h., and submerged on several occasions.

Davies, Peter   Member of the **Loch Ness Investigation Bureau** and skipper of boat *Narwhal*. He sighted something in the Loch through field glasses on 6 August 1967 at 5.20 p.m. A single object of about 10 feet by 3 feet suddenly surfaced and then submerged.

Dawson, Master James   Made a five-minute sighting on Sunday 9 August 1964 at a distance of about 200 yards. Dawson claimed to have seen two dark humps appear in the water, which moved inter-mittently. Without warning, the 'black-coloured' humps sank from view, leaving what appeared to be some disturbance on the water surface.

Dawson, Jay   Reporter with *Aberdeen Evening Express*, who witnessed a mysterious object off **Urquhart Bay** on 13 June 1963. This sighting was also witnessed by members of the **Loch Ness Investigation Bureau**. Miss Dawson later described the experience: 'I have never seen anything like it in the Loch before, and I am convinced it was the monster.' The object was about half a mile from where she stood at **Urquhart Castle**, but was too far away to make out any precise details. As she described it, the 'monster' appeared to be playing in the water and submerged before she could get a better view. One of the Bureau cameras did manage to film it, but the film was largely ruined by a heat haze, which impaired clarity, so no direct evidence was deduced.

Deacon, Mr and Mrs Fred   The Deacons made a surface sighting on 10 July 1968 at about 11.20 a.m. A long black shape partially broke the water and travelled slowly along the Loch, causing a ripple as it did so. It did not seem to have the appearance of either a wave or a boat wake, but looked solid. As the couple continued to monitor its progress it sank from view.

Deans, John   Surface sighting shortly after midday on 30 December 1933. John Deans, a plumber from Inverness, was motoring alongside the Loch, some distance from **Urquhart Castle**.

He gazed out onto the water and there saw a 'great black object'. In his own mind Deans had no doubts 'that it was the monster, about which so much has been written'. This sighting coincided with that of W.U. **Goodbody**.

Death of the Loch Ness Monster   In 1941 the Italian newspaper *Popola d'Italia* reported that the Loch Ness Monster had been killed by an Italian bomber pilot during an air raid. Its carcass was allegedly seen floating on the surface by the pilot who killed it.

Deepscan, Operation   See under **Operation Deepscan**.

deer   According to Steuart (*The Loch Ness Monster – The Evidence*, 1986, p. 112), the **Greta Finlay** sighting of August 1952 could be attributed to 'misperception of a young roe deer', swimming in the Loch.

Demaio, Emalio   One of two South American tourists, the other being Nikhl Banjer, who, while visiting the Loch, both saw a dark hump appear in the water off Invermoriston on 21 July 1996. As is the case with a great many witnesses, Demaio and Banjer both believed that what they saw was a solid object and not any kind of freak wave or boat wave.

Denman, Mr   Surface sighting in the summer of 1935. Accompanied by **Mr Hunter Gordon**, Denman saw what looked like a single hump which looked similar to an upturned 'boat'. The object moved through the water at a slow, almost casual, pace for about 7½ minutes before submerging.
    See also **Hunter Gordon, S.**

Dewar, Mr and Mrs William   As the couple drove towards Fort Augustus on the A82 at 11.45 a.m. on 22 June 1971 they saw a creature with a 'snake-like' head and neck about 300 yards out in the Loch. It was moving rapidly in a southerly direction. Some 4 feet behind the head was a 10-foot-long hump, dark in colour, that stood about 2-3 feet out of the water. After about one minute the animal submerged.

Dickson, Mr & Mrs Robert   The couple encountered something strange on the Loch on 7 July 1966 at around 10.15 p.m. They witnessed a single black hump, approximately 7-8 feet in length, moving through the water at a speed they estimated as being 7-8 m.p.h. As they continued to watch the hump it seemed to dive below the water, rather than sink.

Dieckhoff, Dom Cyril   A Russian *émigré* who was a monk at Fort Augustus Abbey, and who maintained diaries mentioning numerous monster sightings, gathered by practical research in the area. Dieckhoff was a monk at Fort Augustus Abbey, and claimed to have had two sightings of the animal.

The first of these was recorded on 30 August 1934, when, looking from an upper gallery window of the Abbey, he saw what appeared to be a straight neck sticking upright out of the water, some 600 yards from where he stood. Immediately behind this neck he saw a small, dark-coloured, round object, which he believed to be part of a small hump. He was certain that what he saw was a living object and not any mechanically propelled vessel.

Dieckhoff's second sighting occurred on 5 May 1940, when he was in the company of two other monks, Brother Robert MacKay and Brother Robert Murray. Dieckhoff first noticed a wash moving towards **Glendoe**; this was more noticeable because the Loch was dead calm. Looking more carefully, he saw a black-coloured 'perpendicular pole-like' object moving through the water at a 'fairly moderate' speed. He thought this was about 4 feet long. The closer it came to Glendoe boathouse, the smaller and more circular the wash became, until it finally died out as the object creating it disappeared beneath the water.

Dieckhoff initially believed that the creature he and so many others had seen within the Loch was some kind of large fish. He later changed this opinion in favour of the **plesiosaur** theory. He was an avid collector of tales referring to sightings and would seek out eye-witnesses in order to record their impressions. Dieckhoff intended to write his own book upon the case, but died in 1950, before he could do so. Author **Constance Whyte** gained access to his personal diaries and used them in compiling her own work on the subject, *More Than A Legend*, which was published in 1957.

Dinsdale, Tim (1924-1987)   Tim Dinsdale was an aeronautical engineer who turned self-proclaimed monster hunter in or around

1960. He arrived at the Loch for the first time on 16 April 1960 and began his constant 'monster watch'. On 23 April of the same year, at about 9.00 a.m., through his binoculars Dinsdale had spotted an object that he instantly knew to be some unknown phenomenon – its wake was not typical of that caused by a boat, and was too large to be made by any other creature known to live in the Loch. Using a small Bolex camera, he filmed the object moving in a zig-zag in the Loch about 1,300 yards from where he stood, overlooking Foyers Bay. This film – so far as is known, the first-ever movie-film of the animal – was later shown on BBC Television's *Panorama* on 13 June 1960 and also featured in that day's *Daily Mail*.

In 1966 the film was examined by the Royal Air Force Joint Air Reconnaissance Intelligence Centre, (JARIC) which confirmed that the object it showed was not a boat but a living animal. (Dinsdale had in fact filmed a boat in the same area of the Loch in order to prove that such a craft would be identifiably different from the object he had filmed.)

The film as undergone all kinds of further examinations, most recently in 1993, aided by computer enhancement (see **Project Urquhart**). The latest Discovery Channel investigation observed a previously unseen shadow behind and beneath the head of the wake. This forms the distinct shape of what appears to be a large body, lying just beneath the surface of the water and clearly attached to whatever it was that Dinsdale filmed.

After the 1960 sighting, as a result of which he became accepted as something of an 'expert' on the subject, Dinsdale was an inspirational member of a number of expeditions. He directed the **Loch Ness Investigation Bureau**'s surface watch of 1970, and for some time actually lived on the Loch. He wrote authoritatively upon the subject; among his works are *Loch Ness Monster* (1961) and *Project Water Horse – The True Story of the Monster Quest at Loch Ness* (1977).

This most respected monster hunter of them all died in 1987, but his outstanding endeavours ensure that his memory will live on.

See also **Leviathans, The**; *Loch Ness Monster*; **Parliament; Project Urquhart**.

Dobb, Reverend William   Along with his family saw an unusual wave movement at 3.15 p.m. on 13 August 1960. The group initially saw 'several' large waves moving together, along the dead calm Loch. A few seconds later, close to the initial water disturbance on the Loch surface, they were shocked to see a large black hump appear and then disappear. Within moments this was replaced by two black humps, which, again, almost immediately submerged.

Dobbie, Peter   Surface sighting at 11.30 a.m. on 15 July 1967. Dobbie, a service manager, described the weather as being clear and sunny with no obstruction to his view. The object he saw was large, black in colour and gave an impression of being smooth in texture. It appeared to have a tail, which rose and submerged as it propelled itself through the water. It eventually moved out of his field of vision.

dolphins   At one time the **Academy of Applied Science** planned to use dolphins fitted with cameras and strobes activated by sonar to carry out underwater searches of the Loch's depths, but one of the trained dolphins died before this could be done. The plan was eventually scrapped when it was realized that the dolphins involved were not of the type which could adapt to fresh water, and there would have been serious problems in getting them to work in such an alien environment.

Dores   A village on the south-east shore of Loch Ness close to its northern end. The open views from Dores Bay make it an ideal observation point. Notable sightings from this area include those by **Ian Milne** on 14 July 1930; **R.H. Lowrie** on 7 August 1960; **Dick Raynor,** who filmed a large unidentifiable object moving in the water on 13 June 1967; **Graham Hall** on 17 June 1993, and the infamous land sighting of July 1933 by **Mr and Mrs George Spicer**.

Drumnadrochit   Village on the north-west shore of Loch Ness, which is possibly the area's most important tourist centre. It lies about 14 miles from Inverness at the foot of Glen Urquhart. The Drumnadrochit Hotel houses the official Loch Ness Monster **Exhibition,** which incorporates the basic history of the Loch and its surroundings, including data from previous ecological projects. Also in Drumnadrochit is the 'Original Loch Ness Monster Exhibition'.

Notable sightings to occur near Drumnadrochit include those of

Eric H. Bright, who saw a large creature enter the Loch in 1880; **Derek Fowles** on 11 March 1957; **Wallace V. Turl** on 18 April 1968; **David Quinn** on 4 March 1977; **William Wright** on 17 June 1978; and **Derek Quinley** on 14 July 1997.

Drysdale, Douglas   Lecturer in Visceral Physiology at a London college, who in July 1970 suggested that any monsters there might have been in Loch Ness must have been killed by pollution. Drysdale was convinced that the creatures could not have survived in the Loch's waters without suffering the effects of some form of man-made pollution, which, he felt, would cause fatal illness. On the very day that Drysdale made this claim, two separate sightings of mysterious animals were recorded at the Loch.

Dundas, The Rev. N. and Mrs   The Rev. and Mrs Dundas are credited with being the first individuals to believe they had taken a photograph of the Loch Ness animal. Looking through field glasses on 24 November 1933 the couple saw something unusual in the water off Temple Pier, near Drumnadrochit.

The Rev. Dundas later described it: 'An object appeared in the water. There was not much body to be seen, but I saw the tail distinctly. It was causing a great commotion, thrashing the water with much force.' Mrs Dundas believed that 'the tail gave the appearance of thrashing the water like a propeller.'

It was Mrs Dundas who attempted to photograph the creature. However, the shot was taken directly against the sun and the frame could not be successfully processed. The object was also witnessed by the pier master at Temple Pier.

Dunn, James   *See under* **Sigel, Donald.**

Dunton, C.E.   Sighted a curious creature in the Loch on 20 June 1948 whilst in the company of **Mr S. Hunter Gordon.** Two coil-like 'eyebrow-shaped' objects appeared in the Loch, black or dark grey in colour. Each coil/hump was believed to be about 30 feet in length and about 3 feet thick at the surface. The sighting lasted about five minutes.

Durkin, Les   On 22 May 1967 Les Durkin of the **Loch Ness Investigation Bureau** filmed two humps moving through the water near **Invermoriston**. The film, which was approximately 15 seconds long, was later examined by **JARIC** which reported: 'The length of the disturbed areas are 50 feet, 65 feet and 45 feet. Their speed from left to right is approximately 6 knots, and they have portions raised some 2 feet above water level.' Durkin himself claimed that the humps were at a distance of about 800 yards from his position, between 10 and 13 yards in length and about 60 centimetres high, and travelled at about 2 yards per second.

Duthy, Charles   Captain of the Fraserburgh trawler *Tea Rose* who detected on his on-board sonar a large object rising through the water at about 7 knots. He was convinced that it wasn't a wave pattern or any kind of wake. He further believed that what he saw was a solid mass. Duthy later told colleagues that he 'had never seen anything like it before'.

E

Each Uisge *See under* **Columba, Saint; Water-bull; Water Kelpie.**

Eames, Mr and Mrs Roland   Surface sighting on 17 May 1964 at a range of 400 yards. A single, motionless, dark-coloured, 15-foot hump suddenly surfaced, then submerged, creating a large area of water disturbance as it did so. The couple watched the area for several more minutes but saw nothing further which could account for the sighting, and no boats or other objects were in the area at the time the hump appeared. Both were of the opinion that it was a living creature.

Edwards Deep   A depression in the Loch floor just outside Urquhart Bay discovered by auxiliary coastguard and local businessman George Edwards around 1990. Edwards operates the boat *Ness-Hunter* out of the bay. From estimated measurements recorded in 1997, it is believed that the hole/depression is virtually circular in shape and approximately 30 metres in width. It was impossible to estimate the depth of the depression at the time.

Experts were quick to dismiss suggestions that the depression might be an entrance to an underwater cavern, and hence the media view that it could be an access point to the Loch Ness monster's home. Instead, it is believed that the depression has been caused by underwater seismic events which triggered an avalanche causing the Loch floor to slide away. If this was so, however, why does there seem to be no trace of the debris that would have been dislodged by such an event? If such seismic events were reasonably common there would presumably be other such depressions on the Loch floor, but none has yet been located.

George Edwards himself believed that this cavern could lead to a network of caves. He is a firm believer that something unknown lives in the Loch, and that there must be more than one of them.

Further investigation of Edwards Deep will be necessary before all speculation can be dismissed.

See also **cave dwellers.**

Edwards, Margaret   Mrs Edwards, an Inverness housewife, filmed something 'large and solid' in the water in 1966, when a solitary large hump and what resembled a tail surfaced close to Abriachan Pier. Experts who later examined the film stated that it did indeed reveal a disturbance in the water and merely suggested that what was filmed had the presence of something solid. Mrs Edwards was convinced that what she filmed was not a man-made object, but a real living creature. Some experts later claimed that what the film showed was otters at play, others that it was nothing more than a freak wave.

eel   Many sceptics try to rationalize the Loch Ness phenomenon by dismissing the validity of many of the sightings and reaffirming their belief that no unknown species of animal exists in the Loch. Suggestions abound that all sightings have been simple misinterpretations of natural wildlife as unknown creatures. One of the most common theories is that there is a breed of a giant eel in the Loch. The Loch is indeed full of eels, yet no giant eel of a size that corresponds to the sightings of the so-called monster has yet been caught.

elephant   Suggested explanation of species which could be misinterpreted as the Loch Ness Monster by innocent eye-witnesses. This theory was proposed in November 1992 edition of the *British Institute of Radiology Bulletin* by Paul Goddard. *See also* **Goddard, Paul.**

elephant seal   On the last day of March 1972, a team from the Yorkshire Zoo publicly announced that they had found the carcass of a strange animal washed up on the Loch shore near Foyers. They further stated that they were taking the carcass south into England for examination. The half-ton carcass – minus whiskers and with its mouth padded out to disguise its appearance – was packed in ice, placed in a truck and removed from the Loch side for its journey to England. The removal generated much publicity and massive public condemnation in Scotland, along the lines of: 'What right have the English to take our monster from us?' The authorities eventually intervened, stopped the lorry at the Forth Road Bridge and recovered the carcass. Its true identity was then discovered when experts examined the remains. The date? 1 April 1972!

Ellice, Jean and Sandy   *See under* **Ellice, Mrs.**

Ellice, Mrs   In December 1948 Mrs Ellice was walking along the Lochside with her son Sandy and daughter Jean. Looking out over the Loch she was somewhat surprised to see two 'large dark-coloured' humps appear in the water moving very slowly. They eventually submerged, only for a neck and head to appear, before Mrs Ellice finally lost sight of the object.

Elliott, Vivianne and Edward   On 30 September 1965, at about 6.45 a.m., Vivianne and Edward Elliott noticed a mysterious large wash on the Loch. Because no mechanical objects were in the area at the time, the Elliotts were confused by its sudden appearance and scanned the water surface to see what might have caused it, but saw nothing large enough to create such a commotion. About fifteen minutes later a dark grey object broke the surface about half a mile away, and then slowly sank from view. The couple were certain that what they had seen was a very real and solid object, and that this was not a case of mistaken identity.

Ellisford, Captain   According to a report in the *Scottish Daily Express* of 12 August 1933, 'an effort to photograph the Loch Ness Monster is to be made by an ex-Army officer, Captain Ellisford, a well-known amateur photographer.' Unfortunately, the results of this effort are not known, and certainly no evidence was ever forthcoming from the Captain. This may well have been the first recorded attempt by any individual to photograph the animal.

Encyclopaedia Brittanica   In 1969 the *Encyclopaedia Britannica* announced that the 'Loch Ness Monster' was among the leading ten subjects on which they most regularly received requests for information from around the world.

Europa   Name of the Goodyear airship which flew over the Loch in June 1982, packed with £45,000 worth of highly sensitive sonar equipment deemed suitable for picking up any unusual echoes from deep within the Loch's depths. On board was John Blashford-Snell, author of *Mysteries – Encounters with the Unexplained* (Bodley Head, 1983), which covers the story of the Loch Ness Monster. Despite several journeys over the water, nothing of any note was recorded, nor was any aerial sighting of the elusive creature made.

Evening Standard, The   Some time in 1933 this newspaper printed an imaginary tale of an expedition made to the Loch by Messrs Low and Terry, two intrepid 'monster hunters'. The story-line was weak and ineffective and failed to convey any sense of realism for those who had not been to the Loch or knew nothing of its environment. No accurate facts could be gleaned from the tale. It does, however, depict just how big a sensation the news from Loch Ness was.

exhibitions   The first real exhibition relating to the mystery of the Loch Ness monster was originally situated in Fort Augustus, in the late 1970s. This was followed in 1980 by further exhibitions, two at the Drumnadrochit Hotel and one in the Great Glen exhibition at Fort Augustus. In 1984 the Loch Ness Monster Research Exhibition was opened in Inverness. The Drumnadrochit Hotel exhibition pulled in 120,000 visitors during 1984, making it one of Scotland's top twenty attractions.

By 1985 the interest in the phenomenon was so great, the Drumnadrochit Hotel amalgamated with the Inverness exhibition (which moved to the hotel site), the combined exhibition offering a greatly improved information service for tourists and students of the case. Today it provides a full commentary for the visitors who walk through its many rooms and an audio-visual history of virtually everything relating to the Loch. More recently it has concerned itself with the Loch's ecological history.

We are told that the Official Loch Ness Monster Exhibition hopes, in the future, to establish a good source of reference data for the use of students fascinated by the case.

Close by, again in Drumnadrochit, there is a second exhibition, the Original Loch Ness Monster Exhibition, which provides a video show in its cinema and has an excellent souvenir shop.

exorcism   The Loch is reported to have been exorcized on several occasions, most notably on 2 June 1973, when, at the request of author **F.W. Holiday**, a retired vicar from Devon, the **Rev. Donald Omand** carried out the rite. He confessed to having never exorcized anything so vast. Also present at the exorcism was **Wing Commander Basil Cary**.

Within twenty-four hours, further sightings had been made and the team that carried out the exorcism claimed these as 'positive proof that the creature which resides in the Loch is not of an evil kind'.

explanations Over the years, dozens of apparent experts have attempted to justify the mysterious sightings of a large animal in Loch Ness as a number of different known objects or natural phenomena.

The most popular natural explanations identify the creatures as **basking sharks, beluga whales, birds, boat wakes, deer, eels, logs, mines, mirages, newts, otters, seals, sharks,** and **waves.** None of the explanations provides a wholly suitable solution, however. In November 1950 the *Daily Mail* reported that sightings of humps on the waters of Loch Ness could easily be explained away: a string of eight mines had been laid in the Loch by a minesweeper in 1918, so the appearance of humped-backed creatures was explicable as nothing more than the mines occasionally surfacing.

Eye-witness testimonies, most of them describing a familiar pattern of movement, shape and colour, seem to indicate that some large creature does live in the Loch, although without physical evidence, science cannot accept this. Most of the above explanations involve creatures that, in their natural habitat, would be seen with greater frequency – and we are expected to believe that, because they are in Loch Ness, living creatures adopt a totally untypical lifestyle, often acting irrationally and avoiding contact with mankind.

The case for the existence of a monster can be faulted, but the basic evidence for the presence of a hitherto unknown creature in Loch Ness is, in most cases, far more feasible than the explanations so far proposed by amateurs or experts.

F

Falconer, Julie While staying at the Loch Ness Caravan and Camping Park at Invermoriston, Julie Falconer had a very strange experience. At about 3.00 a.m. on the morning of 9 August 1997 she became aware of the agitated splashing of a flock of ducks nearby in the water. Within a few moments she heard a strange humming noise coming from the Loch. Aware that this was no mechanical noise, Julie decided not to investigate any further.

Farrel, C.B. A local man who claimed three separate sightings of a mysterious creature in Loch Ness on the same day. He was a member of the Royal Observer Corps stationed at the Loch. On 3 January 1937 Farrel claimed to have seen an animal at Foyers. Somewhat bemused by this sighting he continued his journey to Fort Augustus and was astounded when he believed he saw a second creature there.

Sometime later, when out walking on the hills behind Culachy House, he noticed a boat on the Loch and stopped to watch it. He claimed that the boat then 'suddenly vanished'. He rushed down the hill to the nearest telephone to report his sighting, and was greeted by his sister Mrs Becket, who, along with others, had been watching the monster through binoculars.

Farrel enjoyed retelling a further sighting of the monster. At 5.15 a.m. on 25 May 1943, he was on Observer Corps duty at the Loch watching for enemy bombers when he saw an unidentified object on the surface. Through his binoculars he saw a creature 25-30 feet long, approximately 250 yards from shore. It projected about 4-feet above the surface, and its skin appeared to be a dark brown-olive shade, lighter underneath. It had large eyes, with a 'graceful' neck that was about 4-feet long, and its body seemed to have a 'fin' attached. 'Every so often it would dip its head beneath the water then rise again, shaking its head from side to side in a violent sort of motion. It eventually slid out of sight beneath the water without causing a disturbance'.

Feltham, Steve A self-proclaimed professional 'monster-hunter', who lives at the Loch so as to search for the elusive creature. Feltham first came to public attention on 1 August 1992, when BBC 2's *Video Diaries* programme studied his decision to sell his house, buy a mobile home and move to Loch Ness in order to chase his dream. As a sideline, and to supplement his income, Steve Feltham carves 'Nessie'-type figures, which are sold in some of the shops around the Loch. He is a most knowledgeable individual. Like many of his predecessors who have left an urban lifestyle in order to chase their dreams, Steve hopes to maintain his vigil at Loch Ness for many years to come.

Ferguson, Hamish A most curious sighting occurred in the River Ness on 30 July 1965, when Ferguson and George McGill saw something moving downstream; both believed it to be a living creature. Along what appeared to be its back were three black, ridged humps with four triangular spikes. It was estimated as being about 15 feet in length.

Field, David At 5.55 a.m. on 18 August 1967, along with Eric Twelves, David Field saw what seemed to be a large hump in the water. It disappeared as quickly as it had appeared. It was estimated as being between 6-8 feet long and rising to 3-4 feet high.

Field Enterprises Educational Corporation Chicago-based company, who sponsored the **Loch Ness Investigation Bureau**, providing somewhere in the region of $100,000 over a four-year period during the 1960s. Sadly, the results from the Investigation team were less sensational than the company hoped, and its sponsorship ceased.

film footage A list of film footage of the Loch Ness creature on the surface, taken since 1933 (further details can be found under the surname of the photographers involved):
1933, 12 December: **Malcolm Irvine**, opposite Urquhart Castle.
1934, 15 September: **Captain James Fraser**, Urquhart Bay.
c. 1935: **Dr Farquhar MacRae**, unknown location.

1936, 22 September: **Malcolm Irvine**, opposite Foyers.

1938, 29 May: **G.E. Taylor**, opposite Foyers.

c. 1938: **James Currie**, opposite Urquhart Castle.

1960, 23 April: **Tim Dinsdale**, Foyers.

1962, 18 October: Seven unnamed members of the **Loch Ness Investigation Bureau**, Urquhart Bay.

c. 1962: Six unnamed members of the **Loch Ness Investigation Bureau**, location unknown.

1963, 6 June: Six unnamed members of the **Loch Ness Investigation Bureau**, Urquhart Castle.

1963, 13 June: **Loch Ness Investigation Bureau**, Urquhart Castle.

1964, 21 May: **Pauline Hodge**, Achnahannet.

1965, 1 August: **Loch Ness Investigation Bureau (Elizabeth Hall)**, Achnahannet.

c. 1966: **Margaret Edwards**, Near Abriachan.

1967, 22 May: **Loch Ness Investigation Bureau (Les Durkin)**, Portclair.

1967, 13 June: **Loch Ness Investigation Bureau (Dick Raynor)**, opposite Dores.

1967, 22 August: **Loch Ness Investigation Bureau (Andrew Chapman, Gillian Christopher)**, unknown location.

1967, 23 August: **Loch Ness Investigation Bureau (Christopher and Jeffrey Hunter)**, north of Invermoriston.

1967, 5 October: **Loch Ness Investigation Bureau (Clem Skelton)**, opposite Foyers.

1968, 4 May: **Lindsay Irvine**, unknown location.

1969, 27 May: **H. Barsky**, opposite Urquhart Bay.

1969, 23 June: **Loch Ness Investigation Bureau (Alison Skelton)**, Achnahannet.

1969, 16 September: **Loch Ness Investigation Bureau (Ian Shields/Gerry Baker)**, unknown location.

1975, 18 July: **Alan Wilkins**, Rubha Ban.

1977, 22 August: **Gwen Smith**, Whitefield.

1983, 6 August: **John Eric Beckjord**, Urquhart Bay.

1992, 21 July: Anonymous, Urquhart Bay.

films   Cinema films based around Loch Ness include *The Secret of the Loch* (1934), starring Seymour Hicks; *The Private Lives of Sherlock Holmes* (1970), starring Robert Stephens and Colin Blakely, directed by Billy Wilder; *Loch Ness* (1995), starring Ted

Danson, a full-length feature film based around the magic of the Loch and its legendary animal.

Finlay, Greta   Sighted an unknown animal in the Loch on 20 August 1952, whilst on a caravan holiday near Aldourie Point, and in the company of her son Harry. Mrs Finlay heard a loud splashing noise coming from the Loch and, looking over to find the source of the noise, saw an animal rise out of the water less than 20 yards away. It had two or three humps with a total visible length about 15 feet, but she was unable to describe the body shape clearly, as her attention was drawn to the creature's hideous head. The head and neck were held erect and rose some 2-2½ feet out of the water, and the neck seemed to be enlarged where it met the water, as though joining a bulky body.

The head itself was about 6 inches long, the same width as the neck, and had two 6-inch-long projections, each with a sort of 'blob' on the end. The skin appeared to have a black, shiny appearance, and the creature itself reminded Mrs Finlay more of a huge snail than anything else. She ran to the caravan to get her camera, but when she returned the creature had moved away and disappeared amidst a great water commotion, which caused waves to crash against the shore.

Finlay, Harry   *See under* Finlay, Greta.

Finola   *See under* Lowrie, R.H.

fish   *See under* identity.

Fisher, Mr and Mrs James   A chartered accountant from Godalming, Surrey. Mr Fisher and his wife Dilys, along with four other holiday-makers, were almost 9 miles south of Inverness, opposite Tor Point, when they saw something in the Loch about 100 yards out from shore. Mrs Fisher described the object as 'a black hump-like object which submerged, but then reappeared within seconds, when two black humps could be seen. One of these appeared to be a tail.'

Fishery Board for Scotland   The Fishery Board of Scotland intervened over an expedition in August 1938, when a private party revealed their intention of setting out to capture and kill the monster with harpoon guns, nets and speedboats. Happily, the expedition was banned before it ever took place.

Fitter, Richard A renowned naturalist and council member of the Fauna Preservation Society. Along with **Sir Peter Scott** he approached **David James MP** in August 1960 to try to get him to seek Government assistance for ascertaining exactly what it was that lived in the Loch. Richard Fitter was one of the founding Directors of the Bureau for Investigating the Loch Ness Phenomena Ltd (the original name of the **Loch Ness Investigation Bureau**).

Flint, Comdr. Francis Russell The one and only alleged physical contact made with the creature in modern times is believed to have occurred in 1969. Commander Francis Russell Flint, in charge of a Royal Navy motor launch, reported to the Admiralty that his vessel had sustained damage while passing through the Caledonian Canal. The launch was travelling at a speed of around 25 knots through Loch Ness when it took a terrific jolt; nothing had been visible above the water immediately before the collision. Shocked by the impact, Flint looked into the water to see what they had struck and saw a very large animal form which disappeared in a flurry of water. Unable to comprehend the situation, he searched the area for any sign of debris, but could find none. He therefore came to the conclusion that what the boat had struck was the Loch Ness Monster.

'flipper' photograph On 8 August 1972, at Temple Pier in Urquhart Bay, underwater photographs were recorded by the **Academy of Applied Science** team headed by **Dr Robert Rines**. After negatives had been developed and further enhanced by digital processing, the photographs received worldwide publicity, since three frames appeared to have captured something unusual in the Loch.

One of them, the notorious 'flipper' photograph, seemed to show a diamond-shaped fin or flipper in murky surroundings. Dr Rines and others at once proclaimed that this was an appendage belonging to what might be some large and hitherto unknown creature that clearly lived in the Loch.

The photographs triggered fierce and widespread debate. Many doubters questioned the enhancement process, believing that it had been interfered with, and claimed that the clearly defined rhomboid object in the newspapers worldwide was not a true representation of what had originally been captured on film. The Academy team vehemently denied all such allegations, claiming that the photographs published were composites that combined a number of separate computer-enhanced reconstructions. It was later suggested that, had any 'touching up' occurred, then it might have been carried out by independent newspapers.

food supply *See under* ITN.

Forbes, Mr and Mrs J.C.   In July 1957 Mr Forbes, manager of the National Bank in Inverness, was in the company of his wife and two friends, Miss Bronard and Miss Mumford, on the Loch side about six miles from Foyers. Forbes was sitting reading while the women watched fish jumping in the Loch. Suddenly, there was an enormous splash about three-quarters of a mile away, and something dark appeared on the surface and began moving in a westerly direction. As it moved, a series of humps was seen, with undulations appearing on the fifth and sixth humps. The group was amazed by the sight but managed to gauge the creature's size and speed by looking at moving buses on the north side of the Loch; Mr Forbes believed it to be at least as big as a coach, and its speed greater. Mrs Forbes estimated its length at around 30 feet and explained that the group had a clear view of the creature until it disappeared behind a promontory in the direction of Foyers. The water was seen dripping off the humps and sparkling in the sunlight. The creature moved across their position from right to left, and at one point seemed to hesitate before turning in towards Foyers. Shortly after it had gone, a series of waves lapped against the shore.

Mr Forbes reported the sighting to the *Inverness Courier*, and this invoked a curious response in late July 1957, in the form of a letter:

Dear Sir,
Although not acquainted with Mr J.C. Forbes, Manager of the National Bank, Inverness, I should like to confirm his statement. From my viewpoint in the Loch I could see Mr Forbes distinctly on the shore with his friends, and I actually saw them leap to

safety from the wash which I caused when racing up the Loch.
Might I ask sightseers to return their empty bottles, for the amount
of broken glass in and around the Loch is very dangerous to us
amphibians.
Yours faithfully,
THE MONSTER

Forbes, John Donald (Jock)   Forbes claimed to have made a land
sighting of some unknown creature when he was twelve years old.
At an unspecified date in February 1919 he was travelling with his
father in a pony cart; when they were two miles north of
Inverfarigaig something large came out of the trees, crossed the
road in front of them and went down an embankment, before
finally splashing into the water. The pony pulling the cart stopped
dead in its tracks, and then panicked, backed away and almost
caused the cart to slide down the sloping bank which ran alongside
the road. Forbes was unable to provide any descriptive details,
because it was pitch-black at the time of the incident, and heavy
rain was falling.

Fordyce, L.   Land sighting some time in April 1932. Fordyce and
his fiancée had travelled to Scotland to attend a family wedding. On
their way back to England, they decided to stop off at Loch Ness.
Travelling from Foyers towards Fort Augustus in their six-cylinder
Morris Isis, they were 'startled' to see an enormous animal emerge
from the woods on their left; it was about 150 yards in front of
them.
    According to Fordyce: 'It had the gait of an elephant, but looked
like a cross between a very large horse and a camel, with a hump on
its back and a small head on a along neck.' He immediately stopped
the car and followed the creature on foot. 'From the rear it looked
grey and shaggy. Its long, thin neck gave it the appearance of an
elephant with its trunk raised.'
    The couple initially thought that the creature must have been an
exotic animal that had escaped from a zoo or menagerie. But, if so,
its size would have made it easy to track down.
    Fordyce refrained from publicizing his sighting until 1981, when
it was published in the *Scots Magazine*. His reason was quite simple:
'Sceptics at that time would have dismissed the story as a hoax, or
an absurdity.' The article, 'Was It The Monster', indicates that

Fordyce now believes that 'Nessie' is an amphibian which lives on land.

Fort Augustus   The largest town on the Loch, located at its southern end, notable sightings to occur here include; **Comdr. Meiklem** (April 1944); **Father Gregory Brusey** (14 October 1971). Fort Augustus has had the unenviable reputation of enjoying the lowest annual hours of sunshine in Britain. It was named in 1742, after William Augustus, Duke of Cumberland. Before that it was known as Kilcumein (the church of Cumein, who was one of **St Columba**'s successors).

In 1867 the original fort, completed by General Wade in 1742, was sold for £5,000 to Lord Lòvat. His son bequeathed it to the English congregation of Benedictine Monks, who converted it into an abbey and college. The rebuilding was completed in 1880, and in 1882 the foundation was raised to Abbey status, with the name of St Benedict's.

Fort Augustus has been the scene of innumerable sightings and is a popular tourist centre.

Foster, David   Surface sighting of strange animal, on 8 June 1961. From Inverfarigaig, Foster claimed that the animal first appeared midway between the west and east shores. The Loch was calm, and visibility was good. Looking carefully, Foster believed he saw a 'long slim neck' and an 'eel'-shaped head well above the water. The animal cruised slowly parallel to the south shore, causing a considerable wash, before angling towards the north shore, holding this route for a couple of hundred yards. It finally resumed its original route before disappearing in a much larger wash.

Fowles, Derek   One of the three witnesses who saw a two-humped monster moving in the Loch near Drumnadrochit on 11 March 1957. Mr Fowles was a teacher at Fort Augustus Abbey School.
See also **Grant, Insp. John**; **Grant, Ian.**

Foyers   Village midway along the south-east side of the Loch. It is renowned for its aluminium smelter, which opened in 1896 and at one time was the largest aluminium-producer in the world. It used hydroelectricity (the first plant in Britain to do so) generated from the River Royers. The works closed in 1967, but a new £10-million hydroelectric station has since taken its place, providing power for Inverness.

The River Royers runs 13 miles across the mountains and has two waterfalls, one of 40 feet and a second of 90 feet. These were once regarded as the most magnificent in Britain, and Robert Burns wrote a poem about them. Tradition has it that General Wade built himself a shelter, known as the 'General's Hut', in this area, but nothing survives and its exact site remains a mystery.

There have been numerous sightings of unidentified objects in the water in and around Foyers, and many believe that this is the ideal place to seek out the mysterious creature of Loch Ness. On 13 June 1996 a total of 16 people, staff and guests of the Craigdarroch House Hotel, witnessed an unusual 'frothy disturbance' close to Foyers in the early evening. One of the most recent sightings recorded here took place on 15 April 1997, when a visitor from the Isle of Skye reported to the staff of the Drumnadrochit Hotel that she had seen 'something strange in the water near Foyers'.

Foyers Bay *See under* **Foyers.**

France, Sid In the company of four friends (Matt Pilgrim, Dennis Williams and **Mr and Mrs Bruce Marshall**) Sid France claimed to have sighted something strange on the Loch some time in May 1971. A large V-shaped wake appeared on the Loch surface, preceded by a large undefinable shape which seemed to be about 20 feet long and 3 feet high. The water around this object was violently disturbed, and the wake it created crashed onto the beach with more force than that thrown up by a motor boat a few days earlier.

Franck, Richard Author of the lenthily titled *Northern Memoirs, calculated for the meridian of Scotland. Wherein most or all of the cities, citadels, seaports are described. Together with various discoveries, remarkable observations, theological notions. To which is added, the contemplative and practical Angler, with a narrative of that art experimented in England, and perfected in Scotland. Writ in the year 1658.* The work was not published until 1694, but it is of interest for the author's mention of a 'floating island' in Loch Ness. Many subsequent commentators have felt that this was a description of a single-hump sighting.

This is a matter which is open to some debate, since 'floating islands' are mentioned in other Scottish topographies, most popularly in connection with Loch Lomond. Without further descriptive detail it would be incorrect to make an assumption about what Franck's 'floating island' represents.

Fraser, Christine   Christine Fraser (the daughter of Samuel Fraser, a **Caledonian Canal** Inspector at **Fort Augustus**) claimed to have had two separate sightings of a mysterious creature in Loch Ness. The first occurred on 8 October 1954, when she was travelling from Drumnadrochit to Fort Augustus on a bus. Just beyond Strone all 27 passengers saw something peculiar moving in the Loch and called for the driver to stop the vehicle at once, which he did. Miss Fraser later described what she saw as, 'a long brown shape with three defined humps, moving in an undulating manner. The middle hump of the three was the largest and was moving back and forth at incredible speed.' At first she thought that this middle hump might be a fin, but after discussing the sighting with other passengers and witnesses she revised her opinion. The creature was about 25 feet long and 18 inches wide at the surface, and its underpart was an orange-brown colour, similar to the stomach of a newt.

Fraser's second sighting, mentioned in a letter to author **Constance E. Whyte** in 1957, occurred in July 1955. Along with a friend, Christine Fraser claimed she saw a large object, darkish brown and lighter on its underside, in the Loch. It was continually rolling over as though taking a bath, but no distinct shape or size could be observed due to its continual movement. Fraser decided not to report this sighting, because of the teasing she had received after her first sighting was reported to the press in October 1954.

Fraser, Dorothy   Dorothy Fraser's hillside cottage home at Achnhannet overlooked the Loch. In April 1967 she was in her garden looking across the water when she saw something suddenly appear about a quarter of a mile away. It was a big grey-black mass which moved out into the centre of the Loch, gathering speed as it did so, and then sank, leaving a wake like a paddle-steamer. Mrs Fraser was well used to the often deceptive sights the Loch can create, but she was convinced that, on this occasion, she had seen something unusual.

Fraser, F.   A resident of Knockie, who corresponded with author

Rupert T. Gould. Fraser told how, on a calm December day in 1903, he was rowing on the Loch with two other men when, about 400 yards from the Knockie shore, they saw in the water an object that looked like an upturned boat. The three men rowed towards it but soon realized that it was a living creature, which was now swimming away from them. Despite their best efforts they could not catch up with it.

Fraser, G. One of a group of people who sighted the monster on 22 September 1933 from **Alltsaigh** tearoom. Mrs Fraser was amazed by the apparent size of the creature, and believed she saw two humps and a tail which seemed to splash the surface.

Fraser, Capt. Iain James Ex-Merchant Navy Captain, James Fraser, was put in charge of a 1934 expedition to the Loch by **Sir Edward Mountain**. At approximately 7.15 a.m. on the morning of 15 September 1934 Fraser was in position below the road, slightly north of Urquhart Castle. Just outside Urquhart Bay, approximately three-quarters of a mile away, he saw what he described as a 'flat-bottomed upturned boat'; he estimated it to be about 15 feet long and dark in colour. Fraser filmed the object on a 16-mm Kodak cine, with a six-inch telephoto lens. The original film is believed to have gone missing shortly after being shown to the Linnean Society in 1934. This in itself has become something of an enigma, as, according to Bauer (*The Enigma of Loch Ness*, p. 57) a still from it was produced in 1970 via The Photo Source! Sadly, all subsequent efforts to trace its whereabouts have proved fruitless.
See also **Mountain, Sir Edward.**

Fraser, Janet With five other people when she saw an animal from the balcony of the tea rooms in **Alltsaigh** on 22 September 1933. The creature was more than half a mile away, but visibility was excellent, and they had a clear view of it. Miss Fraser claimed to have seen a neck and head sticking out of the water. She described the head as like a 'terrier's', and felt it was not much wider than any part of the neck. She also believed that she caught a glimpse of a large, glittering eye on the side of the head closest to their position. Overall, she felt that the beast had the appearance of some mythical creature.
See also **Fraser, G; Hobbes, Rev. and Mrs W.E.; Howden, M.**

Fraser, Jean   Miss Fraser, the daughter of a local police constable, was with Miss Marjorie Rutherford. At around 8.15 p.m. on 5 August 1934 they saw the creature moving through the water in **Borlum Bay**. All they could see before it submerged was a long, sleek, dark-coloured back.

Fraser, William   Fraser claimed to have made a surface sighting in March 1964, when he saw a pillar-like object surface on the Loch. He kept his eyes fixed on the object and was surprised to see it move off. After a short time it apparently dived beneath the water, only to resurface a few moments later. On its second appearance he clearly saw a single 6-8 foot hump before the creature finally submerged.

Fullerton, R.   Sighting in August 1933. At a distance of about half a mile, Fullerton claimed to have seen a single dark-coloured hump which was elongated in shape. The hump suddenly rose to the surface and gave the impression of moving through the water in a zig-zag motion before eventually submerging.

G

Galliford, C. On 30 July 1966 at about 4.00 p.m., she and her two friends, Miss J. Gorton and Miss E. Lewis saw two dark-coloured humps in the Loch; these were estimated as being somewhere in the region of 2-3 feet long. They appeared to be stationary until they disappeared beneath the water.

'gargoyle' head This incredible photograph was obtained by the **Academy of Applied Science** at 11.45 a.m. on 20 June 1975 via an underwater camera placed in an area south-east of **Temple Pier**. With a little imagination the image caught on camera (which is distorted through the murky gloom of the water created by the density of the peat particles which are present in the Loch) seems to portray the head of some hideous beast. If one looks carefully it is possible to imagine horns, or stalk-like objects, protruding from what should be the top of its head. As with the **'flipper' photograph**, the image is indistinct, due to the natural murkiness of the Loch's water.

A large number of expert (and amateur) zoologists have examined this photograph, almost all dispute its authenticity. The general consensus is that it shows nothing more than debris on the bottom of the Loch (although one theory is that it shows the head of the sunken replica monster that was to be used in the 1970 film *The Private Lives of Sherlock Holmes*).

Genuine attempts to photograph the enigma always provoke controversy, but the **Rines** 'gargoyle' head undoubtedly captures the mystery of the Loch.

See also **Rines, Robert; visibility below water.**

Gartrell, Dennis On 22 August 1967, Dennis Gartrell saw a large black flexible object rise out of the water about 1,400 yards from his position. The object was clearly a living creature, and was curling as it leapt from the water. It measured about 8 feet in length and it hit the water with a terrific commotion. It has since been suggested that this may have been an eel.

Gillies, A. A local gamekeeper who claimed two sightings of the creature on 22 October 1933. The first of these was made at about 12.15 p.m. through a stalker's telescope. Gillies initially saw a foam disturbance in the water about one mile from his position. Inspecting this patch of water, he was surprised to see a black, humped object continually breaking the surface. It rose about 3 feet above the surface and seemed to be in the centre of the patch of disturbed water. Gillies thought that there might have been some form of paddling movement on either side of the hump, but was unable to identify this clearly. He left the scene for a few moments, to get a more powerful telescope, but upon his return found the creature had gone.

Later the same day, he monitored a V-shaped wash moving in the Loch. The arms of the wash spread as much as forty feet apart and stood well proud of the surface. He could see occasional splashing some feet ahead of the 'V' and at times thought he saw dark-coloured portions of body breaking the surface. He watched the object moving with what he described as a 'zig-zag' motion for about fifteen minutes before it submerged.

Girl Norma   According to Witchell (*Loch Ness Story*) a Stornaway fishing boat which in March 1964 registered a 30-foot-long object at a depth of about 250 feet with its onboard sonar. None of those on board could account for the reading, though it has been suggested that it may have been caused by sound reflection from the sides of the Loch basin.

Glendoe Pier   Scene of numerous sightings. Glendoe is situated at **Ford Augustus** on the Loch's most southerly tip. The most notable sighting here occurred in July 1934, when **Ian Matheson**, a resident of Fort Augustus, claimed to have seen a large animal on the shore close to the Glendoe Sawmill.

See also **Cameron, John; Dieckhoff, Dom Cyril; Hambro, Mrs Durand.**

Glen More Albyn   Also known as the 'Great Glen of Albyn' or simply the 'Great Glen', it is now more commonly referred to as

Glen Albin. It is a long geological fault, running north-east to south-west from the Moray Firth on the east coast to Loch Linnhe on the west, that completely divides Scotland. A chain of Lochs runs through the Glen – Loch Dochfour, Loch Ness, Loch Oich, and **Loch Lochy** – and these are linked by the **Caldeonian Canal**. General Wade's road traversed the Glen from end to end.

Goddard, Paul   Goddard, a radiologist, stated in the November 1992 *British Institute of Radiology Bulletin* that he believed the Loch Ness Monster was nothing more than an elephant which had apparently escaped from a zoo. Goddard based his belief upon the image of the 1934 **'surgeon's photograph'**. 'Elephant trunks visible above the water look like the head and neck photograph of Nessie.' It is pertinent to add that **L. Fordyce**, who made a 1932 land sighting, indicated that the creature he observed was not dissimilar to an elephant. However, a thorough search of all official records indicates that no elephants were officially reported as lost from any zoo, circus or other such establishment within the British Isles, which casts serious doubt on Goddard's theory.

Goodbody, William Urwick   Proprietor of the Invergarry House Hotel and a member of the Ness Fishing District Board, who reported a sighting on 30 December 1933.

Shortly after 12 noon Goodbody and his daughters were driving along the north shore, about two miles east of **Fort Augustus**, when they saw what at first appeared to be the fins of some kind of large fish. These were moving in a north-easterly direction towards Inverness, and gradually getting closer to the north-west shore. The group had a set of powerful field glasses with them, and as the object came to within about 400 yards of the north shore they saw eight humps; one of the daughters positively believed she saw nine. The humps were raised about a foot out of the water. Mr Goodbody stated:

We saw the head for a brief period twice. The creature had a long, thin neck with a very small head – so small that I was terribly surprised. I did not see the tail (it was under the water), but there was a thrashing movement in the water when the object made a turning movement. The object is not anything like a porpoise or a walrus or a whale, which have been suggested. In fact, I think that all of the guesses made about the monster are wrong. From what I saw of it, the object, as I have stated, is absolutely different from what I have seen in all my world-wide experience.

What is commonly believed to be the same sighting was made by Inverness plumber **John Deans,** who described a similar scene involving 'a great black object in the water', from a position above Urquhart Castle.

Gordon, Andrew   Whilst out cycling with his son on the evening of 5 August 1934, Gordon stopped for a rest at Urquhart Castle, just after 8 p.m.

I stopped to light my pipe and remarked that we were in a fine position to see the monster. I had hardly finished speaking when an object which appeared in the Loch a few hundred yards away caught my eye. It had at least three humps and sped along at a great rate – as fast as a motor launch. The body was easily discernible, and my impression was that the creature's mode of propulsion was by means of fins or something attached to its body. I did not see a head. I watched the creature carefully for a quarter of an hour, and when it disappeared it looked for all the world like a submarine submerging.

See also **Riggs, James.**

Gorton, Miss J.   *See under* **Galliford, C.**

Gough, J.   *See under* **Pharma.**

Gould, Lt.-Comdr. Rupert T. (1890-1948)   Author of *The Loch Ness Monster and Others,* published in July 1934. Lieutenant-Commander Gould began his investigation of the Loch Ness phenomenon on 13 November 1933. On his motorcycle (which he called Cynthia), he made two complete circuits of the Loch, talking to first-hand witnesses.
He later said that he had expected to find that such witnesses had simply misidentified normal objects on the Loch, and mistaken them for a monster. His opinions changed, however, as a realization

dawned that some unidentified creature had been sighted by individuals who were used to the Loch's mysterious ways. Gould also wrote *The Marine Chronometer* (1923), *The Story of the Typewriter* (1949), *Oddities* (1928), *Enigmas* (1929) and *The Case for the Sea Serpent* (1930).

Gourlay, R.R.   One of a group of eight people who, according to the *Daily Express* (14 July 1950) saw three animals on 13 July 1950. The party were at breakfast in a local hotel (name and location unknown) when W. Gourlay Junior suddenly told them to look out on the Loch. Everyone ran to the door and saw something about 300 yards out in the Loch which gave the appearance of three separate monsters. In the centre were two black shiny humps, both estimated to be about 5 feet long, which protruded from the water to a height of almost 2 feet. On either side of these humps were two distinctly smaller creatures, one of which was making a loud, splashing noise as it moved in the direction of the opposite shore. The large creature and the other small one then moved off towards Urquhart Castle.

Graham, Rev. William, CBE., JP   Reported a four-minute sighting of some animal from **Alltsaigh** tearoom in August 1937. It was a clear, warm, sunny day, and Rev. Graham was quite specific in describing what he saw. His first impression was that the object he could see moving through the water 300-400 yards away was like a motor boat with two piles of luggage on board – one at each end, both covered by a tarpaulin. Closer inspection revealed these piles to be two distinct humps, no head or neck was apparent. The distance from the front of the first hump to the rear of the second was estimated at about 30 feet, and each hump sat approximately 4 feet out of the water. The object was swimming at about 35 m.p.h. and the large, clear wake behind it gave the impression of a large, heavy body being propelled through the water. It moved straight across the Rev. Graham's field of view, and he could not see any undulation during the movement. The creature eventually submerged.

Grant, Arthur   A veterinary surgeon from Glen Urquhart, Arthur Grant made a sensational land sighting of the animal at about 1.00 a.m. on 5 January 1934. As he approached a bend in the road near

Abriachan on his motorbike, he saw a dark object close to the bushes on the opposite side of the road. As the animal bounded across the road in front of him and plunged down the embankment into the Loch, Grant made out a small head and a long neck. He described the animal as having two flippers at the front, and two more at the rear. The tail was about 6 feet long, with the end rounded, and the total length of the animal was deemed to be about 15-20 feet. Stopping his motorcycle, he went to the spot where the creature had disappeared down toward the Loch and marked the area, so that he could return in the daylight hours to make a closer examination of the scene.

News of the encounter spread quickly, especially to members of the press. The following morning, when Grant returned to the scene, he was joined by big-game hunter **Marmaduke Wetherell**, and the press had a field day as Wetherell examined broken bracken, wisps of sheep's wool, old bones and the general litter strewn at the Loch side (this included the carcass of a dead goat). Much was made of the scene, but nobody – other than the over-enthusiastic members of the press – took Wetherell seriously, and his personal observations were dismissed. The press, though, made a great deal of the goat carcass, and the 'carnivorous monster' that must have dropped it there.

Serious researchers were also at the scene, however, in the form of a group of students from Edinburgh College of Art, led by H.F. **Hay**, a Fellow of the Zoological Society of Scotland. This group carried out their own investigation of the sighting and the scene, and Grant told them his tale. Hay attached little credibility to much of the debris found in the bracken on the route the creature had allegedly taken down to the Loch. Their researches led them to conclude that the creature Grant had seen had possibly been a mature bull walrus. Hay visited the Royal Scottish Museum in Chambers Street, Edinburgh, where he examined the build of a bull walrus which was displayed there (it is still there). It was, they deemed, possible that in the poor illumination of his motorcycle headlight Grant could have mistaken the size and shape of what could well have been a bull walrus.

More recent research seems to indicate that Grant may have been working in collusion with Wetherell and others to formulate a hoax sighting. Without doubt, Wetherell was quick to attend the scene and gave himself a high profile, identifying the debris which littered the area (the goat carcass could well have been washed ashore from a separate part of the Loch). This sighting must remain questionable, since most things Wetherell involved himself in at Loch Ness are open to great debate. A belief has recently surfaced that Grant was involved in a hoax designed to help Wetherell to enhance his 'news value' during his brief visit to the Loch.

Grant, Barbara Alleged sighting of animal on 21 July 1987. Mrs Grant was in a car with Mrs Mary Appleby, just north of the **Abriachan** turn-off, when she noticed something 'peculiar' sticking out of the Loch's calm waters. It was a pillar-type object, red-brown in colour, which they thought had the appearance of a thin neck.

Mrs Appleby stopped the car in a lay-by, and both women looked out at the point where Mrs Grant had seen the object. No neck was now visible, but a dark shape was clearly seen moving through the water at some speed, throwing up a disturbance as it did so.

Grant, Ian A garage proprietor and one of three men who sighted the animal in the Loch on 11 March 1957. The trio saw a two-humped object moving through the Loch near **Drumnadrochit**, until it eventually submerged.

See also Fowles, Derek; Grant, Insp. John.

Grant, Insp. John Police Inspector and one of three men who saw a two-humped object in the Loch near **Drumnadrochit** on 11 March 1957. No definite features could be seen, but all three men stated that they had 'never before witnessed such a strange spectacle on the Loch'.

See also Fowles, Derek; Grant, Ian.

Grant, Patrick One of the expedition team employed by **Sir Edward Mountain** and **Captain James Fraser** in 1934. At about 10.45 a.m. on 12 August 1934 Grant was observing the Loch from Abriachan Pier when he saw an object appear about 120 yards offshore. He was able clearly to make out the monster's head, which was 'goat-like' in appearance; on top of it, he claimed, were two stumps resembling a sheep's broken horns. The eyes were mere slits, similar to the eye of a darning needle. The neck was about 40 inches long, and where this met the body there appeared to be a swelling which resembled a fowl with a full crop. The animal appeared to have flippers on the front part of its body; these were extended forward and were not being used. It was dark brown in colour and appeared to be lighter on the underside. The skin seemed to be smooth. The creature moved at a speed of about 8 m.p.h. and was about 20 feet long overall.

Grant had also had an earlier sighting at 10.20 a.m. on 27 July 1934, when he and James Legge had seen a 15-foot-long dark-coloured hump move slowly down the Loch for about 50 yards before submerging.

See also **Mountain, Sir Edward; Fraser, Captain James; Legge, James.**

Grant, Col. Patrick The owner of Knockie Lodge, who had a surface sighting whilst driving north out of **Fort Augustus** at about 12 noon on 13 November 1951. Colonel Grant saw a great disturbance in the water about 150 yards off shore and described a 'black-coloured' object about 6 feet in length standing about a foot or so out of the water. The object appeared to submerge and then resurface about 100 yards from where it was originally sighted. The Colonel was convinced that it was a living creature, and not, as had been claimed, a porpoise or a seal.

See also **Kirton, Dr and Mrs J.**

Grant, Ray Miss Grant and **Molly Stewart**, maids at Knockie Lodge, reported a sighting of the monster on the evening of 18 August 1935, from a hill which overlooks the Loch close to Knockie Lodge, Whitebridge. They stated that, 'what seemed to be the creature's tail emerged, lashing the water. Then up came the head, which was something like a cow's, only kind of oval-shaped and smaller.' The creature was dark-coloured all over, and both witnesses estimated its length as being about 20 feet.

The sighting lasted for about thirty minutes, between 7.00 p.m. and 7.30 p.m., when the Loch was calm and the sun bright. During this period the creature submerged just once, only to reappear almost immediately. It was still splashing on the surface, close to the shore, when the two witnesses left the scene.

See also **Stewart, Molly.**

Gray, Hugh British Aluminium Company employee, who took a photograph of what he claimed was the monster on 12 November

1933. The photograph (believed to be the first purported monster photograph to be published) appeared in the *Glasgow Daily Record and Mail* of 6 December 1933. It is far from clear, and recent research alleges that it seems to show a Labrador's head retrieving a stick from the water. There appears to be a lot of spray coming from whatever it is in the water, so the possibility exists that it has been touched up.

Greenpeace   On 9 October 1991, as part of their opposition to the Faslane Nuclear Submarine Base, Greenpeace elected to use a model Loch Ness Monster to promote its cause. Attempts to float the large three-piece model on Loch Long caused more than a little embarrassment for the protesters; the model repeatedly separated into its component parts and stubbornly refused to co-operate. After lengthy discussions the protesters opted to use the head and neck section only. The whole thing turned into a farce when this was attached to a rubber ring complete with outboard motor, and, seemingly out of control, was last seen disappearing down the Loch.

Gregory, Frederick and family   In the summer of 1960, Gregory, his wife and son Ian saw two 15-foot-long humps appear on the surface off **Urquhart Bay** – these both had black, mottled skin. The humps maintained a course parallel with the car in which the family were travelling, and were moving at a speed of around 20 m.p.h. They eventually submerged, leaving a wake on the surface where they had last been seen.

Grimshaw, Mr P.C.   Representative of the Royal Scottish Museum, one of a number of spokespersons who were asked for their opinion of the feasibility of a hitherto unidentified monster living in Loch Ness by members of the press in 1933. 'In our opinion the creature will probably turn out to be a young beluga or white whale.' Other authorities approached by a number of national newspapers keen to cover the story include: **Prof. D.M. Watson**, of University College, London, who believed that the sightings would prove to be no more than a 'large lump of water-logged peat floating round the loch'; Professor Ritchie, who claimed that 'the Loch Ness Monster obviously could not be what it is claimed to be.'

Grummet, Mr and Mrs   On 4 September 1968, at around 11.20 a.m., the couple saw a tubular-shaped hump which they estimated as about 3 feet long and 2 feet tall and described as black and smooth. The hump was stationary, and it submerged twice before reappearing for a third time. Eventually, it disappeared when a boat appeared elsewhere on the Loch.

Guiding Star   Fishing vessel which, according to author **Nicholas Witchell**, claimed to have picked up an unexplainable echo-sounding of some large object moving in the Loch in November 1959.

gypsy   According to a local belief, an unknown gypsy woman reported a sighting of some strange creature in the Loch in the 1890s.

H

Ha-Burn   A fishing trawler which operated on Loch Ness in April 1969 and was captained by **James Runcie**. The on-board echo-sounder detected a large object about 700 feet down. The crew who witnessed the recording on the machine were undecided as to what it could be, except that it was a very large and seemingly animate object. Its size and shape did not correspond with anything which they had previously ever recorded.

See also **Runcie, James.**

Half-Way House, Alltsaigh   Tearoom situated on the west side of Loch, and the scene of numerous sightings. On 22 September 1933 a party observed the animal from the upper storey; in June 1938 John MacLean saw an animal's head and neck less than twenty yards from shore; and in August 1934 when Count Bentinck saw an animal's head with steam emerging from its mouth. After the Second World War the tearooms became the Alltsaigh Youth Hostel.

See also **Alltsaigh; Bentinck, Count; Fraser, Janet; MacLean, John.**

Hall, Elizabeth   Elizabeth Hall was a member of the **Loch Ness Investigation Bureau** team that was deployed around the Loch shore, monitoring any surface movement. From the **Achnahannet** expedition site, she filmed nine seconds of footage of two wakes moving virtually parallel to each other through the Loch; there was no sign of any solid object at the head of either wake. The film was submitted to **JARIC**, who examined it closely, but the results proved inconclusive because of the distance of the objects from the camera, 3,864 feet. The only information which could be gleaned from the film was that: the wakes were approximately 9 feet from each other; one of them was about 7½ feet in front of the other; and both were travelling at a speed of around 2 m.p.h.

See also **film footage.**

Hall, Graham A former police officer who sighted something in the Loch on the evening of 17 June 1993 at about 8.15 p.m. Approaching **Dores** from **Inverness,** he saw a black buoy in Dores Bay, about 400 metres from shore. Immediately to the left of the buoy he caught a glimpse of something moving in a south-south-westerly direction. The object was in silhouette and he believed he saw a thin neck with what appeared to be a head on top. Comparing this to the size of the buoy, Hall thought that it might have been 6-7 feet tall. He lost sight of the creature before he was able to stop the car.

Hallam, Mr and Mrs Y.H. A couple from Filey in Yorkshire. In June 1936, whilst travelling on a pleasure boat, they saw a head and two humps which moved quickly down the River Ness, towards the sea. The head was most clearly visible, and the animal's length was judged to be about 20 feet overall.

Hambro, Mrs Durand Victim of a drowning accident on the Loch. In the Autumn of 1964 Mrs Hambro, the wife of a London banker, was on board a pleasure boat near the **Glendoe** boathouse, close to the coastline area known as **Horeshoe Scree,** when the boat collided with something unknown, which caused an explosion and a fire. Mrs Hambro jumped off the vessel into the water and was drowned.

Her husband later claimed that when she leapt from the boat she had been wearing jewellery worth £100,000 and made an insurance claim to recover the loss. The insurance company employed a professional diver to try to recover the body and the lost jewellery.

The experienced diver went down to a depth of around 150 feet, but after just a few minutes he returned to the surface, without the body or the jewellery, but clearly shocked and looking very pale. He refused to go back down due to the murkiness of the water created by the density of peat particles which made visibility virtually impossible. It is also claimed that he stated that he would never dive in Loch Ness again; some writers have since claimed that the shock he received in the Loch turned his hair white.

Local talk at the time was of treacherous currents, attack by giant eels, and huge underwater caverns. Mrs Hambro's body was never recovered, and the insurance company never did pay out on her husband's claim.

See also **visibility under water.**

Harden, Donald   In 1969 Harden, who was from the London Museum in Kensington, was a guest lecturer to businessmen in Tokyo representing the British Council for Tokyo's 'British Week'. He told his hosts that he would speak on any British subject they wished; the Japanese asked to hear about 'Nessie', which stumped Mr Harden. Eventually the Board of Trade intervened and explained that the 'Monster' was regarded as a myth and was not the sort of cultural subject that Harden was used to discussing. He eventually talked about the history of the Tower of London.

Harper-Smith, J., OBE, LL B   Mr Harper-Smith, the Town Clerk of Lincoln, was on a fishing holiday to Loch Ness in June 1951. At about 9 p.m. his son pointed to something which he thought looked like a periscope sticking out of the mirror-calm water. Looking round, Mr Harper-Smith saw a black head and similarly coloured neck standing about 5 feet tall, and 1 foot in diameter rise out of the water. This began to move very quickly through the water, followed by a huge wash, and he could see some oscillations of the head and neck. Eventually, when it was about 800 yards away, it turned and went back up the Loch, before submerging. Mr Harper-Smith described the incident as 'the greatest thrill of my life'.

Harvey, Patricia   Alleged land sighting of an unknown animal, on 22 February 1934 on the shoreline of **Inchnacardoch** Bay by Patricia Harvey and **Jean MacDonald**. The creature crossed a stream heading out towards the Loch. It was said to have a thick body which tapered towards its tail, and the underside of its neck was white, although the rest of its body was decidedly dark. It moved on four short legs. The two women believed the creature to be somewhere in the region of 8-10 feet long and some 6 feet tall.

See also **Inchnacardoch; MacDonald, Jean.**

Haselfoot, Capt. F.E.B.   A naval colleague of **Rupert Gould**, who sighted an animal near **Fort Augustus** on 12 July 1934. As a maritime surveyor, Haselfoot was accustomed to the ways in which water can deceive the naked eye, and he was able to perceive distance and shapes in the water with some degree of accuracy.

He claimed to have seen a 'spade-pointed' head on a long thin neck which projected something like 4 feet above the water surface about 400 yards out in **Borlum Bay**. Behind the head and neck were two dark-coloured humps that rose about 1 foot out of the water and seemed to be moving slowly towards the shore. Haselfoot also believed he saw a wash of 'white-feather' pattern produced from the front hump area, as the creature moved in the water; this, he claimed, indicated that 'the creature has a broad body'. Haselfoot, confirmed that what he saw was a living creature, the like of which he had never before witnessed. He communicated his sighting in a letter to *The Times* that was published on 16 July 1934.

Hasler, Lt.-Col. H.G., DSO, OBE 'Blondie' Hasler is best known as the man who conceived and led the canoe raid on Bordeaux Harbour in 1942, in which a number of German ships were damaged by limpet mines. For two months from 4 June 1962 he led an expedition of forty volunteers who carried out observations on the Loch from the yacht *Jester* and from the shore.

A number of low-frequency tapping noises, which appeared 'animal-like' in nature, were recorded on hydrophones. Apart from this and two fleeting sightings, no other useful evidence was gathered.

Hay, H.F. A Fellow of the Zoological Society of Scotland who in January 1934 returned with **Arthur W. Grant**, to the spot where Grant had seen an animal cross the road in front of him, close to the **Abriachan** turn-off.

Hay found evidence that something large had indeed been present in the area where the creature was said to have done down the bank to the water. No body drag marks were evident, but the marks of the feet or flippers, appearing as skids or scrapes in the soft earth, were about 5 feet apart; they were too indistinct to be identified as made by a known species. More exciting was what appeared to be a set of foot or flipper prints about 70 yards further along the beach. These measured 24 inches from toe to heel and 38 inches wide and were 30 inches apart, measured from heel to heel. Close by was a heavily crushed area of bracken, which had clearly been flattened by some large animal. Hay believed that it was unlikely that any known farm animal could have reached such a secluded spot, although other people examining the area had clearly made the evidence unreliable. Hay proceeded to carry out research into the sighting. He visited the Royal Scottish Museum in Edinburgh, measuring a bull walrus which was on display there and comparing its measurements with those he had recorded at the scene. There was a close match between them, and Hay concluded that it was possible that Grant had seen a mature bull walrus cross the road in front of him.

Hay, Taylor   Associate and friend of **Lachlan Stuart**, who assisted in the hoax photographic sighting of 14 July 1951. Hay claimed that the animal was travelling past them at a speed of about 10 m.p.h., its three humps, head and neck clearly visible. He further stated that the head and neck were moving in a bobbing motion, as though hunting fish.

See also **Stuart, Lachlan.**

Hayward, A.E.   Surface sighting, on 21 September 1967, at approximately 3.10 p.m., close to Dores. A 20-foot humped object, dark brown in colour and rough in surface texture, surfaced on the Loch about half a mile away. It appeared to be extremely flexible in its movements and it created a wake in the water before submerging. The hump was also witnessed by two other men in the group, a Mr Birnic, and Alexander Massie.

Heal, Mr and Mrs Ronald   Tourists who had a surface sighting made through a telescope on 23 July 1968. A single 25-foot dark brown hump appeared near Inverfairgaig and was estimated to project about 2-3 feet out of the water. The hump moved through the water at some considerable speed before the couple lost sight of it.

Heathcote, Dr J., and family   Reported two separate sightings of an object in the water in Urquhart Bay on the same day. The first (seen by Dr Heathcote only) occurred at 10.30 a.m. on 20 August 1966, when a large rock-like object appeared in the Loch, creating a linear wash. The second sighting (viewed also by Felicity and Martin Heathcote) was at 3.50 p.m., when something black and similar to a 'large car inner tube' continually broke the surface again in Urquhart Bay. It disappeared when a boat came into the area.

Hedgeley, John   On 10 April 1996, Hedgeley saw a dark object moving down the centre of the Loch with its head and neck visible above the surface. He followed it in his car for about 4 miles before he finally lost it from view.

Henderson, Col. E.G.   Member of the Inverness Scientific Society and Field Club, who saw an unknown animal in the middle of the Loch on 17 June 1934, while travelling on a coach near **Abriachan**. The coach stopped to allow the party a better view of what, at first, appeared to be a pile of debris; it was then observed that it was moving against the wind and waves. It was very large, and Henderson and the rest of the coach party were convinced that it was a huge living creature.

Henderson, Insp. Henry   On 13 October 1971, Inspector Henderson and **Sergeant George MacKenzie** of the Inverness Police were part of a group who saw two humps move up through the Loch near **Alltsaigh** Youth Hostel. The animal was estimated to be about 30-40 feet long, and travelling at around 10-15 m.p.h. Henderson wrote in his official report that 'it was clear that the two humps were part of one animate object'.
See also **MacKenzie, Sgt George.**

Hepburn, Austin   On 11 August 1996 Austin Hepburn took a photograph of a 'solid black object' in the water. At about 4.00 p.m. he stopped his car beyond Dores to take a couple of photographs of the waterscape which confronted him. He was pointing his *Praktica* camera towards **Urquhart Castle** about two and a half miles away when he noticed a large wake moving up the Loch towards Dores. Through the viewfinder he could see 'something black' breaking the surface. Behind the wake and halfway across the Loch Hepburn spotted a boat with its sails down, but it was clear to him that this could not have created the wake, because the water around it was perfectly calm. As far as he could see, no other boats were present on the Loch at the time. The incident was also witnessed by a group of European tourists in a camper van, whom Hepburn spotted pointing to the same wake.

Hepple, Rip   Founder of the **Ness Information Service**. In 1974 he issued the organization's first ever 'Nessletter', to 'fill the void' created by the closure of the **Loch Ness Investigation Bureau**. Hepple claims that his interest was aroused by reading **Constance Whyte**'s *More Than A Legend*, which he felt was impressive for its lack of 'hard sell', and for 'allowing the reader to come to their own conclusions'. After he visited the Loch for the first time in 1964 his interest grew so avid that he became an enthusiastic and active member of the LNIB, and his enthusiasm has never waned.

Higgins, Jackie   *See under* **Pyman, Col. D.**

Hill, Mrs Stanley   *See under* **mass sightings**.

Hinton, M.A.C.   *See under* **hippopotamus hoax**.

hippopotamus hoax   Alleged footprint of the Loch Ness animal found on Loch side by the self-proclaimed big-game hunter **Marmaduke Wetherell**. A cast of the footprint was made and sent to the **British Museum of Natural History** in London, where it was examined by **Dr William Thomas Calman** and **M.A.C. Hinton**. It turned out to be nothing more than the imprint of the right back foot of a hippopotamus, presumably placed at the Loch side for Wetherell to discover.

Hitching, Hilda D.   Surface sighting on 21 April 1966 at 10.30 a.m. Hilda Hitching was a member of the Women's Voluntary Service and its organizer for Ayrshire. She and Mrs V. King were motoring on the east side of the Loch, four miles north of **Foyers**, when they saw some strange animal about a quarter of a mile out into the Loch. Three grey humps were clearly visible.

hoaxes   *See under* **crocodile claw**; **elephant seal**; **hippopotamus hoax**; **Spurling, Christian**; **'surgeon's photograph'**; **Wetherell, Marmaduke**.

Hobbes, Rev. and Mrs W.E.   While staying in Glen Urquhart on a family holiday with his wife and sister-in-law, the Rev. Hobbes, from Wroxeter in Shropshire, had a surface sighting of the animal on 22 September 1933. Visiting the **Alltsaigh** tearoom, he looked out across the Loch from an upstairs balcony and saw a 'snake-like' head and neck which seemed to move up and down and from side to side. Behind this were two low humps and what looked like a tail. The sighting lasted about ten minutes before the creature sank from view.

The Rev. Hobbes was amused by the 'calmness' of his fellow witness, **Miss Janet Fraser,** in that ten minute sighting, during which everything from glittering eyes to two low humps were identified by different witnesses. Miss Fraser later revealed to Hobbes that she had seen the monster 'three times before, hence found it difficult to get as excited as the rest of the witnesses'.

See also **Fraser, Janet.**

Hodge, Mr and Mrs Peter   Alleged sighting at 8.15 a.m. on 21 May 1964, at **Achnahannet.** Peter Hodge was on a private expedition with his wife, Pauline, when he saw a pole-like object sticking out of the water. He called for her to come and look, and ran to get his camera from his nearby car. In his excitement he slammed the car door shut, and he believes that the sound alerted whatever it was out on the Loch, for it immediately disappeared from view. A few minutes later a wash began to move along the Loch with what appeared to be a black dot at the head of it. It moved right across the Loch before turning left. Mr Hodge estimated the neck as being about 4 feet long, and the speed of travel at somewhere in the region of 5-8 m.p.h. The object's movements in the water were also witnessed by a number of students camped close by, who had heard Mr Hodge's excited calls to his wife.

When reporting the incident at the **Loch Ness Investigation Bureau** headquarters later that evening, Mr Hodge had a further sighting in company with Bureau member **Ivor Newby.**

See also **Newby, Ivor.**

Holiday, Frederick W.   Journalist, writer on angling topics and author of *The Great Orm of Loch Ness* (1968) and *The Dragon and the Disc* (1973). Holiday suggests that the monsters are invertebrates. He claims that two films of the monster exist in bank vaults, and, in his second book, he speaks of monsters being organically related to the creatures controlling UFOs. He claimed to have been investigating the Loch Ness phenomenon for some 35 years when *The Great Orm of Loch Ness* was published. In 1977 Holiday wrote the *Dyfed Enigma*, discussing alien beings and extra-terrestrial occurrences in Wales. He died in February 1979.

Holmgren, Lena   One of the few recorded incidents when a human scream has apparently frightened off the animal. On 20 June 1966, at 10.30 a.m., Lena Holmgren was startled when a single dark grey object surfaced in the Loch. The shock caused her to scream and the animal instantly submerged.

Horan, Brother Richard   Surface sighting of animal on 26 May 1934. Horan was a monk at St Benedict's Abbey, **Fort Augustus**. While working on a pump in the Abbey boathouse, he heard a noise coming from the water. He ignored it and continued with his work, but glanced up a few moments later to see the animal looking at him from a distance of about 30 yards. He described it as having a graceful neck with a broad white stripe down the front. Its head and neck stood about 3½ feet out of the water, at an angle of about 45° to the water surface. The animal moved about slowly in the water, until it apparently sighted a rowing boat some distance away. This seemingly caused it to stop and swing round, before finally plunging back into the water. As it moved off up the Loch in a north-easterly direction it created a trail beneath the water similar to that of a torpedo. Horan noted a curious motion in the water behind the creature as it moved, almost as if a propeller was working. The sighting was also witnessed by James Fraser, William Macintosh and a woman golfer watching from a different location.

Horseshoe Scree   Situated in the south-east part of the Loch, about three miles north of **Fort Augustus**, it was the sight of an alleged land sighting by **Torquil MacLeod** in 1960. The Horseshoe is easily identifiable: formidably steep, it drops dramatically into the waters of the Loch and continues to drop away beneath the water. A depth of 236 feet is said to have been recorded only 100 feet from the shore.

Howden, Miss M.   Sighting on 22 September 1933. In company with **Janet Fraser** at the tearooms, **Alltsaigh**, Miss Howden saw what she described as two humps in line with a head and neck which were in the water over half a mile away; visibility was good.

Another member of the party claimed to have been aware of the animal's 'two shining eyes'.

See also **Fraser, Janet.**

Hughes, Hector, MP   An enthusiastic believer in the existence of an animal in the Loch, he felt that it was in the interest of science to locate such a creature. In the House of Commons in May 1957 he asked the Secretary of State for Scotland, John Mackay, whether he would be prepared to authorize the use of the latest underwater viewing and listening devices to locate the animal. He referred to **Constance Whyte**'s book *More Than A Legend*, and asked 'Does not the Secretary of State realize that he owes an obligation to science in this matter, and that recent learned works have indicated that such a survey might reveal the existence in Loch Ness of a prehistoric or unique monster, fish or reptile, of some kind, the discovery of which might add considerably to science?' The response was negative; the Secretary of State declined all such proposals and closed the debate. It is said that Mr Hughes was told by another member of Parliament to 'go and jump into the lake and look for the monster himself'.

In 1958 Hughes expressed his real fear for the animal's safety, and again asked the Scottish Secretary what action he proposed to take to protect this valuable Scottish asset. His request met with a similar response and was all but ignored in Parliament.

Hunter, Christopher and Jeffrey   The Hunter brothers were both members of the **Loch Ness Investigation Bureau.** On 23 August 1967 they were on a surface watch about two miles north of **Invermoriston**; the weather conditions were good, although views across the Loch were difficult due to a heat haze. Both witnesses observed something unusual in the Loch: a dark object, which gave the appearance of moving 'up and down'. This movement was causing some amount of water disturbance, which was filmed. When examined, the film image was affected by the heat haze, which reduced its clarity. After close scrutiny, it was claimed that the object sighted and filmed was nothing more than diving birds.

See also **film footage.**

Hunter Blair, Sir David   This man, who was to later become Abbot Oswald of Dunfermline, was quoted in the magazine

Universe in 1934 as believing in the Loch Ness Monster:

> I became, and remain, absolutely convinced on the testimony of a veritable cloud of credible eye-witnesses, which it would be absurd to flout or ignore, that a weird and mysterious creature does really and truly haunt these deep waters, not as a casual visitor, but as a resident. I hazard a conjecture that it belongs to no existing species but to a period dating back some hundreds of millions of years.

Hunter Gordon, S.   Mr Hunter Gordon, a director of Resistance Welders Ltd, Inverness, claimed to have had three separate sightings of the creature. The first occurred in the summer of 1935. With a **Mr Denman**, he was driving alongside the Loch, between **Aldourie** and Loch Ashie, on what was described as a beautiful clear day. They stopped the car to admire the view of Loch Ness and **Meallfuarvonie**, and Mr Hunter Gordon noticed an object in the centre of the Loch. His friend initially suggested this was a boat, but Mr Hunter Gordon pointed out that it was a Sunday and boats were rare on the Loch on Sundays. 'We monitored its slow movement through the Loch for around two and a half minutes, before it suddenly and quietly sank.'

Hunter Gordon's second sighting occurred in 1939, when he was driving past the Loch with **Mr Dale Bussell**, Deputy Director of contracts for the Admiralty. Both men saw two humps appear on the Loch surface about 200-300 yards from the shore at **Brachla**. The humps, which were smooth in texture and seemed to be several yards apart, broke the surface every 200 yards or so as the creature travelled along at a speed of about 20 m.p.h. Tracks appeared in the water, indicating the creature's route. No other identifying features were noted during the sighting.

The third sighting took place in the company of a fellow businessman, **C.E. Dunton**, on 20 June 1948. Two 'eyebrow-shaped' coils suddenly rose to the surface of the Loch and showed above the water. These were dark brown or black in colour and light grey shadows appeared between the parts that were out of the water. Hunter Gordon estimated each coil as about 30 feet long, and 2-3 feet thick at the water surface. The two coils remained in view for about five minutes. One then sank from view, but the other remained clearly visible for a further ten minutes, until it, too, slipped beneath the surface.

See also **Bussell, Dale; Denman, Mr; Dunton, C.E.**

Hutton, Stephanie On 9 August 1996, while holidaying in the area, Stephanie Hutton managed to photograph an 'unidentified object' in the water opposite **Urquhart Bay**. She could not say exactly what it was that she saw, but she believed it to be something that was different to the natural Loch environment. To date no evidence of the photograph has been published.

hydrophones One of the tools used by scientists and monster-hunters at Loch Ness. A hydrophone is basically a listening device – a water-tight container containing a highly sensitive microphone – which is lowered into the water to record noise. The first organized expedition to use hydrophone equipment was the 1960 Oxford and Cambridge team.

I

identity Perhaps the most controversial of all the subjects relating to the Loch Ness phenomenon is the identity of the species the creature may belong to. The characteristics recorded in many eye-witness sightings create anomalies which cause zoologists to question such reports, as they conflict with the species known to science. What science and the public in general fail to appreciate is that the creature in Loch Ness could be uniquely adapted. Science deals with facts, a new species would not be known to them until caught and studied. Zoologists dismissed reports of the giant squid as being 'mythical' until one such species (with 35-foot-long tentacles) was caught off the cost of Peru in the late 1970s, providing evidence that science is not infallible.

The most popular theory is that the creature is a reptile, but this is problematic. A reptile would be forced to the surface to breathe. This would indicate that a greater quantity of surface sightings would be recorded. The water temperature of the Loch would also appear to be too cold for any reptile to remain active.

A mammal would seem a more likely alternative. They are warm-blooded so remain at the same temperature no matter how hot or cold it is. Clearly such a group could exist within the Loch, surviving from the fish population.

If the creature is a fish, then judging from descriptions of recorded sightings it must be a most peculiar species, with a long thin neck or some form of limb, unless it is from the eel family. Bottom-dwelling fish (such as the European pond loach) are believed to surface in calm, hot weather. This activity tends to support surface sightings of the creature in Loch Ness, which has also been seen to surface in such conditions.

A further alternative is that of the amphibian group, which live and give birth in fresh water. To further the case for the amphibian, members of this group do not need to breathe often, so would not be a common sight on the water surface, justifying why the creature in Loch Ness is not seen with any regularity. The main argument against the proposal is that, so far as records can be traced, there have never been any marine amphibians. Bearing in mind that the most popular belief is that the creature in the Loch arrived there from the sea, then this species seems highly unlikely, unless it can first be answered how it got there.

Idle, Christopher   Idle and school friend **John Coulton** were fishing on the Loch north or Urquhart Castle on 22 August 1977. Idle left his friend on the shore and went out in their boat. When he returned Coulton told him that, while he had been away, he had seen something surface and dive in the Loch several times. (This was close to the location of the sighting by **Gwen and Peter Smith** on the same date.) Idle then told his friend of seeing a 'large black thing' surface so close to the boat that he could have 'hit it with an oar'. It had actually risen out of the water to a height of about 1 metre. Idle further described the object as having a neck that was about 45 cm wide at surface level and about 22 cm where it joined the head. There was no obvious demarcation between neck and head.

There are those who claim that Idle and Coulton had prepared a hoax, which in turn caused the Smiths to have their sighting. It has been further claimed that a wooden timber post, for example, could easily be manipulated to give the appearance this sighting created. Peter Smith discredits such theories and having spoken to both boys at the time of the incident believes them to be telling an accurate account. Both Idle and Coulton later informed author **Tim Dinsdale** (who interviewed them about their sighting) that they were at the Loch side carrying out a school project. Author Steuart Campbell claims that contact was made with the boys' school, which knew nothing of the project, and that Idle had not replied to his enquiries.

Inchnacardoch Bay   *See under* Inchnacardoch.

Inchnacardoch   Situated in the south-western corner of the Loch and close to **Fort Augustus**, Inchnacardoch has both a bay and a forest of trees. The most infamous sightings here have occurred on land. Just after the First World War **Margaret Cameron** and her two brothers saw an animal come out of the trees and into the bay. And in February 1934 **Jean MacDonald** and **Patricia Harvey** saw a creature on the shoreline.

Independent Television News (ITN)   Mounted an expedition that carried out an echo-sounding sonar search of the Loch in September 1969. Some 50 people were employed by the expedition, using underwater devices and cameras, and teams were deployed around the Loch, maintaining a surface watch. A vertical blanket sonar screen was directed down into the Loch's depths, providing complete coverage across its whole width. It seemed like a comprehensive exercise. In order to tempt the creature to the surface, food consisting of anchovy, blood meal and gelatin was tossed into the water. It has long been believed that any creature such as the Loch Ness Monster must be carnivorous, since the paucity of vegetable matter in the Loch is such that it would be highly unlikely to be able to support any kind of large herbivore. Scientists have different opinions about the food supply available in the Loch, but it was recently ascertained that there are enough fish to satisfy a large creature's appetite. The food supply question has caused some controversy over the decades among those who seek the monster.

Since a number of reports indicated that the creature disliked 'above-surface' noise, a team of boats deliberately created underwater noise, in the hope of forcing it to swim away from this and directly into the sonar screen.

Despite all these efforts, the expedition did not record a single success – no large readings on the sonar and no appreciable sightings. Mike Fiddell, who worked as part of the team, said later 'The search was ninety per cent effective. I don't see how it could have escaped our sonar beams.'

Ing, Bruce   A member of Cambridge University expedition of 1960, Bruce Ing had a brief sighting of an 8-10 foot lump which projected between 12-18 inches above the surface at **Achnahannet** on 10 July 1960. He had a second sighting four days later, when, at the same location, on a calm Loch at 5.30 a.m., he saw a similar size hump just over half a mile away through binoculars.

Inverfarigaig   Situated on the south-east shore of the Loch, close to the mouth of the River Farigaig. An alleged land sighting was

made near here by **John Donald Forbes** in February 1919.
See also **Forbes, John Donald.**

Invermoriston   Situated on the north-west side of the Loch, by the
River Moriston, in what was once the traditional country of the
Grant clan. Close by, a small cairn at the edge of the road leads to
mysterious footprints. It is said that in 1827 an itinerant preacher,
Finlay Munro, was interrupted while holding an open-air service.
The preacher declared that he spoke the truth, and to prove it the
very ground would bear witness to him; his two footprints are
permanently embedded by a larger cairn near Torgyle.

Inverness Courier   Since 1933, this one newspaper has aroused
much of the media interest in the Loch Ness phenomenon, and it
can claim to have published the first full-length article on alleged
sightings. The *Courier* was the first newspaper to publish a sighting
of any real significance: its edition of 2 May 1933 carried an item
under the headline 'Strange Spectacle on Loch Ness', in which **Alex
Campbell**, the Loch's water bailiff, told the story of **Mr and Mrs
John Mackay**'s sighting.
See also **Campbell, Alex.**

Irvine, Malcolm   Malcolm Irvine, of Scottish Film Productions,
deployed a small team of cameramen around the Loch over a two-
week period in late 1933. On 12 December, whilst on a hillside
opposite Urquhart Castle with colleagues Stanley Clinton and Scott
Hay, he shot two minutes of film of what he claimed was the
monster – the first film of the animal.

Irvine claimed that he observed two humps gently rising and falling
as the creature propelled itself across the lake at a speed of around 9-
10 m.p.h. He estimated it as being over 16 feet in length and grey in
colour, but virtually black at the tail. The witnesses claimed that the
monster swam past them at a distance of just 100 yards.

Unfortunately the Irvine film cannot be located – although it was
apparently shown to the Linnean Society a couple of years after it
was taken – so its existence is open to debate. Without evidence of
its existence the Irvine film cannot be categorized as evidence; a
couple of unclear still photographs have emerged in recent years,
allegedly from the Irvine footage, but the existence of these still
does not validate its authenticity.

On 22 September 1936, shortly after 3.30 p.m., Irvine filmed further footage of something strange in the Loch, opposite **Foyers**. A dark object appeared on the surface amid a disturbance of foam and spray, much of the spray apparently coming from what Irvine described as 'the rear'. The object, which remained submerged just beneath the Loch surface, moved very slowly, before sinking without trace.

See also **film footage.**

Irvine, Lindsay   Filmed an object in the Loch at 9.00 p.m. on the evening of 4 May 1968. A long, dark-coloured, 'log-type' object appeared to surface and break into two separate heavy humps. These moved off at speed. The image is hardly discernible on the film, and lacks any clear definition. This is mainly due to the type of equipment being used, which was totally inadequate for such a task.

See also **film footage.**

ITN   *See* **Independent Television News.**

J

James, David Guthrie, MBE, DSC, MP A Conservative Member of Parliament, and a man with a distinguished record of service in the Second World War, he was the leader of the **Loch Ness Investigation Bureau**. James was a man who refused to accept defeat. He greeted all the volunteers joining the Bureau and introduced them to Loch Ness. He would explain exactly what was required and expected of each and every individual with almost military precision, yet he was always amenable to positive suggestions.

James took it upon himself to find financial backing for the Bureau and did everything in his power to promote the investigations at the Loch. On the afternoon of 19 October 1962 he, along with seven other people, claimed to have had a surface sighting: 'Eight of us saw a length of back, 6-8 feet long, break the surface about 200 yards away and cruise slowly after fish. We shot about fifty feet of film, and eyewitness statements were taken from all concerned that evening.'

Curiously, in the foreword to William Owen's tourist brochure *Scotland's Loch Ness Monster* (1980) James says: 'I have spent many weeks by the Loch side and many blood-chilling hours drifting around Urquhart Bay on flat-calm nights praying for (and dreading) a close-up surfacing, without ever seeing anything.' Here he seemingly disregards the 1962 episode, though for what reason remains unclear.

What is clear, though, is that James was enthusiastic about his role with the Bureau, and was often prone to exaggerate facts. In June 1963, when the Bureau filmed a dark, log-shaped object in the Loch, he stated 'the head and neck are in the can'. The film was subsequently scrutinized, and the object found to be some 2½ miles away – too far to determine details such as head and neck. James died in 1986.

See also **Parliament**.

Jamieson, G.   Surface sighting on 27 December 1933. Jamieson, a local fruiterer, stated:

> I was driving a small car towards **Invermoriston**, near Jack's Quarry, when I saw in the water a 'tremendous creature' swimming rapidly towards Fort Augustus. The head and the face of the thing appeared to me to be the size of a large dog's, but the shape was definitely snake-like.
>
> The neck, which was rather thick, stood three feet out of the water and joined, just at the water level, a large hump which protruded about two feet above the surface. Behind this, and joining the first hump, was another and larger hump three or four feet out of the water. The whole length of the strange creature was between fifteen and twenty feet. Its skin seemed to be rough and of a 'knobbly' texture. The colour was almost black.
>
> I watched for about a minute and then, noticing a small boat near the opposite shore, I sounded my motor horn to attract the attention of the people in the boat. Immediately I did so, the creature, with a quick turn of its head, dived below. It had disappeared in a second or so, leaving behind a heavy wash. This is the first time I have seen anything resembling a 'monster', although I travel along the Loch road three times a week. I am positive there was no optical illusion about this thing I saw.

This sighting was recorded in the *Daily Mail* of 31 December 1933.

Japanese expedition   This took place in September 1973 amid great media excitement. The expedition leader was **Yoshio Kou**, an impresario; more curiously, his female sonar expert was believed to be a Tokyo nightclub singer! The expedition carried out sonar traces of the Loch, but was shocked by the sheer size of the expanse of water, and divers brought along to carry out underwater studies were similarly shocked at its murkiness. Sonar tests were carried out, but in the main the expedition was a failure. The team left Scotland after just two months, with Kou, the expedition leader and sponsor, greatly disillusioned.

JARIC   The British RAF's Joint Air Reconnaissance Intelligence Centre is internationally respected for its experience in analysing photographic and film footage. Its authority is unquestionable when examining evidence presented by those seeking out the unknown creature in Loch Ness. Using scientific methods, JARIC can enhance photographic picture quality to guage height, distance, depth, and even direction of travel of objects when filmed in the water. Computers can estimate camera angle thus providing important information for further research.

See also **Dinsdale, Tim; Raynor, Dick; Loch Ness Investigation Bureau.**

Jenkyns, Richard A retired farmer from **Invermoriston**, who had a sighting at 11.45 a.m. on 10 November 1973. This occurred close to the Invermoriston shore. Jenkyns started his tractor and then noticed a large commotion in the nearby Loch. It seemed to him that the noise of the tractor had frightened some creature, causing it to jump into the water. Watching the water he initially saw nothing, but then about 10-15 yards out, he saw a fish-like object slowly surface until he could see about 18 inches of it above the water. It remained motionless, before eventually moving forward and sinking without trace.

Jenkyns described the creature as being a black or grey-brown colour, with a matt texture to its skin. The head profile was similar to a snake's, with a small black eye or blow hole, and a 'great gash of a mouth' which he estimated to be about 9 inches long. He estimated that the creature measured about 9 inches in diameter, with the general appearance of a tube.

Jobes, William Jobes was with **Bruce Marshall** when, at 10.45 a.m. on 7 April 1969, he saw a single hump rise in the water. This was quickly followed by the appearance of a second 'in-line' hump. The object was grey with a glistening effect. It moved at a great speed before sinking out of sight.

See also **Marshall, Mr and Mrs Bruce.**

Johnstone, Mr and Mrs George The Johnstones witnessed a single, dark-coloured, humped object moving through the water at 7.50 a.m. on 14 June 1966. Before they had a chance to study the object, it had disappeared, leaving a large wake on the water surface as it did so.

K

Keay, John   A surface sighting on 6 October 1974. Keay was an Army recruiting sergeant, who was driving along the Loch side when he spotted something about 20 yards out in the water. He first saw a black dome about 1 foot tall and 4 feet long. Keay believed that this was too big to be a seal or a dolphin. (When interviewed about the sighting, Keay humorously stated that he had not had a drink for three weeks, and so wasn't hallucinating!)

Keith, E.M.   Headmistress of Rothienorman School, who had an alleged sighting of an animal on 30 March 1965. From a site close to **Dores** she saw a black creature about three-quarters of a mile away, paddling out across the Loch in the direction of Dores. As it came more fully into view it changed direction and began moving down the centre of the Loch, and 'some feet of black body' could be seen.
   See also **Ballantyne, James.**

Kerr, Craig   On 18 August 1996 Craig Kerr saw what he thought was the head and neck of a creature rising above the water off the **Invermoriston** camp site. He allegedly managed to photograph it, but to date this photograph has not appeared in print.

Keyes, Prudence   Prudence Keyes was a maid at Fort Augustus Abbey. On 5 August 1933 at 2.30 p.m., from a distance of about 740 yards, she claims to have seen a large dark object moving in the water on the flat calm Loch. This was off Fort Augustus, in the same place as **Nellie Smith**'s sighting and just half an hour earlier. Miss Keyes described the object as having a dark brown or blackish-grey granulated type of skin. There was one hump, estimated as being around 4-6 feet long, with ridges moving back and forth in the water.

Prudence Keyes claimed to have had a total of six separate sightings of the creature. On another occasion in 1934 she saw the creature close to shore, splashing about in the water, and she believed that during this sighting it was splashing water over its back, using its legs or flippers.
See also **Meiklem, Comdr. and Mrs R.A.R.; Smith, Nellie.**

Kilmany, Lord Member of the House of Lords who asked Her Majesty's Government in 1969 whether 'any harm' would come to any monsters which might be found to inhabit the Loch by expeditions mounted there. Lord Hughes, Joint Parliamentary Under-Secretary for Scotland, replied that he was satisfied that 'no harm' would come to any creatures located.

Kinder, Bill and family Surface sighting on 9 April 1996. The family, who were on holiday at the Loch, saw a 'shiny black' object moving through the water just north of Fort Augustus. It left behind a 30-foot trail in the water.

King, Mrs V. *See under* **Hitching, Hilda D.**

Kirton, Dr and Mrs J. Three sightings of the monster in two months. Dr Kirton was a medical practitioner from **Fort Augustus**.
The main sighting occurred when the doctor and his wife were crossing a wooden bridge over the River Oich, with their young granddaughter, on 13 November 1951. Mrs Kirton saw a black 'boat-like' object moving at a tremendous pace through the water, creating a huge commotion on the flat-calm Loch as it turned this way and that, before sinking from view. Her testimony totally corroborated the sighting made by **Col. Patrick Grant**, who also reported seeing a hump in the same area on the same day.
Also in November 1951 Dr Kirton and his wife were coming down the path behing **Invermoriston** village. Just over a mile away he saw moving away from them in the direction of Knockie boathouse, a creature dark brown in colour, which 'in shape looked like the rear view of a duck swimming in a pond'. Through binoculars, he estimated that it had an overall width of about 3-4 feet, and a little less than 3-4 feet was showing above the water surface. The sighting lasted about ten minutes until the creature disappeared into the shadow of the hills opposite.

On 26 December 1951, Dr Kirton had a further sighting when driving from **Fort Augustus** to Invermoriston with his son and another child. They were close to Innislaurne in Fort Augustus when they saw a black object in the water, half a mile or so away from them in the direction of Gorrie's Cave. They continued on their journey, monitoring the object in the water which sank as they passed Cherry Island. No head was visible, although a dark body like an 'upturned boat' was evident, which was about 10 feet long. The sighting lasted two minutes.

Klein, Dr Martin   Sonar expert in the **Rines** team which carried out an expedition at the Loch in September 1970. Klein was the designer of the Klein Associates high-frequency side-scan sonar that was used.
   See also **Rines, Robert.**

Knapp, H.   On 28 July 1966, Mr Knapp claimed to see a dark brown and green hump moving slowly in the Loch for a short distance before sinking from view. He could not determine what it was, other than it was 'large'.

Kou, Yoshio   *See* **Japanese expedition.**

Krane, John   On 21 September 1997, at around 4 p.m., John Krane claimed to see a large, black, animate object moving swiftly in the Loch just north of Urquhart Castle, creating a considerable wake as it did so. He said it was clearly a 'living creature', about 20 feet long, with 2 feet of body clearly visible above the surface. At one point the creature's head rose from the water and jerked upwards, as though swallowing. The sighting lasted two minutes before the animal submerged.

L

Lamb, William   *See under Arrow.*

land sightings   It is virtually impossible to determine with any accuracy the number of sightings either on land or in water. Most researchers have subjective views about the authenticity of those recorded, either verbally or in print, and this leads to disagreement about numbers, which vary according to which source one consults.

The following is a full list of all known land sightings, in which the creature has been seen clearly out of the water. Further details can be found in relevant entries.

1879: Group of children playing on north shore in an unnamed graveyard.

1880: **Eric H. Bright**, near Drumnadrochit.

1890s: **Gypsy.**

1912: **William MacGruer** and other children. Inchnacardoch Bay.

1919, February: **John Donald Forbes** and father, north of Inverfairgaig.

1919, September: **Mrs Peter Cameron** her sister and two brothers, Inchnacardoch Bay.

1923, April: **Alfred Cruickshank**, north of Invermoriston.

1926: **Ronald MacLeod**, Sandy Point.

1930s: **Alec Muir**, near Inverfarigaig.

1930s: Schoolchildren near Drumnadrochit.

1932, April: **L. Fordyce**, near Abriachan.

1933: **Mrs Eleanor Price-Hughes.**

1933, 22 July: **Mr and Mrs George F.T. Spicer**, Whitefield.

1933, 6 August: **Mrs M.F. MacLennan**, near Whitefield.

1933, December: **Mrs Reid**, Inverfarigaig.

1934, 5 January: **Arthur Grant**, near Abriachan.

1934, February: **Doreen Taylor**, near Foyers.

1934, 22 February: **Doreen Taylor**, near Foyers.

1934, 22 February: **Patricia Harvey/Jean MacDonald**, Inchnacardoch Bay.

1934, 3 June: **Margaret Munro**, Borlum Bay.

1934, 4 July: **Ian J. Matheson**, Glendoe.

1960, 28 February: **Torquil MacLeod**, between Invermoriston and Fort Augustus.

1963: Unnamed members of **Loch Ness Investigation Bureau** from Achnahannet.

1971, 15 May: near Foyers.

1979, 8 July: **Donald MacKinnon**, Foyers.

Lane, Lt.-Col. W.H.   Alleged sighting in May 1945 by Lt.-Col. Lane, his wife and two neighbours, from their homes at Tigh-na-Bruach just south of **Invermoriston**. The animal was described as a huge black object, which remained on the surface for about two minutes. Lt.-Col. Lane studied it through his binoculars and believed that there was a slight curve in the wake, which he described as moving through the water like a torpedo.

Leddy, Peter   Member of a camera team from BBC Scotland were travelling between **Fort Augustus** and **Inverness** on 3 September 1969 when they saw something peculiar swimming in the Loch. Cameraman Peter Leddy captured a 10-minute film of the object, which was about half a mile from shore. Because of the distance from the shore to the object, it was impossible to estimate its size accurately, but whatever it was created a reasonably-sized wake as it moved off towards Fort Augustus.

Legge, James   *See also* **Grant, Patrick.**

Lewis, Miss E.   *See under* **Galliford, C.**

Lichtervelde, Count Emmanuel de   Sighting on 28 September 1966. The Count was being driven around the Loch by Guy Senior, a former naval officer and Chairman of the Inverness Unionist Association, and his wife. A few miles to the south of **Dores**, they spotted a large dark object moving slowly in the water and watched it for around six minutes. They claimed to have seen two distinct humps, travelling at a speed of about 8 knots. Lichtervelde later said that the sighting was the most wonderful thing that could ever have happened to him.

Ling, Yorang, and family   Whilst on holiday at the Loch on 9 April 1996, the Ling family had a surface sighting of two humps rising from the water, just north of **Fort Augustus**. As the humps moved forward they left behind a trail in the water.

Loch Lochy   The most southerly of the three fresh-water Lochs which form the **Caledonian Canal**; it is situated to the south-west of Loch Ness. In 1997 a belief has been recorded that this Loch may well have underground tunnels which lead directly into Loch Ness, providing a route for any living creature to pass between the Lochs. Further scientific exploration of Loch Lochy is anticipated in the immediate future to confirm or dispel such beliefs.

Loch Morar   Loch near Mallaig, on the west coast of Scotland. 'Monster' sightings of a similar nature to those at Loch Ness have taken place over the years. The Loch Morar creature is commonly known as 'Morag'.
  See also **Loch Ness and Morar Project.**

Loch Ness   The Loch lies at the northern end of the Great Glen fault (*see* **Glen More Albyn**), which cuts across the Highlands of Scotland. It was formed around three hundred million years ago, when ancient Scotland began to split in two. During the Ice Age the fault line deepened beneath four thousand feet of ice, and when the ice thawed, about twelve thousand years ago, the Loch was born. The surrounding mountains rise to a height of two thousand feet. Loch Ness is part of the **Caledonian Canal** which connects it to Inverness at its northern end and with Loch Oich at its southern end. It is also connected to the sea at the northern end by the River Ness. The Loch contains the greatest volume of fresh water in the UK (an estimated 263 billion cubic feet), lies some 52 feet above sea level, and is 24 miles long and about 1 mile wide, giving it a surface area of 14,000 acres, or 21¾ square miles.
  According to sonar measurements taken by the Vickers submersible *Pisces* in 1969, the Loch is some 975 feet deep. It is estimated to contain 27 tonnes of fish, more than enough to provide food for a large predator, according to some scientists. The

main food sources to be found within the Loch (to identify these might provide some intimation as to what type of creature might well dwell in the Loch) are plants, plankton, detritus (organic constituents of sediment which are present on the Loch floor) and fish. The fish population generally consists of salmonids – salmon, trout (sea and brown) and char. The consistency of the water, which is peat-filled, and the Loch's steep sides, restrict the growth of rooted plants below a depth of about 10 feet.

The Loch is fed by eight rivers and somewhere around forty streams (burns). Its level rises during periods of heavy rain, or when snow thaws on the surrounding countryside. A rise of 2 feet is not uncommon, and rises of some 7 feet have frequently been recorded.

Loch Ness Investigations   The changed title of the **Loch Ness Investigation Bureau** which took place in 1970 when the Bureau believed a change of title would cause the work they carried out at the Loch to be taken more seriously.

See also **Loch Ness Investigation Bureau.**

Loch Ness Investigation Bureau   Formed in November 1961 as the Bureau for Investigating the Loch Ness Phenomena Limited, but formally incorporated on 20 March 1962 with **David James, Peter Scott, Richard Fitter** and **Constance Whyte** as its directors. A registered charity, it elected to donate any profits accrued to the World Wildlife Fund and the Council for Nature. In October 1962, 24 volunteers with war-surplus searchlights, which had a range of 6 miles, carried out a night-time search of the Loch for two weeks from a base at **Temple Pier.** On 18 October **Michael Spear** spotted a finger-like object, standing 6-8 feet out of the water and the same afternoon, seven members of the team together witnessed and filmed a long, dark shape cruising through the waters of **Urquhart Bay**, at a distance of about 200 yards. Analysis of this film by **JARIC** confirmed that the shape had some solidity and was dark in colour, with a glistening effect. This shape was estimated to be '6-8 feet long, 3 foot high and 6 foot wide' and was confirmed as being neither a boat, nor a submarine.

On 6 June 1963 six unnamed members of the Bureau filmed a curious water disturbance on the Loch, some 2 miles or so from their position at **Achnahannet**, which gave the appearance of a large dark object on the water's edge. On examination of the film, this was believed to have been caused by a group of mergansers. Further film was shot the same day, and this showed a dark cylindrical object, which lay in shallow water. The witnesses claimed to see a 'serpentine head and neck', and the object gave the impression of moving slowly up and down a small area against the wind and the waves. This footage was sent to JARIC for more detailed examination, and the experts were at a loss to determine just what the object was. They said it was impossible to determine whether its movements were independent, or caused through wave movement. A totally separate panel of experts checked the film, but they simply stated that the film corresponded with the eyewitness testimony.

During a third sighting on the same day, the Bureau filmed a 'dome-shaped' object which moved through the Loch, appearing to leave behind it some kind of trail or slick. This film was examined by experts including **Dr Maurice Burton**, who were at a loss to determine what it was. They noted that it seemed to make distinct progress in the water, with a turbulence around it, yet no one could identify it. They eventually conceded that, 'if it is an animate object, then it is a species unknown to any of us.'

On 13 June 1963 further footage of something moving in the Loch was taken by six members of the Bureau. When the film was later examined within the Bureau it was believed to show birds on the water and not any suspicious creature.

By 1968, the Bureau had enlisted the support of American sponsors and technicians and mounted a serious underwater investigation of the Loch. In 1970 the words 'phenomena' and 'bureau' were dropped from the title of the organisation in an effort to arouse greater interest through the use of a more professional-sounding name. As time progressed, however, Loch Ness Investigations found it increasingly hard to fund serious investigations. Interest had dwindled, and the cost of advanced technical equipment was rising, so that eventually it could not afford to maintain such expeditions. At the end of 1972 it was forced to close down field operations, due to lack of funds.

See also **JARIC; Mackal, Prof. Roy.**

Loch Ness Monster Fan Club   Formed in early 1996, after Gary Campbell (now Club President) sighted something 'unexplained' at the Loch and could find no official body to which he could report the occurrence. The fan club has numerous aims: to act as the first point of contact for those interested in the Loch Ness Monster phenomenon; to attempt to compile a comprehensive list of sightings and issue regular 'latest sighting bulletins'; to liaise between the various organizations and societies that have an interest in the phenomenon; to put members with specific interests/expertise in touch with others with a similar background. It now has an international membership, and it issues a six-monthly newsletter, *The Nesspaper*.

Loch Ness and Morar Project   In 1969, reports were received by the **Loch Ness Investigation Bureau** of a number of monster sightings at **Loch Morar** on Scotland's west coast. A team was deployed to the Loch in order to investigate these, however, as was the case with Loch Ness, no firm evidence was gathered by such expeditions. It was felt necessary to maintain an active interest at Morar, thus a small band of Loch-watchers volunteered to investigate the sightings there – this became known as the Loch Morar Expedition.

In 1979 the work carried out by the Loch Morar and Loch Ness Expeditions became known as the Loch Ness and Morar Project, in an attempt to raise interest and funds for both causes both of which were dwindling. The object was to continue research and expeditions in search of evidence of unknown animal life in the two Lochs (Loch Morar has its own monster, known as Morag). In 1981 the project discovered a population of Arctic char living in Loch Ness at a depth in excess of 700 feet. In relation to the monster phenomenon, the project offered very little new evidence; several sonar traces were recorded, but nothing which warranted any special attention. By 1985 the project was all but complete and was slowly disbanded, so that further research expeditions could propose their ideas.

logs   Some of the commonest objects to be mistaken for the creature are floating logs or tree trunks. With so much woodland surrounding the Loch it is common for such items to be seen floating on the surface. From a distance these can give the impression of being something rather more suspicious. Peter Baker commented, in an article published in the *Scotsman* (13 September 1960), how his expedition initially claimed a sighting of the creature, only to discover it to be a floating fir-tree.

Love, Robert, jnr   Love recorded a sonar trace of something large in the Loch on 10 October 1969 from the motor vessel *Rangitea*, which was fitted with a Honeywell Scanar II-F sonar. During a six-week spell at the Loch, Love covered 256 kilometres in patrolling the Loch. He claims that on 10 October 1969, at a point 2 km north-east of Foyers, he tracked a large target which moved along a looped path 190 m ahead and to one side of the boat, which was travelling on a straight course; he calculated from the sonar readings that the target was 67 metres deep.

Ten further searches of the area proved negative. It has since been claimed that there are certain inconsistencies in observation time and the boat's speed, and that the sonar being used was not capable of giving precise depth measurements, so that Love may have been tracking inanimate debris.

Lowe, Gordon   A 16-year-old boy who was out climbing **Meallfuarvonie** with **Robin Ward** in April 1955. From a height of approximately 1,500 feet, Lowe looked down toward the Loch and saw two dark humps swim out of **Foyers** Bay at great speed and disappear behind some trees. They reappeared a few seconds later, looking closely there seemed to be a third 'smaller hump' behind the first two. The creature moved in a straight course before disappearing from view.
See also **Ward, Robin.**

Lowrie, R.H.   The Lowrie family were aboard the 40-foot motor yacht *Finola* near **Aldourie** when, at 4.15 p.m. on 7 August 1960, they observed a curious form coming up astern, 3-5 metres away. Initially it looked something like a couple of ducks. The *Finola* was forced to change course to avoid a possible collision. The object was seen to submerge intermittently and had a neck-like protrusion breaking the surface. It moved quickly, causing a considerable disturbance and showing a green and brown skin coloration as it did so. The Lowries estimated the object's length as 12 metres. After about 10 minutes it swung away towards Aldourie Point, and some photographs were taken. When developed, these showed very little, other than two long lines of disturbed water.
See also **MacLeod, Torquil; Parliament.**

Lundberg, Sven, and family   Surface sighting on 27 June 1968, from a distance of around half a mile. A single black/green-coloured object like an upturned boat appeared on the surface and submerged without trace.

M

MacConnel, Robert   An engineer on board the vessel *Scott II* which on 20 October 1933 was towing the steel barge *Muriel* from **Fort Augustus** to Inverness. MacConnel saw a large wave mound moving out from the side of the Loch, until it eventually took station behind the *Muriel* and then followed the two boats for a time, providing MacConnel with the opportunity to ascertain that it was in fact something solid, and not some kind of freak wave motion. The engineer shouted across to the men of the *Muriel*, pointing and telling them to look at the object, but as he did so it seemed to veer off and submerge. MacConnel estimated that the object was about 2 yards long, and about 18 inches high.

MacDonald, Alexander   An **Abriachan** crofter who regularly travelled the Loch on the mail steamer between Abriachan and Inverness. In 1802 MacDonald claimed to have sighted something strange in the Loch on several occasions at different locations. He referred to it as 'the Salamander'. On one occasion, he saw it from a distance of just 50 yards; it turned out into the Loch and submerged some 500 yards from shore, with a great commotion.

MacDonald, Miss C.   Alleged sighting on 22 October 1933, at about 12.45 p.m., of a single dark-coloured hump, with a definite splashing movement on either side towards its front portion, moved slowly across the Loch creating a V-shaped ripple as it did so.

MacDonald, Mrs C.   Mrs MacDonald from **Invermoriston** had what she believed was a sighting of the creature one August evening in 1933. From a distance of about 600 yards she saw a black/grey-coloured object which she could only describe as being similar to a 'great eel', but much thicker. The thickness of the body showing above the surface was about 3 feet, and the length that was visible varied as the creature moved. There was definite side-to-side rolling movement noticed as it progressed slowly towards the shore. It remained in sight for a period of about 3 minutes before sinking from sight.

MacDonald, Douglas On 1 July 1996 between **Dores** and **Invermoriston**, MacDonald saw two black humps rise out of the water and submerge again within a few seconds. He could find no explanation for what he saw, but clearly believed it to be something unusual.

MacDonald, Duncan Curious tale of a diving incident said to have taken place in 1880. MacDonald was a diver sent to examine a sunken ship off the **Fort Augustus** entrance to the **Caledonian Canal.** He entered the water and was lowered into the murky depths where the wreck lay, but within a few minutes he signalled to his team on the surface to pull him clear. When he reached the surface MacDonald was pulled from the water a 'gibbering wreck', his face as white as chalk. His service crew could make no sense of his ramblings, but he eventually told how he had been examining the keel of the ship when he suddenly noticed a large animal lying on the shelf of rock where the ship was lodged. He claimed it was an 'odd-looking beastie', almost like a huge frog. It is said that MacDonald never dived in Loch Ness again.

MacDonald, Jean Land sighting of the animal on 22 February 1934 recorded in the *Glasgow Herald* of 3 March 1934. The two girls from **Fort Augustus** were walking along the road close to the town where **Inchnacardoch** Burn runs into the Loch. Under a full moon they saw an animal cross the burn on the shore below them and disappear in the direction of the Loch. Both described the animal as being 8-10 feet long, with four feet and a head which stood about 6 feet from the ground. The body was thickest at the shoulder and tapered towards the tail. The creature was very dark in colour, but perfectly white under its neck. Its legs were very short, and it moved rapidly yet silently.
See also **Harvey, Patricia.**

MacDonald, Capt. John A former captain of the MacBrayne's steamers which travelled the length and breadth of the Loch for half a century. On 12 May 1933, he wrote to the *Inverness Courier* in connection with the sighting by **Mr and Mrs Mackay**:

While I have no doubt that the parties, when motoring along Loch Ness, saw something that to them was unusual and perhaps uncanny in the great disturbance of water, I am afraid that it was their imagination that was stirred, and that the spectacle is not an extraordinary one. I say that from close and intimate experience of the Loch for well nigh seventy years. In the first place, it is news to me to learn, as your correspondent states, that 'for generations the Loch has been credited with being the home of a fearsome monster'. I have sailed on Loch Ness for fifty years, and during that time I have made no fewer than 20,000 trips up and down Loch Ness. During that half-century of almost daily intercourse with Loch Ness I have never seen such a 'monster' as described by your correspondent.

I have, however, seen what at first sight might be described as a 'tremendous upheaval in the Loch' but which to myself became a very ordinary occurrence as the years rolled on. On a day when the Loch was calm as a mill pond, reports reached me of what was described as an 'awful commotion in the Loch' perhaps three-quarters of a mile or so distant. As the steamer drew nearer to the place it was plainly seen that it was sporting salmon in lively mood who, by their leaping out of the water and racing about, created a great commotion in the calm waters, and certainly looked strange and perhaps fearsome when viewed some distance from the scene. While I do not desire to question the credibility of those who witnessed the spectacle, might I suggest that what they saw was nothing more or less than salmon at play, and that the occurrence was merely what I have seen many hundreds of times in voyaging up and down Loch Ness?

Sir John Murray of the Survey Department, and his able staff, made a thorough survey of the entire Loch some years ago, and made a minute chart of its surroundings. The survey was carried on for three years. Every part of the Loch was carefully sounded. Nothing in the way of abnormal fish or beasts were seen. I have no desire to kill a good yarn that adds to the romance of a beautiful Loch, but as I have been asked, or rather twitted, by many of my friends about the great monster I felt it was my duty to tell in

as plain a way as possible my own experiences of unusual experiences in Loch Ness.

MacDonald, Miss K.   Perhaps one of the oddest sightings yet to
be reported. In February 1932 Miss MacDonald saw, in the River
Ness, an animal which she described as being 6-8 feet long with a
short neck and toothed jaws. It looked not dissimilar to a crocodile.

She had a further sighting on 1 May 1934, when she saw an
animal in the Loch raise its head. Behind this was a single hump
which seemed to flatten out, although at times it seemed as though
there was three humps. Splashing motions seemed to be coming
either side of the humps, and the creature held its neck and head at
an angle to the water. It was described as drab brown in colour.

MacDonald, Miss Margaret   Surface sighting of an animal on 12
July 1954. She and **Kenneth MacKintosh** were out on the Loch in
a rowing boat. MacKintosh was rowing when he saw a series of
humps in the water a few hundred yards away. Miss MacDonald
also saw a three-humped creature cross the bay towards **Temple
Pier**, and further claimed to have seen a head, which remained in
view for about three minutes.

See also **MacKintosh, Kenneth.**

MacDonald, Sir Murdoch,   Surface sighting on 8 August 1934.
When driving south from **Invermoriston** in company with his son,
and having travelled some four miles, MacDonald saw two humps
in the water, about equal in length. He estimated that the total
length of the creature was about 15 feet, and it moved slowly in the
direction of **Fort Augustus**. The pair viewed the animal through
binoculars and said it was a greyish black colour.

MacDonald, William   Surface sighting of a creature on 29 April
1952. Macdonald was driving from **Fort Augustus** to Inverness with
a work colleague, when he spotted a wash about 150 yards long in
the Loch. At the front was a head, which stood about 3 feet out of
the water. The neck was about 8 inches in diameter, the head about
the same size but tapering to a point like a 'snake's head'.

MacEwen, Robin   An Inverness solicitor who reported two independent sightings of a creature in the Loch sometime in late 1930s,

both from **Brachla**. On the first sighting he described what he saw as being like an upturned boat, measuring 12 feet by 4 feet, and standing about 4 feet out of the water. It made an up and down motion. This very dark hump was about 200 yards from the Brachla shore. 'To say that it was twelve feet long would be an understatement,' claimed MacEwen.

His second sighting began with a big water commotion, followed by the appearance of a 'thick periscope' which then moved off moving from right to left across his position. Again there was a great disturbance of the water around the periscope object and behind it. The object, which was a few hundred yards away from him, travelled about 100 yards before disappearing. Both sightings, it is claimed, were witnessed by other persons who were not known to MacEwen.

MacGruer, Bella   See under **Chisholm, Duncan**.

MacGruer, William   One of a group of children who claimed to have had a land sighting of a 'strange animal' at **Inchnacardoch** Bay in 1912. MacGruer related the story in an article in the *Inverness Courier* of 10 October 1933, so the passage of time must have clouded his memory, causing his description of events to be somewhat vague. The group were apparently just a few yards from the creature, which MacGruer compared to a small camel. It had a long neck, a humped back and reasonably long legs, and it was a sandy pale yellow colour. It moved forward into the Loch and almost immediately disappeared without trace.

MacInnes, Edna   Eyewitness interviewed on satellite television's Discovery Channel and on BBC Radio Four's *Today* programme. On 17 June 1993 Miss MacInnes and her boyfriend **David Mackay** saw what looked like a head appear from the water. This, she believed, was about one foot above the surface. The creature was dark brown in colour and swam around waving its long, giraffe-like neck as it did so; its movement sent waves inshore. 'It was a definite living creature,' stated MacInnes. This initial sighting lasted about ten minutes.

Some forty minutes later, after running to a relative's house to fetch a camera, the couple had a second sighting and photographed the creature as it moved along the Loch, apparently just 200 metres from shore. Sadly, the published photographs show a white line moving from right to left creating a clear wake, but no defined outline of the monster.

See also **Mackay, David.**

MacIntosh, James and James jnr   On the evening of 17 June 1993 the two were returning from a fishing trip and driving along the Loch side. James junior looked out onto the Loch and exclaimed, 'Dad, that's not a boat.' James senior looked out over the Loch and saw what he described as 'a brown thing with a neck like a giraffe. It was swimming quite swiftly away from the shore.' The pair described the object they saw as being about 20 foot long. Its neck was some 6 feet tall and the body beneath it seemed to rise as the creature moved along. Both witnesses were interviewed by satellite television's Discovery Channel.

MacIver, Mr and Mrs Donald   When motoring alongside the Loch in the direction of **Foyers** in July 1947, the couple saw a large object moving at great speed near Inverfarigaig. 'At first we thought it was a motor boat, but there was no sound of engines, and no motor boat could attain such speed. Also, the Monster's head was held high out of the water. We were amazed at the amount of spray, and watched it for about ten minutes.'

Mrs MacIver recalled: 'I have motored alongside the Loch hundreds of times and until now was sceptical. We were convinced that it was a very big object. Two cyclists had stopped a little further along the road. I spoke to them and we all agreed as to what we had seen.'

See also **MacKinnon, Mrs A.**

Mack, A.   Surface sighting of something unusual in the Loch on 25 December 1933 at a distance of about 30 yards. A dark-coloured 10-foot-long hump was seen slowly moving in the water. It did not stay at the surface for very long before it submerged.

See also **Cameron, John; Christmas day; MacKintosh, D.**

Mackal, Prof. Roy   Author of *The Monster of Loch Ness* (1976), Mackal was for over twenty years an Associate Professor of Biochemistry at the University of Chicago, and Director of the **Loch Ness Investigation Bureau** between 1966 and 1972. He began his

dedicated research at the Loch in 1965. According to the *Sunday Telegraph* of 1 November 1981, he had abandoned it in favour of searching out dinosaurs in Central Africa. He does, however, re-visit the Loch and maintains a great interest in activities which occur there.
See also **Parliament.**

Mackay, David   Had a double sighting of a creature in the Loch in June 1993, along with his girlfriend, **Edna MacInnes**. Mackay attempted to photograph the creature, but the resulting frames showed only a wake on the water, with no clearly defined outline of what had created it.
See also **MacInnes, Edna.**

Mackay, Mr and Mrs John   According to **Alex Campbell**, correspondent for the *Inverness Courier*, the story of this sighting is basically as follows. The Mackays, tenants of the Drumnadrochit Hotel, were returning from Inverness on 14 March 1933. Driving along the old narrow road, they were close to the seven-mile stone opposite Aldourie Castle, at the very northerly tip of the Loch, Mrs Mackay suddenly shouted to her husband to stop the car and look at the Loch; she told him she could see an enormous black body rolling up and down. Mr Mackay stopped the car, but all he could see were ripples in the water which he estimated to be about 1½ miles away. He knew that something big must have caused these. The Loch is in fact only approximately five-eighths of a mile wide at this point.

Later, Mrs Mackay allegedly told author **Rupert Gould** that the creature was about 100 yards from shore. It moved towards Aldourie Pier, showing two black humps moving in line, the rear hump somewhat larger. These humps rose and sank in an undulating manner, before turning sharply to port in a semi-circle and then sinking.

Curiously, at the time of the sighting the Mackays simply claimed to have seen a violent commotion in the water like two ducks fighting.

Mrs Aldie Mackay was interviewed on BBC Radio on 3 April 1983, when she repeated the statement of her sighting. This failed to clarify which, if any, of the facts were most accurate, and with the passage of time the story of the sighting had changed. (Basically, it is now so full of ambiguity that one wonders just how much can be taken as an accurate version of events.) During this interview Mrs Mackay pointed out that many previous commentators on the case have mistakenly dated the sighting in April 1933; she confirmed that it occurred in March of that year.

Mackay, Brother Robert   *See under* **Dieckhoff, Dom Cyril.**

Mackay, John   Carpenter from Inverness, who had a sighting on 7 July 1968 near **Invermoriston**. MacKay saw a black hump in the water, which, he thought, was about 16 feet long and 8 feet high. The creature's head was similar to a sheep's, only bigger.

Mackay, John   MacKay, the chief reporter for the *Inverness Courier*, along with **Kenneth Cottier** and **J.W. McKillop** and his son Norman, had a surface sighting of the monster on 4 April 1947. MacKay claimed: 'I saw the dark head held high very distinctly, there can be no denial by even the most rabid scoffers that in Loch Ness there is something very abnormal.'
   See also **Cottier, Kenneth; McKillop, J.W.**

MacKay, William, DL, OBE, FSA   Chieftain of the Glen Urquhart Games, and ex-Dean of the Faculty of Lawyers in Inverness. He claims to have had two independent sightings of the animal in the Loch. The first was in 1937, when he was returning home from **Fort Augustus** in his car with some boys. In between **Temple Pier** and **Abriachan**, everyone in the car saw two dark humps about 3 feet high, which were stationary in the Loch.
   MacKay's second sighting took place just before the end of the Second World War. Returning from **Foyers** at about 5.00 p.m. one evening he saw two humps about 600 yards out in the Loch across from **Urquhart Bay**. He stopped his car and at once took out his telescope and began to watch the animal. MacKay described what he saw as being about 30 feet long, with a long neck that was kept flat in the water. The two humps were dark elephant grey in colour, and the creature appeared to have hair all over it. MacKay further mentioned seeing two flippers, which were paddling to help it change course.

MacKenzie, D.   MacKenzie from Balhain, allegedly had a sighting some time in October 1871 or 1872. He was apparently standing

on a rock off **Abriachan** when he saw what looked like a log floating across a flat-calm Loch. Without warning, the rigidity of the log
changed, as it suddenly seemed to come to life. MacKenzie thought
it looked like an upturned boat, but it seemed to wriggle, and
churned up water as it progressed towards **Urquhart Castle**.

MacKenzie, Sgt George   A police sergeant from Inverness who on
13 October 1971 was with **Inspector Henderson** in a group of
people who saw two humps in the water near Alltsaigh Youth
Hostel.
   See also **Henderson, Insp. Henry; Halfway House.**

MacKenzie, Miss Rena   Invermoriston woman who saw the
animal at about 3.00 p.m. on 22 December 1935. She claimed to
have seen the head and neck of the creature rise out of the water,
and described the under-part of the body as white and the head
small in comparison to the length and thickness of its neck. A passing steamer sounded its horn, which caused the creature to shake its
head agitatedly and then plunge out of sight.

MacKenzie, Torquil   Eyewitness interviewed on satellite television's Discovery Channel. Claimed to have seen a 'brown/black
slimy green object' surface on the Loch then submerge. He
described its appearance as being 'a neck as thick as a thigh, seven
feet tall'.

MacKinnon, Mrs A.   Surface sighting late one afternoon in July
1947. It is strongly suspected that this is the same sighting, from a
different location, as that of **Mr and Mrs Donald MacIver**. From a
distance of about 20-30 yards Mrs MacKinnon saw five dark-brown
humps appear on the surface and move through the water at great
speed.

MacKinnon, Donald   Whilst out walking at the Loch side near
Foyers in the late afternoon of 8 July 1979, Donald MacKinnon
claimed to have made a land sighting, observing a strange creature
appear from a wooded area, walk down to the Loch and slither
into the water. MacKinnon, who estimated that he was about 100-
150 yards away from it, described the creature as grey in colour,
about 24 feet long, with a long neck and small head. Four feet were

clearly visible, with what he described as 'three fingers' on each foot.

McKinnon, J. *See under* **MacRae, C.**

MacKintosh, Hamish Automobile Association patrolman who had a sighting at about 4.20 p.m. on 2 February 1959. A few hundred yards out into the Loch was a tall thin neck and a broad and very big 'humped body' moving slowly towards the Brachla shore. The head and neck, which appeared to project about 8 feet above the water and were greyish in colour, seemed to be moving from side to side. MacKintosh and a group of people who joined him, later saw the animal disappear from view, sinking vertically.

MacKintosh, J. Alleged sighting through field glasses on 16 July 1934. Two humps, about 3½ feet apart, rose about 3 feet out of the water. The overall length of the creature was somewhere in the region of 15 feet, and MacKintosh believed it was similar in colour to an elephant.

MacKintosh, Kenneth Saw an animal whilst boating on the Loch with **Margaret McDonald** on 12 July 1954. MacKintosh was rowing the boat when he saw a series of humps surface a few hundred yards from their position. He at once stopped rowing in order to look at the creature, which moved slowly towards **Temple Pier**. Throughout the 5-minute duration of the sighting, a head and three humps were visible before the creature submerged.
See also **MacDonald, Margaret.**

MacLean, Donald Captain of the Peterhead drifter *Rival III* which, on 2 December 1954, detected odd traces on the chart printed by its on-board sonar equipment.
Experts who analysed the readings estimated that the object had been at a depth of 480 feet deep and about 120 feet above the Loch bottom. It was moving from left to right on the chart and was about 50 feet long.
See also **Anderson, Peter;** *Rival III.*

MacLean, Jack   Sighting on 12 June 1963, whilst driving a bus on the Foyers-to-Inverness route. From just above Foyers Pier MacLean saw two humps: a large one and a small one. In front of them was a long, stretched-out neck with a head which resembled that of a dog or a sheep. A passenger on the bus, who also witnessed the incident, said that the humps were contracting and expanding like a piston as the animal moved through the water. The front hump was twisting backwards and forwards.

MacLean, John   In June 1938, John MacLean saw the animal less than 20 yards away in Alltsaigh Burn. Initially, only the head and neck were visible; the small and pointed head reminded him of a sheep without ears; a pair of narrow eyes were evident at the front, and the skin was dark and glistening. The neck was rather thin. The creature opened and closed its mouth several times quite quickly and kept throwing its head backwards, as though swallowing. Two humps appeared on the surface, as did about a 6-foot length of tail. The entire visible length of the creature was between 18 and 20 feet, and there was no sign of any limbs.

After a couple of minutes the creature lowered its head before diving, and as it did so the first hump rose twice as high out of the water. The creature submerged, only to reappear further out into the Loch. During the initial dive MacLean noticed that its underside was lighter in colour than the upper part; the underbelly seemed to be a straw colour. He told a reporter, 'I was petrified with astonishment.'

MacLean, William   Alleged sighting recorded in **Nicholas Witchell**'s *Loch Ness Story*. At Christmas time in 1933 MacLean apparently caught sight of a large animal basking on a gravel-covered beach half a mile south-west of **Dores**. After a short time it slithered off into the Loch, creating a large wash behind it.

MacLennan, M.F.   Land sighting on 6 August 1933. The MacLennan family, from **Drumnadrochit**, had crossed the Loch to attend church and were about to make their way home. Mrs MacLennan wandered down to the Loch side to their boat near Whitefield, where she came across a dark grey animal resting 6 feet above her on a ledge. Alarmed, she shouted out for her family to come and see. However, hearing the cry, the creature lurched and slithered off the other side of the ledge and splashed down into the water; as a result the rest of the family failed to see anything but water disturbance. The animal was described as being 'hunched up, facing the water'. It was about 20-25 feet long and had short, thick, clumsy legs with a kind of hoof, very like a pig's (the feet were later described as being more like the cloven feet of a dinosaur). The rear legs did not appear to support the body, because it slithered along, almost like a seal. The creature had no ears on its head, and its back appeared to be ridged 'something like an elephant's' and was humped.

Mrs MacLennan reported a further sighting on 25 February 1934, when at about 4.20 p.m. she saw a 6-foot-tall, black, round column, with a small and pointed top. It seemed to turn from side to side before submerging and leaving a wash.

MacLeod, F. On 30 October 1933, from a distance of 450 yards, F. MacLeod saw a black hump in the water. This appeared to undulate, which made it difficult to assess its size; however, Mr MacLeod believed it to be a maximum of some 9 feet in length. The hump moved at about 6 m.p.h. and changed direction before submerging.

MacLeod, Isobel Alleged sighting on 31 August 1979 along with **Muriel Clark**. A snake-like head and coil appeared in the water. Both women were convinced that beneath this head and below the water there was a huge body. It sank in a manner similar to a submarine.

See also **Clark, Muriel.**

MacLeod, J.M.F. At 8.30 a.m. on 6 November 1968, from a position close to **Dores**, MacLeod saw a 4-foot neck protruding from the water at an angle of about 70°. In his eagerness to get out to look at the object he slammed his car door – this seemed to frighten off the creature, which sank causing ripples that moved towards the centre of the Loch.

MacLeod, John Sometime in 1908 MacLeod was fishing near a pool on the River Moriston where it joins the Loch, when he noticed a large creature lying in the water just below the surface. He cast his line at it, and the creature, which looked like an eel with a 40-foot-long tapering body, swam off. This report was not recorded until December 1933, when it appeared in the *Weekly Scotsman* and *The Times*.

MacLeod, Ronald According to Mrs Ann MacDonald, her brother Ronald MacLeod had a land sighting of the creature at Sandy Point, some time in 1926. Through his telescope he allegedly saw a long, rough-necked animal move out of the water onto land. He claimed it had a large broad head and a wide mouth, and along its back were seven 'sails', the largest of which was in the centre.

MacLeod, Torquil Allegedly sighted the creature on two separate occasions. On 28 February 1960, at about 3.30 p.m., whilst travelling from **Invermoriston** to **Fort Augustus**, he saw what he thought was a slight movement on the opposite Loch shore. Stopping his car, he peered through his binoculars and saw a large black/grey mass basking on the shore. At the front there appeared to be what looked like outsize elephant trunks, although MacLeod was unsure whether he was looking at the animal's head and neck, or its tail. It looked as if it was scanning the shore in both directions. MacLeod watched the animal for about 8-9 minutes before it turned, exposing a large squarish end flipper which was situated in front of big rear paddles or flippers. The animal then flopped into the water and disappeared from sight. MacLeod later stated that he thought the animal must have been anything between 45 and 50 feet long.

MacLeod's second sighting occurred at **Aldourie** on 7 August 1960 at around 4.15 p.m. He and his wife and Mr and Mrs Seddon-Smith, an Australian couple, were looking through binoculars and saw rhythmic splashes in the water, as though made by a paddle motion. Whatever made the splashes was estimated to be moving at 8-9 knots. This coincided with the **Lowrie** sighting.

Torquil MacLeod was allegedly a sick man, suffering from a blood disorder. Together with his Australian wife, he had moved to the area with the sole purpose of searching for the creature, which he wanted to see before he died. The couple sold the two-masted ketch *Airy Mouse* in which they had been living and bought a large war-surplus radio vehicle, which they converted into a mobile home and base for monster watching. Sadly, for all his enthusiasm and belief, Torquil MacLeod's retelling of his initial sighting threw up inconsistencies in the basic facts of his story, and this in turn led to some concern about its authenticity. It is difficult to conceive that anyone, whether or not they were sick, could forget precisely what the creature looked like, or what the weather conditions were on the day in question. MacLeod apparently did, which has cast doubt over much of what he claimed.

See also **Lowrie, R.H.**

MacMillan, Duncan   Alleged sighting on 28 October 1936 about 1½ miles south of **Urquhart Castle**. This is the most witnessed sighting on record – something like fifty people in different locations claimed to have seen a similar incident – but MacMillan, it is claimed, was the first of them. Standing in the doorway of his cottage, on the road above Lennie, he saw what appeared to be a head and neck rise out of the water, about 500 yards out into the calm Loch, then the animal slowly moved along with its head and neck visible above the water. The head was described as 'small' with a greyish appearance. Behind this two distinct humps appeared, one a short distance behind the head, and the second some distance behind that. MacMillan called to his wife and her father and sister to come and see. Other independent witnesses recalled seeing a tail/flipper-like object behind the second hump below the surface, which gave the appearance of propelling the animal.

See also **mass sightings.**

MacMillan, Peter   Sighting on 17 August 1954. Peter MacMillan, who was Head Keeper on the Glenmoriston estates, claimed to have watched the creature near the mouth of the River Moriston. Using a telescope, he saw that the animal had two humps and that its skin was rough and crinkly, like an elephant's. It set off at high speed towards the **Fort Augustus** end of the Loch, sending out a terrific wash as it did so. MacMillan estimated its total length to be 35 feet and said it was the most agile and powerful creature he had ever seen.

MacNab, Peter A.   An Ayrshire councillor and bank manager who photographed something off **Urquhart Castle** on 29 July 1955. Standing on the road above the castle, he noticed a movement in the water and, thinking of the monster, he changed the lens of his

Exacta 127 camera and took a photograph. Within seconds he had taken a second photograph with a Kodak fixed-focus camera. The creature then submerged.

A great deal of mystery surrounds this image. Allegedly, only one of the photographs is now in existence. Furthermore, the surviving print has apparently been rephotographed, as object angles differ in the various reproductions. There is now a belief that the MacNab photograph is in fact a fake, with the humps having been superimposed over an image of a 14-foot Loch boat – hence the suitable wake.

MacNaughton, Helen   Sighting on 8 September 1964 from a range of about 230 yards. A 6-foot-tall head and neck surfaced and appeared to turn from side to side. The head looked to have protuberances at the top, and was held at a 45° angle to the water.

MacPhail, Hector   Alleged sighting towards the end of August 1933 at about 8.00 p.m. on an overcast evening. MacPhail claimed that about 100 yards out into the Loch, a long hump gradually surfaced and moved slowly in the water before disappearing. It was described as being about 18 feet long, and 2 feet in diameter, with a brown, smooth skin.

MacPherson, John   Commercial photographer from Drumcharrel, Cawdor, Nairn, who developed and printed **Lachlan Stuart's** photograph in 1951. MacPherson stated that the film appeared to be perfectly normal and that the low light level was correct for a picture taken at 6.30 a.m.

MacRae, C.   Sighting through a telescope on 10 November 1933, at about 2.00 p.m., on a flat-calm Loch. Mr MacRae and J. MacKinnon saw a reddish-brown hump, similar to an upturnd boat, appear about one mile from their position. There was a great deal of splashing in the water around the object, which dived and surfaced two or three times before finally disappearing.

MacRae, Dr Farquhar   Born at Lochalsh on 14 November 1855, he matriculated at the University of Aberdeen and took degrees on Bachelor of Medicine and Master of Surgery in 1887. He practised as a medical officer at the Rio Tinto Mine at Huelva, Spain, in July

1887 and registered as a doctor on 13 March 1888. In February 1889 he resigned from his position with Rio Tinto and returned to Great Britain. From 1892 to 1904 he practised at a number of surgeries in London before retiring in 1925 and returning to Scotland where he took up residence at Ratagan on the south shore of Loch Duich, buying the old Ratagan farmhouse and renaming it Selma.

At some time, believed to be around 1935, early in the morning, he is said to have captured the creature on film for around 4-5 minutes. His reason for being at the Loch so early was presumably the hope of filming the beast. The **film footage** is said to have been shown to three other persons (Col. Sir Donald Cameron of Lochiel and Alastair Dallas), who were to act as trustees. The creature it showed was described as having a long neck, a pointed head with narrow eyes, small horns and three humps, and an estimated length of about 10 feet. The original film of the sighting was then allegedly placed in a London bank vault, where it was to remain until mankind took the subject of the Loch Ness Monster more seriously.

The story of this sighting and the footage was first recorded by author **F.W. (Ted) Holiday** in *The Great Orm of Loch Ness*, who failed to mention his source for the information. The whereabouts of this film and the authenticity of the tale surrounding it are extremely dubious. Along with Dr Mike Dash, the author has spent several months tracking down and identifying Dr MacRae and others associated with the story. All first-hand witnesses are dead. Author Ted Holiday interviewed one of the three alleged trustees of the film, Alastair Dallas, at his Kirkudbright home, but despite his efforts, Holiday failed to produce any positive evidence of the film's existence.

Born in Berlin in 1898, Alastair Dallas was a distinguished painter of landscapes in oil and watercolour. He died in 1983. Private research carried out by the author located his son, also known as Alastair. An interview with him on 21 May 1998 confirmed that he did not know the whereabouts of the MacRae film, and that Alastair Dallas senior apparently had a personal sighting of the creature in the 1930s, as he had lunch by the Loch. The alleged MacRae sighting was always something of an enigma to the rest of the family; indeed, it was family knowledge that Dr MacRae himself did not know where the film was kept.

I was told by Alastair Dallas junior that the identity of the alleged third trustee was never known, and – since, to the best of his knowledge, all three trustees were now dead – the film, if it ever existed, or if located, could not be released without all three signing the release papers. Dallas junior felt that further research into the MacRae film was likely to lead to a dead end, and remained sceptical about the creatures existence, and hence about the existence of the film. Furthermore, he could not recall his father having any close personal contact with any Dr MacRae. Presumably, to have been nominated as a trustee, he must have been a close personal friend of MacRae, and there is no evidence of such a friendship. Moreover, if the film remains in a security box in a bank, then someone somewhere would have to be paying a fee for this. If Alastair Dallas junior knows nothing of this, then the question that must be asked is, Who, if anyone, is paying the fees for the security box? Nor is anything known of any other trustees. Checks of London banks popular during the era when the film was said to have been shot revealed no direct trace of any vault in the name of Farquhar MacRae, and none of the MacRae family knows anything of a London bank vault or any film. If the film exists at all, its safekeeping must be financed by someone, yet no family members are aware of it! Neither the author nor Dr Mike Dash, both of whom have researched the subject extensively, have been able to confirm the film's existence. It seems that the Farquhar MacRae film was little more than another fanciful tale which has until now been accepted as fact.

See also **film footage.**

mammal *See under* identity.

Man, Mysteries and Monsters Half-hour television programme shot in 1969 by a film crew from the Walt Disney Film Company. The result could hardly be described as serious research. It involved a cartoon monster questioning its own authenticity with the programme's commentator. In 1949 Walt Disney had considered using the Loch Ness creature as a feature in one of his films, but for some reason elected not to follow this idea through.

Marshall, Mr and Mrs Bruce Alleged sighting in May 1971 when in the company of Sid France, Matt Pilgrim and Dennis Williams. Jean Marshall believed she saw a flipper-type action on a large, indefinably shaped object which moved through the Loch.

Bruce Marshall, in the company of Bill Jobes, had made a previous sighting on 7 April 1969 at around 10.45 a.m. The two men first saw a single hump appear in the water. This was quicklly followed by the appearance of a second hump; they estimated the total length of both humps as being around 20 feet. The humps moved at great speed through the water, submerged, reappeared and then sank again.

See also **France, Sid; Jobes, Bill.**

mass sightings

1933

Three witnesses on the Foyers to Dores road had a sighting on 24 August. They saw a disturbance on the surface of a calm Loch virtually opposite them and about halfway across. A drifter, the *Grant Hay*, was steaming along the Loch toward Inverness, and the disturbance was about 500 yards astern of it. (The water between the steamer and the disturbance was flat calm, causing the group to believe that the disturbances could not have been created by the drifter's movement.) Several humps were seen to rise and fall in line, with what was described as an undulating motion. The size and number visible at any one time varied, but they maintained a constant speed, and appeared to create their own wakes. After a short time the humps appeared to turn round and travel in the opposite direction before eventually submerging. The crew of the *Grant Hay* were later asked about the incident, but no one on board had seen anything unusual on the Loch that day.

1934

Sometime around 1934, a group of schoolchildren claimed to have spotted a 'most peculiar and horrifying animal' in the bushy swamp in the Urquhart Bay area. The creature observed apparently bore no similarity to anything they had ever seen before. It has been claimed that there were pictures of prehistoric animals located on the walls of their classroom, and they later identified the long-necked plesiosaur as closely resembling what they had seen.

1935

Two Benedictine fathers, several lay brothers and three schoolboys claimed to have seen a strange animal on the Loch through a telescope on 21 January 1935. The Loch was calm at the time, and the group said that the creature had three humps, each one about a foot high. It disappeared after several minutes.

1936

As many as fifty people are recorded as having witnessed a sighting lasting for 13 minutes on 28 October 1936. An initially unnamed cottager, now known to be Duncan MacMillan, who lived just above the shore road close to Urquhart Castle, saw two humps appear in the Loch about 500 yards from shore. Within minutes two tour buses and several car-loads of observers had stopped to witness the same incident, some through telescopes and binoculars. All unanimously described what they saw as being black humps lying behind a long neck and a small head.

1948

A forestry worker and several of his workmates claimed to have seen an animal on the Loch for 15 minutes on 15 July 1948. The creature broke the surface off Alltsaigh Youth Hostel before turning towards the shore and plunging out of sight.

A bus party on a tour from Strathpeffer had a sighting on 29 August 1948. They saw an animal in the Loch for approximately 15 minutes, as it travelled at great speed towards Urquhart Castle. One of the party said that its head was about 2 feet out of the water. No tail was seen, although the creature created a very large wash.

1953

Five employees of a building contractor and wood merchant reported a sighting through binoculars on 15 December 1953 in Urquhart Bay. They said that at the front it looked like a huge horse and that there was a great splashing about 20 feet behind which seemed to indicate a tail. The front part of its body was initially held high out of the water, and it seemed to shake itself. It then disappeared below the water, only to resurface further away, until it eventually moved out of their sight.

1954

Two women sighted an animal in the Loch on 22 July 1954, when they saw a long neck and three humps moving across towards Borlum Bay. The humps had an undulating movement as the animal picked up speed, and it created a large wash before eventually disappearing below the surface.

1958

On 21 May 1958 a bus driver, his conductor and two passengers had a sighting as an unknown animal swam across the Loch from Urquhart Castle towards Temple Pier. The animal moved across the water at a moderate speed leaving a wake behind it. It resembled a pair of dolphins.

Two female employees of the Lovat Hotel in Fort Augustus also believed they had a sighting on 16 July 1958. In Borlum Bay, near Fort Augustus, they saw a disturbance in the water that involved abnormally large ripples. Then, they claimed, an animal with a huge head resembling a camel's emerged and travelled up the Loch at about 10 m.p.h. It was dark grey, almost black, in colour and had a large snout.

1959

A busload of tourists from Inverness believed they saw the monster near Foyers on 26 June 1959. It followed a zig-zag course across the Loch. One witness said the head resembled a dog's.

Six people believed they saw an animal cruising along the surface of the Loch in the early morning sunshine, near Drumnadrochit on 8 July 1959.

1960

Three members of a scientific expedition claim to have had a sighting for around 20 seconds on 11 July 1960, near Drumnadrochit. They saw a dark shape break the surface, until eventually there was a hump about 1 foot to 18 inches above the water surface. This was thought to be about 10 feet long. The hump was near the middle of the Loch, about a mile away and moving against the current.

Two people, one of them a monk, had a sighting on 27 November 1960. They were part of a funeral procession making its way to St Benedict's Abbey, and saw something which looked similar to a 'periscope' break the surface of the Loch, rise about 1 foot above the water and move about 300 yards across Borlum Bay.

On 5 December 1960 a party of schoolchildren from Fort Augustus Junior Secondary School and three members of the school's canteen staff saw a hump cruising past the mouth of the

River Oich. It turned eastward then disappeared. Earlier that day two schoolboys in this party claimed to have seen two humps, the head and what appeared to be a tail. The canteen staff were impressed by the size of the wash the creature created.

1961

On 11 August 1961 some fourteen people, including Mrs Stanley Hill, made a sighting from the windows of the Clansman Hotel. According to Mrs Hill:

> It was a very fine day and the Loch quite calm. When we saw the monster it was just quietly lolloping along through the water 25 yards from shore, which made it 70 yards from us. We saw three humps, each about six feet long, and twice we saw its two near side flippers come out of the water in a paddling motion.
>
> We didn't see any head or neck, but I could make out the shadow of the submerged part of the body about 2 feet deep in the water. It was going as fast as a rowing boat, going a good pace – but very leisurely, with no wash or fuss at all. The humps were very dark charcoal grey in colour and rose about 2 feet above the water line. I am sure they were solid humps, like a camel's, and not undulations. We watched it for five minutes and then it submerged.

1964

Three forestry workers had a sighting near Invermoriston on 26 March 1964. They claim to have seen a large black object break the water, and cruise slowly towards the opposite shore. It was estimated as being about 15 feet long and grey in colour. Ten minutes before this sighting there had been a massive explosion at the side of the Loch, due to rock-blasting operations on the road. It is thought that this may have disturbed the animal.

1966

Three independent groups of people had separate sightings of a strange animal in the Loch, on 26 September 1966. Something large, black and heavy was seen by two different groups close to the Falls of Foyers, and another sighting was made by three members of the **Loch Ness Investigation Bureau**.
See also **MacGruer, William.**

Matheson, Ian J. Land sighting on 4 July 1934. Ian Matheson stated:

At 9.00 a.m. I was working at Glendoe sawmill, and looking down towards the Loch I saw a curious wave break the calm water about 100 yards from the shore. The wave increased in size as it rolled shorewards, and presently there emerged from the shallows a beast like a horse, but with a body in the form of five humps. With the air of flippers, it propelled itself right onto the beach, the body moving with the motions of a wriggling worm or eel. While the beast was actually worming its way ashore, twelve distinct humps were in view. The head was smaller and thicker than a horse's' and the neck was heavily maned. The beast shook the water from the mane as a horse does on a wet day.

The beast, which was seen to feed on weeds and water plants growing at the shore, where the ground is soft and swampy, had a body fully 30 feet long, but not very thick. When it was wriggling out of the water I thought it would never end. The eyes were small. It was the queerest looking thing I ever saw.

I thought, being alone, of running to the nearest house, but feared that if I turned my back the beast would vanish. I had no camera. I must have watched the creature for just about an hour, because the monastery clock struck ten as the beast wriggled back into the Loch and disappeared with a great splash.

Matheson, Roderick Alleged sighting in the summer of 1895, according to a report in the *Glasgow Herald* of 18 December 1933. Matheson described the object as 'the biggest eel I have ever seen in my life'. It had a neck like a horse and a mane.

McAfee, Andrew A story printed in the *Glasgow Sunday Post* of 27 July 1952, which indicated that many sightings were in fact, optical illusions. McAfee apparently sighted three dark humps in the water at a distance of 300 yards. Using this theodolite, he was able to determine that the humps were shadows, and that ripples and the wash of water moving past them gave the impression that the humps were moving. The story was repeated in a 1956 British Museum of Natural History booklet, *Scientific Research*, which stated that 'McAfee witnessed something "odd" through a theodolite at a distance of around three hundred yards. What he saw was three humps. However, closer inspection of the humps through binoculars revealed them to be shadows of the water.' McAfee therefore supposed that the phenomenon of 'monster sightings' would appear to be one of waves and water currents.

McCulloch, William   Cyclist who met **Mr and Mrs George Spicer** shortly after their land sighting of 22 July 1933. William McCulloch, from **Foyers**, cycled to the place where the Spicers had told him the creature had crossed in front of them. Examining the ground both above and below the road he deemed that it had been flattened by something large and heavy – he likened it to the flattening caused by a steamroller.

McDonnell, B.   Alleged sighting on 25/26 August 1933. Mrs McDonnell and **Mrs Sutherland** saw a brownish-black hump in the water, with a disturbance about 20 feet behind it. The hump was moving in an undulating manner and then submerged.

McGill, George   *See under* **Ferguson, Hamish.**

McGillvray, D.   Reported a sighting of a hump, believed to be the size of a horse's body, at 9.30 a.m. on 29 August 1923. The whole episode was viewed through a telescope. The hump was black/dark in colour and remained motionless before sinking with a splash.
   See also **Cumming, Mrs.**

McGillvray, James   Sighting of object at 7.30 a.m. on 10 May 1923, McGillvray and William Miller saw a 10-12-foot hump like an upturned boat. It remained stationary for a short time, before moving off in an arc and submerging.

McGowan, Dr C.   From the Department of Vertebrate Paleontology, Royal Ontario Museum, Canada. McGowan was part of the presentation who spoke upon the phenomena to Parliament in 1975. He said:

> Having assessed the photographic and sonar evidence collected in 1972 and 1975 ... and having considered other data pertinent to the Loch Ness phenomenon, I have arrived at the following ... I am satisfied that there is a sufficient weight of evidence to

support that there is an unexplained phenomenon of considerable interest in Loch Ness; the evidence suggests the presence of
large aquatic mammals.
See also **Parliament.**

McIntosh, D.   Alleged sighting on 26 December 1933, at about
10.15 a.m. McIntosh, **A. Mack** and **John Cameron** sighted an inanimate object about 30 yards from their position on the Loch. The
object was black and shiny and began to move around slowly; it had
a hump which was approximately 10 feet in length and 3 feet high.
About 6 feet in front of this was a further dark object, believed to
be the animal's head. Without causing any fuss the animal then
submerged.
See also **Cameron, John; Christmas Day; Mack, A.**

McIntosh, Dan   Alleged sighting of animal 200 yards off Tor
Point, whilst fishing with **James Cameron** from a boat at about 10
p.m. on a July evening in 1963. The head and neck reared 4-5 feet
out of the water only 20-30 yards away. Behind this was a small
hump. McIntosh described the head as being brownish-black, wide
and ugly, and the neck as a continuous curve; the creature appeared
to have a hairy mane.

McKay, William   Alleged sighting on 12 July 1934 at about 10.30
a.m. Through binoculars, McKay saw a slow-moving streak on the
water surface. It was a singular black object, which then disappeared. McKay had a second sighting at 4.30 p.m. the same day,
when he and **William Campbell** saw two 6-foot humps, which were
about 6 feet apart, surface five times before moving away.
   McKay seems to have had two other sightings on consecutive
days: 18/19 July 1934. On 18 July he claimed to see a single black
hump moving through the water, estimating it as being about 15
feet long and 1 foot deep. The next day he saw a head and neck,
black with white on the underside, which splashed into the water.
See also **Campbell, William.**

McKillop, J.W., CBE   Sighting on 4 April 1947. McKillop was the
Chief Administrative Officer of the Inverness County Council and
a well-respected member of the community; his sighting of something unusual in the Loch was accepted by all who knew him as

authentic. He was in a car with three other men, travelling to Oban, when, about a mile short of **Drumnadrochit**, he claimed to have seen a very fast wake travelling in the water.

> I saw a large object at the head of the trail of rough water and foam. One of the party suggested that perhaps it was a motor boat, but there was no sound. I was sorry that I had no binoculars with me. There was a leading object like a head held high out of the water and part of a blackish body behind it. I watched it very carefully for 4-5 minutes. Then the head disappeared, but the long trail on the surface of the water continued.

The group moved on to **Urquhart Castle**, where they again stopped and looked out across the Loch for a further view, but all that could be seen was a water disturbance where the creature had apparently passed.

Such was the interest aroused by MacKillop's sighting that at the next meeting of the Inverness County Council he was asked to give a statement of what he had seen.

> I confess that I had certain doubts about it myself, but these were largely removed by the fact that several men on whose word I could place reliance had already seen the object. But any doubts that remained were completely dispelled on the afternoon of Good Friday, when I had the good fortune to witness what is regarded as the Loch Ness Monster.

This same sighting was in fact witnessed by an unnamed independent party of motorists who had seen a 'long dark form moving very slowly in the Loch; after two minutes it sank leaving a great wash'.

See also **Cottier, Kenneth**; **Mackay, John C.**

McLennan, Mr and Mrs Alleged sighting of animal in May or June 1933. The creature's head and neck reared up out of the water, creating a large water disturbance. Further disturbance indicated to the couple that the creature's full length must have been about 30 feet. Two humps were clearly visible above the water, a short distance in line behind the head and neck. The creature appeared to have wool or hair on the back of its neck.

McQueen, G. Two claimed sightings. The first was in August

1933. In mid-afternoon, at a distance of about 500-600 yards on a calm Loch near **Foyers**, a 12 foot by 4 foot dark-coloured hump appeared on the water; it appeared to be moving slowly and was causing ripples in its immediate area. The second sighting was 22 October 1933, a sunny day, when at about 12.15 p.m. Mr McQueen again saw a single hump in **Urquhart Bay**. This one was brown in colour and about 5-6 feet long and about 2 feet in circumference. It moved in a zig-zag across the Loch, causing a V-shaped wash as it did so.

McSkimming, J.M. Alleged sighting in September 1933 near **Dores**. At around 3.45 p.m., a single dark-brown 30-foot hump surfaced about 2,000 yards from the shore. It moved slowly towards the shore, passing out of Mr McSkimming's field of view.

Meallfuarvonie Mountain 2,284 feet high on the north-west shore of the Loch, some 4 miles north-east of **Invermoriston**. It is conspicuous, as it stands alone, and is used as a point of navigation by many ships in the Moray Firth. From its peak, there are fantastic views of the natural fault of Glen More Albyn.
  See also **Lowe, Gordon**.

Meiklem, Comdr. Mrs and Richard Alleged sighting at 3.00 p.m. on 5 August 1933. At a distance of around 740 yards the Meilklems observed the humped back of an animal in the dead calm Loch off Cherry Island. Comdr. Meiklem watched it for a few minutes through binoculars. He described the hump, which was end on to him, as dark brown or grey in colour, with a darker-coloured ridge along it that appeared to taper down towards the water. The skin was knobbly and warted. Meiklem claimed that he saw this hump on no less than six occasions within a 90-minute period.

Comdr. Meiklem was a firm believer in the continued survival of plesiosaurs and also a close neighbour of **Alex Campbell**. Both men were interviewed by journalist **Philip Stalker** for the *Scotsman* in October 1933, and it was perhaps the publication of their tales that prompted so much interest in the mystery.

According to **Nicholas Witchell** in *Loch Ness Story*, Meiklem had a further sighting in April 1944. A report of this was included in a news bulletin sent out to prisoners of war in Europe.
  See also **Keyes, Prudence; Smith, Nellie**.

Miller, Mrs William   On 14 July 1908 Mrs Miller saw a large, dark-coloured hump rise above the water. It remained stationary for a few seconds before suddenly swimming off and creating a terrific wash as it did so.

Miller, William   Gamekeeper from Caigellachie, who claimed to have seen the monster on the clear morning of 10 May 1923. The creature was lying on the surface of the water near Abriachan pier. At first it lay motionless and looked like an upturned rowing boat, then it swam in an arc before disappearing beneath the water.
   See also **McGillvray, James.**

Milne, Ian   One of three young anglers who were out on the dead calm Loch off Tor Point, **Dores,** at about 8.15 p.m. on 14 July 1930. Milne heard a great noise and saw a commotion in the water about 600 metres south of them. Spray was thrown into the air as the commotion moved to within 300 metres of their boat before apparently turning aside into the bay above Dores; the boat rocked violently as a 75-centimetre wave passed. Milne claimed that he saw two or three shallow humps and that the object moved with an undulating motion, similar to a giant conger eel, and appeared to be propelled from its tail end. He was certain it was neither an otter nor a seal.

mirages   It has been claimed that many sightings are of everyday objects magnified by mirage distortion, when temperature inversions in the air over the water disturb the refraction of light during the spring and summer. A mysterious haze does often appear over the Loch on a warm, sunny day, and this does cause visibility to deteriorate. The main causes of the mirage effect at Loch Ness are generally attributed to the light on any specific day; similarly on warm days a haze is often present over the water surface which does cause confusion over sightings. The shore-to-object distance and reflection from the water do often cause misleading portrayals of events to the naked eye, not only of the casual visitor but those of experts also. Finally, it has to be said, that taking all these things into account, and the fact that all too many people who visit the Loch possess a desire to see the monster, there is perhaps, an element of 'seeing what you want to see' involved.

Moir, Marjorie   With **Mrs Grant Shewglie** had an alleged 14-minute sighting one afternoon in October 1936. A dark grey creature with three humps appeared, stationary on the surface of the Loch, with its head and neck clearly visible. The long, slender head and neck appeared to be dipping into the water before the creature turned and resurfaced, before again submerging. It then moved off quickly in the direction of **Urquhart Castle**. In *More Than A Legend*, **Constance Whyte** recounted how Mrs Moir had told her that, as a child, she recalled her grandfather warning local children not to play near the water's edge because of the 'water kelpie'.
See also **water kelpie**.

Moir, W.D.H.   Mr Moir, from **Fort Augustus**, was out walking towards Point Clair at about 9.15 p.m. on 26 August 1933; the evening was sunny and the Loch dead calm. About 200 yards out into the Loch he noticed an object moving towards Inchnacardoch Bay, passing the far side of Cherry Island, and he moved to a better vantage point to watch it.

The creature was rolling slightly from side to side in what appeared to be relatively shallow water. Mr Moir estimated the part of it that was visible above the water surface to be about 40 feet long, rising abruptly at one end to a height of about 5 feet; the opposite end seemed gradually to taper. The animal was a brown colour, although it seemed to be lighter along its sides, near the water. The sighting lasted for about 5 minutes and ended when Moir left the scene to get a camera. When he returned he found that the creature had left the area.

Monster Hunt Weekend   All comers were invited to Loch Ness for the weekend of 5-7 October 1990 to find the monster. Bookmakers William Hill offered a £250,000 reward to anyone providing first-class evidence of the monster's existence that would satisfy an expert from the **British Museum of Natural History**. Sponsors offered further rewards: £1,500 for the most original search method, and £1,000 for the best sighting.

Teams from all over the world arrived at the Loch side to try their luck, and television crews from Japan set up satellite links to beam home live transmissions. One unusual contribution came from Screaming Lord Sutch and his henchman Baron Von Thunderclap of the Monster Raving Loony Party (renamed The

Monster-raising Loony Party for the weekend). Lord Sutch yelled to the monster below the water, through a megaphone, demanding that it come out of its lair. He also attempted to coax it to the surface with a haggis steeped in 'loony stew' and sprinkled with magical dust. This he threw into the water, in the vain hope that the creature would surface and give him time to catch it in his net!

Despite the often light-hearted atmosphere of the weekend, there was the occasional incident which evoked serious excitement. A team from Aberdeen-based Oceanscan chartered two boats, complete with sonar equipment, and set out on the Loch. Without warning there was an unexplained blip on the sonar screen witnessed by four members of the ITV children's programme *Motormouth* as well as a Japanese film crew. The trace appeared to indicate something large moving at speed at the bottom of the Loch; it was too deep to be fish and moving too quickly and purposefully to be attributed to sonar error. Experts were at a loss for a reasonable explanation. As one witness said later, 'It's just another one of those mysterious happenings that seem to occur on Loch Ness with some frequency. I don't think it was anything other than a large creature. That, I'm afraid, is the only explanation I can come up with.'

The Oceanscan team won the £1,500 reward for the best search method. London-based journalist, Daniel Isted, joined in the search using a 'psychic crystal' attached to a fine chain, which, he claimed, would swing clockwise and anti-clockwise, to provide positive and negative answers to questions. His search was unsuccessful, but he did however make the headlines by proposing to his girlfriend on the shores of the Loch (the media recorded this as 'Catch of the Day').

Moran, E.J.R.   One of five witnesses who, on the evening of 27 July 1973, watched one of the animals swim across the Loch at speed. The sighting was made from the drive of the Foyers Hotel. Moran later stated that his scepticism had now dissolved and he was a firm believed in the animal's existence.

See also **Shaw, J.**

Morgan, Mary   Mary Morgan was one of a number of witnesses who saw something strange in the Loch at 8.30 p.m. on 4 April 1967. A single, 10-foot-long hump appeared on the surface, approximately 300-400 yards from where she stood, and then eventually submerged. It was clearly discernible, despite the fact that the Loch's surface was 'rippled' that evening.

See also **Breaks, Michael; Cary, Mrs E.W. and Heather.**

Morrison, Bobo   Claimed to have sighted an animal in March 1987. Morrison, a postman from **Drumnadrochit**, was driving to Inverness with three friends. Approaching Lochend, the group saw what appeared to be a large wash being thrown up out of the water, approximately 100 yards into the Loch. They parked the car and looked out into the Loch where they saw something 'big' churning up a lot of spray. It initially travelled in a southerly direction before circling, then heading north. After a period of about two minutes it submerged. Within five minutes it had resurfaced, displaying a long, low hump, with what looked like a second hump just in front of this.

Morrison, D.W.   One of a number of people who had a surface sighting of the monster off Balnafoich, near **Dores**, at 3.00 p.m. on 29 September 1933. It was a clear day and the Loch surface was calm. The creature moved across the witnesses' field of view, from right to left at a rate of about 15 knots. It was about half a mile away when first seen, but after five minutes it was believed to have moved to over a mile away. Morrison described what he saw as being like a 'giant caterpillar', with an up-and-down movement. He further thought he counted seven humps, the central ones rising higher than the others. The neck of the creature was not visible throughout the sighting, but when out of the water it was held vertically and appeared serpent-like. The head was of the same diameter as the neck.

Morrison, George   Assistant at Inverness chemist Messrs Ogston's who received the undeveloped **'surgeon's photograph'** from Lt.-Col. R.K. Wilson. It was Morrison who recommended to Wilson that he sold the copyright of the best photograph to the *Daily Mail*.

Mountain, Sir Edward   Chairman of the Eagle Star and British Dominion Insurance Company. On 13 July 1934, along with the company's Publicity Manager, **Captain James Fraser** of Inverness, he launched an expedition to the Loch. Twenty unemployed men from the area were signed on to stand watch on the Loch side between 9.00 a.m. and 6.00 p.m., five days a week, for five weeks. This saturation provided 11 clear reported sightings of 'something mysterious' within the Loch and a number of printable photographs. Most of the photographs have since been claimed to show the wakes of boats or waves caused by wind; experts claimed that just one photograph was of an anomalous object. The photographs were reproduced in the *Illustrated London News* of 8 August 1934, and cine film shot by Captain Fraser was shown to the Linnean Society's 1934 Annual Meeting, where those who saw it identified the object depicted as a seal, otter or whale.

Mountain was the author of an article, 'Solving the Mystery of Loch Ness', published in the *Field* of 22 September 1934.

See also **Fraser, Captain James; Grant, Patrick.**

Moyse, R.A. Witnessed a 'black three-humped' object appear on the Loch on 1 August 1969, at 8.30 p.m. The object, which was about 100 yards away, seemed to be 20-30 feet long and projected between a foot and eighteen inches above the surface. It moved very slowly in the water, creating a wake as it did so; its estimated speed was 3 m.p.h. At the time of the sighting, the Loch was flat calm, and visibility was good.

Muir, Alec Alleged land sighting recorded in Captain Alastair MacIntosh's memoirs (*No Alibi*, 1961). In the 1930s, whilst out in his car, Muir, a carpenter at the Foyers Aluminium works, claimed that a 'monster' crossed the road in front of him close to **Dores**. So startled was he that he could not appreciate what he had just seen. He stopped his car and returned to the area from where the creature had emerged. There he saw a depressed area of moss where he believed the creature must have been lying. It had left a visible trail to the Loch. No further relevant details of this sighting are known.

Mumford, Miss *See under* **Forbes, Mr and Mrs J.C.**

Munro, Capt. D.J. In 1938 Munro proposed setting up a limited company, Loch Ness Monster Limited, and selling blocks of one-shilling shares to finance a serious expedition. The expedition plans that were drawn up involved three fixed camera stations around the Loch, to be manned by one naval officer in charge, one marine and two others. Munro believed that somewhere in the region of £1,500 was needed to implement them. His scheme was hardly appealing to potential subscribers, since, he explained, 'No divident can be expected'. Just £90 was raised and the whole scheme collapsed.

In 1937 Munro privately published a paperback book, *Loch Ness Mystery*, which was based upon his private opinions. He was a keen writer to the press on the subject; a typical example is a letter he wrote to the *Inverness Courier* in late September 1933 in response to a feature based upon monster sightings:

> It may be dismissed at once that any large animal of a new species has appeared in Loch Ness. The animal in question is probably a large otter or seal. Otters frequenting the sea coast attain a much greater size than those found in inland waters, and one may have found its way into the Loch from the sea, or a pair of them. Otters are great travellers, and think nothing of a twenty-mile jaunt during a wet night.
>
> Lately in a Loch in New Galloway, a motor driver saw what he thought was a large animal playing in the middle of the Loch. A closer view proved this to be a male and female otter, with three half-grown ones, gambolling and playing.

Munro, Hugh Inverness lorry driver who believed he had a sighting on 23 August 1968, near **Foyers**. Munro described a 'strange' animal he had seen in the Loch as being about 50 yards long with two fins at the rear.

Munro, Margaret On 3 June 1934, at about 6.30 a.m., Miss Munro, a housemaid with Mr and Mrs Arthur Pimley at Kilchumein Lodge, was looking through binoculars towards Borlum Bay, abaout 200-300 yards away. She claimed to have seen a strange animal rolling on the shingle beach in the sun for about 25 minutes. The animal, much of which was clear of the water, had a giraffe-like neck and an absurdly small head out of proportion to the size of the body, which was dark grey in colour. The under part of the chest was white, and the skin was like an elephant's. Two very short forelegs or flippers were clearly seen. The animal kept turning itself in the sunshine, and it was able to arch its back into large humps. Finally it lowered its head and quietly entered the water and disappeared.

Murphy, Jonathan   On 14 May 1996 Murphy claimed to have taken a photograph of what he described as 'something spooky' in the Loch. It is claimed that this photograph has been submitted to NASA for further examination, but so far there have been no further developments.

Murray, Brother Robert   Surface sighting on a flat calm Loch near Fort Augustus, on 5 May 1940, along with Brother Robert MacKay and **Dom Cyril Dieckhoff**. A pole-like object estimated to be about 4 feet tall, seemed to surface and move through the water at a moderate speed before submerging.

Murray, Sir John, KCB, FRS   *See under* bathymetrical survey.

Museum of Natural History   *See under* British Museum of Natural History.

N

Nan   See under Academy of Applied Science.

Natural History Museum   *See under* British Museum of Natural History.

Ness Information Service   Formed in 1974 by enthusiastic monster watcher Rip Hepple as a news information service to replace the defunct **Loch Ness Investigation Bureau**, which had ceased to exist in 1973. The Ness Information Service issues regular bulletin-style newsletters to its worldwide membership, aptly titled *Nessletters*, which are aimed at filling the news gap created when the LNIB ceased issuing quarterly reports. This is the longest-running newsletter service relating to Loch Ness currently in existence.

Ness, Loch   *See under* Loch Ness.

Ness, River   Flows from the northern end of the Loch to the sea at Inverness. It is not uncommon to see seals in the river. In 1965 two businessmen claimed to have seen a 15-foot-long body, complete with humps, swimming out towards the sea. Many believe that this river is the access route that the creatures may have taken to enter the Loch. It should be noted that the River Ness is, in the main, fairly shallow, so that any large animal would find it difficult to swim up to gain access to the Loch. According to legend Saint Columba did encounter such a creature there in 565.
    See also **Columba, Saint.**

Nessie   The affectionate term most commonly used to refer to the alleged creature in Loch Ness. (Hence such terms and phrases as 'Nessie hunters' – those who take to the waters of the Loch in search of the creature – and 'Nessie watchers' – shore-based observers).

For some unknown reason, it has been deemed that 'Nessie' is in fact, a female. Most likely this is because the name Nessie is a diminutive of Agnes. Whatever the reason, the creature in Loch Ness is now well known as The Lady of the Lake.

Nessiteras rhombopteryx   Scientific name given to creature by **Sir Peter Scott** (then Chairman of the World Wildlife Fund); translated, it means 'Ness wonder with a diamond-shaped fin'. The name, first quoted in the 11 December 1975 issue of *Nature*, alludes to the Academy of Applied Science **'flipper' photograph** of 1972. **Nicholas Fairbairn** derived from it the anagram 'monster hoax by Sir Peter S'; **Dr Robert Rines** produced another in reply: 'Yes, both pix are monsters. R'.
See also **British Museum of Natural History.**

Newby, Ivor   Alleged sighting of animal on the evening of 21 May 1964 from the **Loch Ness Investigation Bureau** headquarters at **Achnahannet.** Two dark objects were sighted about 200 yards out into the Loch, where the water is estimated to be about 100 feet deep. Each was believed to be about 10 feet in length. Newby attempted to film the objects, but because of the loss of light nothing came out on the film. **Peter Hodge** also witnessed this sighting as he was standing with Newby.

news   Virtually everything to do with the Loch Ness Monster makes its way onto television or radio or into the press, but the coverage is not always sensible. One of the first ever 'news' features was filmed in 1933 by British Movietone News. A short clip shown in cinemas bore the title 'Expedition Still Combing Loch Ness'. It was in fact a report on **Marmaduke Wetherell's** expedition to the Loch and his finding of a 'monster' footprint, and it went on to explain that this was a hoax and that Wetherell was the butt of much hilarity. Further footage by the same company portrayed 'monster-hunting parties' flocking to the Loch to catch the beast. A mock creature was even filmed swimming in the Loch and was classed as 'unique footage'. Such reporting did little to justify reasonable sightings, although it did however bring the subject into the limelight and create a great deal of interest in it.

newt   Suggestion as to possible **identity** of the Loch Ness Monster. *See under* **Burr, Dr Malcolm.**

number plate   On 1 September 1992 the motor vehicle registration plate NES 1E was auctioned by the Driver and Vehicle Licensing Authority. It was sold to an intrepid monster fan for the sum of £4,500.

O

O'Connor, Peter O'Connor was a 26-year-old fireman from Gateshead who announced in 1960 that he had gathered a team of 60 volunteers from the Northern Naturalists Association to carry out an expedition to the Loch with the intention of trying to catch and destroy the monster using Bren guns and a bomb. The expedition never materialized, but O'Connor gained a small amount of media attention.

Then, in May 1960, he visited the area with his girlfriend, living in a tent beside the Loch. He revealed that he had had two sightings of the creature in the space of four days. The second and most notable occurred early in the morning of 27 May 1960, when he awoke and left his tent at 6.30 a.m., to see the animal swimming past his camp site. Grabbing his Brownie camera, he claimed to have waded into the water and taken a flashlight photograph of the creature from a distance of around 25 yards. (He later explained that he was able to get so close to the creature without alarming it thanks to his training as a marine commando and frogman, which enabled him to move through water without making any splashing or noise.)

The photograph which looks very much like a large boulder or stone was ridiculed by experts from the outset. According to **Dr Maurice Burton** the incident was faked, and the object photographed was little more than an inflated polythene bag weighed down with stones. Burton claims to have visited the camp site within two weeks of O'Connor's revelations and found the remains of the polythene bag, as well as stones and sticks which had been used in the hoax. Despite this, O'Connor went on to announce that he and his organization had titled the object in the photograph 'Nessiesaurus O'Connori'. An article about O'Connor's claims was published in the *Weekly Scotsman* of 16 June 1960.

O'Flynn, Henry Ardan   Claimed to have a sighting in autumn of 1933, along with a student named McBride. A single, rounded, 'black mass' appeared, moving through the water on the Loch, and then submerged. O'Flynn claimed that shots were fired at the object, which caused it to dive.

Ogilvy-Wedderburn, Sir Peter   In 1962 allegedly sighted three small humps which appeared on the Loch surface of **Urquhart Bay,** at a distance of about 50 feet. He was certain that humps were not the result of any kind of wave action but were solid objects. They disappeared after a few seconds.

Oich, Loch   Smallest and most central of the three fresh-water Lochs that make up the **Caledonian Canal.** Four miles long, it is located to the south-west of **Loch Ness,** and the **River Oich** and a stretch of canal connect the two.

Oich, River   Various sightings of the Loch Ness animal have been made around the mouth of the Oich, notably those of **Alex Campbell** in April 1933 and **Mrs Kirton** in 1951.

Old Fourlegs: The Story of the Coelacanth   Book by J.L.B. Smith (Longmans, 1956). Discusses the discovery of this prehistoric fish and how it survived for so long. It is a useful source of reference for proponents of the notion that a prehistoric creature may reside in Loch Ness. If the coelacanth can survive, then what else can?

Omand, Rev. Dr Donald   Carried out exorcism of the Loch on 2 June 1973 at the request of author F.W. Holiday. Omand said of the monster phenomena:

> The many honest folk who have beheld Nessie have been mistaken. What they saw was not something which was actually taking place at that precise moment. They possessed the same mysterious receptiveness I inherited from my mother. The gigantic creature which they were so privileged to see was no longer in the land of the living. It was something seen out of time. The so-termed Loch Ness monster is not physical but psychical.

See also **exorcism.**

Operation Deepscan   Sonar echo-sounding expedition in October 1987, led principally by **Adrian Shine**. A team of 19 motor cruisers lined up across the Loch, each fitted with echo-sounding devices. The idea was to sweep the full length of the Loch with the cruisers deployed in line across its full width. This, it was felt, would not only determine the presence of any large animate objects but also identify the habits of the Loch's fish and clarify other biological matters.

The operation captured the imagination of the world's press, which flocked to Loch Ness, and avidly awaited the daily briefing at the operation headquarters in the New Clansman Hotel. A number of large indeterminable contacts were made on initial forays, none of which could be scientifically explained, yet ultimately the news that the media longed for – that Loch Ness was home to some Jurassic-style animal – was never forthcoming.

A large portion of the Loch was swept, but not all of it, and the results of Deepscan were, from a media perspective, uninspiring. However, no one who saw the operation in progress can say that it was anything less than impressive.

otter   A further theory as to the **identity** of the Loch Ness Monster, which has been proposed by countless authorities writing upon the subject over the years. The case for the otter being some kind of unknown creature swimming in the Loch is a common one, notably made by Binns in *Loch Ness Mystery Solved* (1983, pp. 186-91), where he proposes a case for Monster sightings being nothing more than otters playing and swimming.

Oudemans, A.C.   Author of *The Great Sea Serpent: An Historical and Critical Treatise* (1892) and a pamphlet, *The Loch Ness Animal* (1934). Although well respected for his work upon the legend of the sea serpent, Oudemans' ideas about the Loch Ness animal seem strange – he held that the creature would be hairy.

P

Palmer, A.H. Made a surface sightong on 11 August 1933 at about 7.00 a.m. While camping near **Achnahannet**, Mr Palmer saw an animal from a distance of about 100 yards. Hearing a sudden disturbance, 'as though a gale of wind had struck the Loch', he rushed down to the shore and found that for some distance around the water was covered in large amounts of foam. He looked out into the Loch but could see nothing which could have created this. Returning to the scene about an hour later, he again looked out across the water, and saw what appeared to be a dark-coloured head travelling towards him. It was set low in the water and had an antenna set on each side. The mouth, which was opening and clos-ing, was about 12-18 inches wide and opened about 6 inches; it was clearly red inside. The animal then submerged.

Parliament Due to the apparently increasing evidence indicating the presence of some unidentified creature living in Loch Ness, and mainly as a result of the publication of the 1975 **Rines** photographs ('**gargoyle head**' and **underside view**), a presentation of the available evidence was given to both Houses of Parliament in the House of Commons on 10 August 1975. Those present included **David James MP**, **Tim Dinsdale**, **Dr Robert Rines**, **R.H. Lowrie**, **Prof. G.R. Zug**, **Prof. Roy Mackal** and **Dr C. McGowan** – a collection of academics and witnesses. Both McGowan and Zug categorically stated that it was now their belief that some form of large animal resided in Loch Ness, although there was as yet insufficient evidence to indicate precisely what the creatures were. Roy Mackal discussed the zoological aspect of the sightings, David James the conservation of the area, and Rines, Dinsdale and Lowrie all presented the evidence from their respective experiences. The outcome of the presentation was predictably negative (no government in the world would be prepared to confirm its belief in a real-life fairy tale – 'the existence

of a monster'), but the case for the existence of a large creature in the Loch had at least been given an official airing.
See also **Kilmany, Lord.**

Paterson, Sylvia   On 31 May 1966, at 11.15 a.m., Sylvia Paterson saw three dark-coloured humps moving quickly in the water. These seemed to streamline before submerging, but the disturbance they created in the water caused what seemed like a terrific wave motion.

Patience, Donald   *See under* **Sigel, Donald.**

peat   *See under* **visibility under water.**

Petrie, Provost, D.   Perpretrator in November 1935 of the infamous quote which led to sightings of the creature not being taken seriously. He said: 'The town of Inverness, had a reputation for bad drinking habits, all because it is said that anytime the Loch Ness monster is seen it is associated with persons intoxicated.'

Pharma   According to **Nicholas Witchell** (*The Loch Ness Story*) the *Pharma* was a motor yacht which belonged to the British Medical Association. On 22 August 1966 it tracked a moving object on its surface radar for almost 30 minutes. This object was estimated to be about 30 feet long. Observers from on board the vessel saw five humps, about three-quarters of a mile astern. The captain of the *Pharma*, J. Gough of Bridlington, later told reporters, 'What I saw has me completely puzzled. It looked like the belly of a huge horse breaking the surface.' G. Ralph of Inverness, the vessel's pilot, who monitored the sighting on its radar scanner, reported: 'It was sharp in the nose and tapered to a point at the other end. The part above the water measured about 30 feet.'
See also **Amery, Mike, B.Sc.**

Pilgrim, Matt   *See under* **France, Sid; Marshall, Mr and Mrs Bruce.**

Pimley, Mr and Mrs Arthur   The Pimleys visited the beach area of **Borlum Bay** on 3 June 1934, having heard of **Margaret Munro's** sighting (Munro was their housemaid). They found a large indentation in the heavy shingle which they thought might have been caused by a huge body. In the centre was a branch which had seemingly been crushed into the gravel.

See also **Munro, Mrs Margaret.**

Pisces   Submarine used in the production of *The Private Life of Sherlock Holmes*. *Pisces* also carried out underwater searches of the Loch and made a number of discoveries of ancient artifacts.

See also **underwater searches.**

plesiosaur   The most popular suggestion for the species of animal that may live in Loch Ness. A fish-eating dinosaur with sharp teeth, the plesiosaur had a long neck, a broad flat body without fins on its back, a stubby tail and oar-shaped flippers. It would occasionally swim into bays, or along the coast in search of its prey (mainly fish and squid), though it is believed to have preferred more open waters. The proposal that the alleged creature in Loch Ness might be a plesiosaur originated from **Dr Denys Tucker.**

The plesiosaur is thought to have been extinct for somewhere in the region of 70 million years, and the main argument against the animal in Loch Ness being a plesiosaur is that the Loch has only existed for somewhere around ten thousand years.

Point Clair   According to **Alex Campbell,** he visited gypsies camped on the Loch side at Point Clair, who had a sighting of an animal in the Loch in the mid-1940s. They told him that a pony tethered at the site became restless early one morning, causing one of the male members of the camp to get up to quieten it down. On looking out into the Loch he saw, about forty yards off shore, a large black 'swan-like' neck and head, rising and dipping into the water as it swam by. This, he believed, was the cause of the pony's uneasy condition.

Pommitz, Mr and Mrs   On 29 May 1966 at 10.05 a.m., Mr and Mrs Pommitz saw a single shiny hump rise in the water about half a mile away. The hump moved in 'jerk-like' motions, creating a wake as it did so. They believed it was part of an animate object, the majority of which lay hidden just beneath the water surface. The hump then suddenly sank from view – they said it 'dropped out of sight'.

Pool, M. Saw waves breaking against a stationary hump-like object at 9.20 a.m. on 5 September 1966. The object resembled an upturned boat, was about 6-7 feet long and 4 feet tall. It submerged, leaving a disturbance in the water.

Portland, Duke of Wrote to *The Times* in 1933, recalling that in 1895, when he became the tenant of the salmon-fishing on Loch Oich and the River Garry, the forester, the hotel keeper and the gillies used to talk of a 'horrible great beastie' which often appeared in Loch Ness.

Pratt, Howard Sighting of a single 10-12 foot grey-brown hump moving quickly through the water on 5 May 1968, at 10.00 a.m. in the evening.
See also **Bull, Phillip.**

Price-Hughes, Mrs Eleanor In 1933, shortly after the initial excitement of the first batch of sightings of something 'queer' in the Loch, a high proportion of 'rogue' sightings were reported, although many of these were verbal appraisals of incidents and cannot therefore be verified. The Price-Hughes land sighting is one such case.

Mrs Price-Hughes claimed to have first seen the monster in 1933. It appeared from some bushes on the Loch side carrying something pink in its mouth, plunged into the Loch and disappeared. No further details of this sighting are known.

Project Rosetta Scientific survey that examined the ecology of Loch Ness, based upon core samples taken from the bottom of the Loch, where layers of silt that have formed over centuries provide what has been described as 'a calendar of events'. Twelve-metre-long tubes were lowered to the bottom of the Loch, penetrating the layers of silt and collecting a sequence of them. The tubes were then brought to the surface, and their contents – a virtual time capsule of silt – dried out and examined.
See also **bathymetrical survey; Shine, Adrian.**

Project Urquhart An expedition that took place in 1993, involving satellite television's Discovery Channel, and co-founded by **Nicholas Witchell** and led by **Adrian Shine.** The results were filmed and produced by Yorkshire Television and directed by Colin Nobbs.

A team of invited scientists examined wildlife in the Loch and looked at some of the evidence so far produced. Modern computer-enhancement methods were applied to a number of the better-known historical photographs of alleged sightings of the creature, including the **'surgeon's photograph'**. When magnified and enhanced, this showed a 'white' object in front of the head and neck of the alleged creature with the appearance of tiny ripples emanating from it. This was thought likely to have been a separate object pulling along what is now almost certainly a fake monster behind it. The **'flipper' photograph** was also enhanced from its original format and despite every modern photographic technique available, could not be reproduced as the image that is most commonly known – which aroused speculation about the authenticity of the image.

The **Dinsdale** film was closely examined and, again, enhanced. The best possible still from the film was scrutinized and clearly shows some kind of shadow following the head of the wake, just beneath the surface. Closer examination of this revealed an object that, in the experts' opinion, looks like a body shape not too dissimilar to that commonly associated with the plesiosaur. The expert examining this stated, 'I never believed in it [the Loch Ness monster] before I did this enhancement, but now I am not so sure.' The item identified in the Dinsdale film is an exciting find and tends to indicate that it was an unknown object which Dinsdale filmed – rather than any mechanical object, such as a boat, as has previously been alleged.

Sonar tests were carried out on the Loch, twenty-four hours a day. On the night of 19 July 1993 Dr Colin Bean monitored the on-board sonar screens and saw an underwater storm caused by atmospheric conditions on the Loch. The following day, when examining the sonar charts of this incident, he noticed two large underwater contacts which were followed by a wake. It was confirmed from the readings that these could not have been shoals of fish (which do not cause a wake). Whatever the objects were, they were large, and the scientists could offer no logical explanation for their presence. The evidence deduced by the team seemed to indicate that at least one large unidentified creature may live within the Loch.

Pugh, Roger A visitor from London who saw what he termed 'the monster' on 14 October 1971. Whilst walking by the Loch with

Father Gregory Brusey, Pugh saw a disturbance in the water out of which rose a head and neck, which stood about 10 feet tall. Whatever the creature was, it appeared to swim towards them before sinking from view.

See also **Father Gregory.**

Pullen, Fred   Surface sighting on 18 May 1964 from a position about 2 miles from the object. Pullen saw a single 15-foot hump surface, remain stationary for a few seconds, and then submerge. Pullen later told others that he felt it to be part of some great animal and that, whatever it might be, it was much larger than he ever anticipated it could be.

Pyman, Col. D.   Along with A.G. Taylor, Jackie Higgins and P.M. Christopher, Col. Pyman saw, through binoculars, two linked water disturbances which were followed by the momentary sighting of a dark-coloured hump cruising on a curving course. The sighting occurred on 28 May 1967 at 10.10 a.m. in pleasant weather conditions. The hump was estimated to be around 2½ miles away.

Q

Quincey, Joseph Surface sighting on 31 January 1997 at 11.30 a.m. From a distance of around 100 yards in **Urquhart Bay**, Quincey saw a large brown object that he thought 'was about twenty feet long, with what appeared to be three feet of head and neck clearly visible at front'. The creature, which was most certainly a 'living beast', created a large V-shaped wake as it moved through the water. It submerged leaving a terrific wash behind.

Quinley, Derek A serving senior police officer who saw a 'pole-like' object rise from the water near **Drumnadrochit** on 14 July 1997 at about 6.00 a.m. Quinley believed this to be the head and neck of some animal, and he estimated its height at around 6 feet. He thought the skin was a deep brown, turning to a lighter brown, on the creature's underside. The head and neck appeared to be moving in a 'dipping' motion, and as the creature gathered speed the head and neck dropped to a more horizontal position, and a wake was created. The head returned to a more vertical position about 30 yards from where the initial sighting occurred, before finally submerging.

Having taken everything into account, Quinley came to the conclusion that there had to have been a large body behind and beneath the head and neck. The water immediately surrounding the visible parts was foaming as the creature progressed.

> I still cannot believe what I have seen. I, of all people, have actually seen the Loch Ness Monster. I know that people won't believe me, but who cares? That moment will live with me for the rest of my life.

Quinn, David Car mechanic from Leeds who was on holiday at the Loch, and sighted a dark coloured pole-like object rise out of the water on 4 March 1977 near **Dores**. The object was in sight for about 30 seconds, and was, in Mr Quinn's own words:

> A living object which stood about 3 feet above the water which looked very much like the top of a lamp-post in shape, which I took to be its head and neck. It was apparently turning as though looking around. It then dived under the water, arching its neck as it did so. I was only about 100 yards from it but couldn't make out any distinguishing features. It was incredible really. I didn't believe in the monster before, but I do now.

R

Ralph. D.   On 24 July 1934 Ralph claimed to have seen a solitary black hump, which he thought to be about 8 feet long and 18 inches high. Many claimed that what he saw was simply a boat wake, but he remained certain that his eyes had not deceived him and vehemently maintained that it was a large and solid living creature which had surfaced.

Raynor, Dick   Surface sighting and film of animal on 13 June 1967. From his position close to **Abriachan,** Raynor (a member of the **Loch Ness Investigation Bureau**) filmed a large V-shaped wake moving out of Dores Bay. As he was filming, the pleasure boat *Scott II* came into view and continued to travel on a parallel course with the object.

Raynor's film was sent to **JARIC** for further examination. There the film was magnified 38 times, and it was concluded that the object was travelling at not less than 5 m.p.h. and that the part of the object clearly breaking the surface may have been around 7 feet long. Since nothing in the Loch is known to be of that size, Raynor believes that some unknown large creature does reside there.

Reid, Mrs A.   Claimed land sighting of an unknown creature in mid-December 1933, first recorded in the *Inverness Courier* of 20 December 1933. Mrs Reid was the wife of the **Inverfarigaig** postmaster. While travelling along the road to Inverness, just outside Inverfarigaig she believed she saw an odd-looking creature lying in the bracken. It was about 10 feet long, dark in colour, and had a hairy mane on its neck (Mrs Reid recalled that 'its entire body seemed to be covered in hair'). Its body was described as similar in shape to that of a hippopotamus, and it had a large, round head and four short, thick, stumpy legs.

Since the sighting was obscured and took place at a distance of about 100 yards, some researchers have wondered whether this could have been a case of mistaken identity. **Mackal** dismissed the sighting and suggested that the creature could have been some form of 'congenitally deformed specimen of the Highland cattle common in the area'.

reptile   *See under* identity.

rewards   A number of rewards for the animal's capture have been offered over the years. The first came from Bertram Mills **Circus** which in 1933 offered £20,000 for its capture alive. So did the New York Zoo (which offered £5,000) who wanted the creature taken to America as part of this deal, and a private individual offered £1,000 to keep it in Scotland. Substantially higher sums were offered during the **Monster Hunt Weekend** in 1990.

Riggs, A.   Riggs, a butcher from Inverness, had a surface sighting on the evening of 5 August 1934 from **Urquhart Castle.** He told the *Scotsman* newspaper:

> I watched the object intently for a time, and when it was out of the bay a long thin neck with a pointed head appeared. I had an excellent view of the monster. As it moved along there seemed to be several humps appearing and disappearing, and the only thing that puzzled me was whether or not the humps were the peculiar wriggling motion of the large body as it moved along. I also saw, as the object was moving, something white, which I took to be the under-part of the creature.

See also **Gordon, Andrew.**

Riley, Comdr. And Mrs Quintin   Sighting on 6 September 1964, from a distance of about 400 yards. The couple saw what looked like a single 'dome-shaped' hump appear on the Loch surface and then submerge. They were at a loss to know what they had seen, but firmly believed that it was part of something very much alive.

Rines, Dr Robert H. Head of the **Academy of Applied Science** team which first investigated the Loch in September 1970. Rines proposed to lure the creature to the surface by means of sexual attractants, but all attempts failed. He and his team returned in 1971, but no sonar traces were found. Rines did have a surface sighting though, along with his wife Carol, when, on the evening of 23 June 1971, they saw a 20-foot-long hump surface in **Urquhart Bay**. This moved through the water for a distance of about two-thirds of a mile before submerging.

In 1972, using sonar equipment and underwater cameras off **Temple Pier**, Urquhart Bay, Rines and his team produced alleged photographic evidence of the mysterious creature's existence. This was in the form of an underwater photograph that, after computer enhancement, revealed the clear shape of a flipper (the **'flipper' photograph**). Initially there was much media hype about this image, but more recently its authenticity has been brought into question (specifically it has been suggested that the photograph may have been 'touched up' after the computer enhancement, in order to emphasize the flipper shape). Experts also claim that if it is part of the mysterious creature, then it is too small to be a flipper that would be adequate to propel through the water an animal as large as the monster is believed to be. The problem with any photographic evidence taken beneath the water surface is the presence of peat particles, which greatly reduce visibility beneath a depth of around 30 feet and can cause a cloudy barrier between the object and camera, hence distorting the image. The debate will long continue.

In June 1975 Rines and his team returned to the Loch, and once again produced dramatic underwater photographs allegedly confirming the creature's existence. These depicted what Rines claimed was to be the animal's **'gargoyle head'**, and a second frame which was purported to be the creature's underside. Again the media seized on these images, and again, their validity has been questioned. Experts believe that the 1975 photographs show nothing more than a decomposing tree trunk on the Loch bed, which gives the appearance of a monster head.

See also **Klein, Dr Martin; Nessiteras rhombopteryx; Parliament; Temple Pier.**

Rival III The Peterhead drifter which recorded a large object on its echo-sounder trace close to **Urquhart Castle** on 2 December 1954. The object that appeared on the screen appeared to be about 50 feet long and was about 480 feet down. The trace charts were later submitted to the boat's owners for examination, and it was then confirmed that the reading was genuine and could not have been faked in any way.

See also **Anderson, Peter.**

Rose, James   Shopkeeper from **Fort Augustus**, who, along with several other local people, is said to have seen a large hump-like object moving at speed through the Loch in 1896. Rose apparently said that what he saw took the familiar form of 'an upturned boat.' He died in 1904 and is buried in Fort Augustus cemetery.

Rose, D. Murray   Wrote to the *Scotsman* in October 1933, claiming that he had found a reference to the monster in an old book dealing with Fraser of Glenvackie's slaying of the last known dragon in Scotland (said to have occurred in about 1520). The reference read: 'No one has yet managed to slay the monster of Loch Ness, lately seen.' Rose went on to suggest that the monster was seen twice between 1600 and 1700, and appeared again in 1771, when locals were convinced that it was a **Water Kelpie.** Unfortunately, he failed to provide any source references in his correspondence. Until such references can be located, these tales cannot be classed as reliable evidence. Rose himself believed that the Loch Ness monster was simply 'sharks', which could have entered the Loch at some time in the past.

Ross, A.   Mr Ross claimed to have a multiple sighting in June 1933. He described the creature he saw as a giant eel some 25 feet long and with a diameter of around 5 feet. As it swam along the Loch, it used its tail powerfully, and its back curved into a series of humps. He saw this on fifteen separate occasions that day at different locations.

It would appear that Mr Ross had a further sighting on 17 July 1934. At 8.20 a.m. he spotted a single hump, estimated to be about 20 feet long and 2 feet deep, which turned over and dived in **Urquhart Bay.**

Ross, Duncan   Sighting on 8 February 1935. Whilst driving over the Oich bridge at the southernmost tip of the Loch, he spotted a huge, dark-coloured object which rose to the surface of the Loch near to the entrance to the **Caledonian Canal**. He said that the creature's back was 'decidedly humped'. Mr Ross was with an unidentified friend, who was certain that the object they had seen was part of something which he had never before witnessed in his life.

Ross, Pheomie   *See under* **Tait, Mrs Jessie.**

Rowand, Hugh   Hugh Rowand was the proprietor of the Foyers Hotel in the spring of 1958, when, along with others, he saw an unexplained sight on the Loch. With his wife and two friends, Rowand was sitting on the lawn of the hotel, which overlooks the Loch. A triangular 'fin shape' appeared in the water a few yards off Sand Point. Initially it remained stationary, then it suddenly burst into life and 'literally rocketed' across the Loch towards **Drumnadrochit** for about 400-500 yards before submerging. Neither Rowand nor any of the other three witnesses could hazard a guess as to what it was they saw.

Runcie, James · Captain of the Loch trawler *Ha-Burn*. In April 1969, the boat's sonar detected a very large object over 700 feet below the surface of the Loch. Runcie, from Cullen, later commented, 'There was definitely something unusual down there. I don't know what it is; I wouldn't like to hazard a guess. But I know what our sonar picked up, and I have not seen anything like it before.'
   See also **Ha-Burn.**

Russel, Mr B.A.   A master at the Fort Augustus Abbey School, who had a sighting at about 10.30 a.m. on 1 October 1933, at a distance of approximately 800 yards. What appeared to be a dark-coloured neck and head, something like 5 feet in height, appeared out of the water. The head was not much thicker than the neck and was grey-brown in colour. The creature moved along the Loch, creating a V-shaped ripple, before submerging. At the time of the sighting Russel assumed that what he saw must have been a 'seal' which had somehow found its way into the Loch, but he later felt that it was much larger than any seal he had previously seen.

Rutherford, Miss Marjorie   *See under* Fraser, Jean.

S

Saint Benedict's Abbey   *See under* **Fort Augustus.**

Sanderman, Patrick W.   A witness who believed he saw a V-shaped wake moving way from him on a flat calm Loch on 20 August 1966. Sanderman was unable to make out the size and colour of the object that made it, because it was moving just beneath the water surface.

Scottish Film Productions   *See under* **Irvine, Malcolm.**

Scott, Mrs E. Garden   Sighting on the Loch on 16 August 1933 at about 11.00 a.m. On a fine, clear day, with the Loch waters calm, Mrs Scott saw a hump which she likened to an 'upturned boat' at a distance of about 800 yards. She described it as being 'mostly grey in colour with a definite blotchy appearance'. There was also a defined 'dark ridge' running along its back which showed up against the background colour.

Mrs Scott claimed five separate sightings of the creature. Once she believed she saw two forelimbs or flippers. Again it had a rough-looking skin which appeared to have blister-like marks.

Scott, Sir Peter Markham, CBE   English artist and ornithologist, born in London in 1909. Scott represented Britain at the 1936 Olympic Games (dinghy sailing) and served with distinction in the Royal Navy during the Second World War. He became a popular television presenter, introducing wildlife programmes, and was created CBE in 1953 and knighted in 1973. Sir Peter was a firm believer that some large animal existed in the Loch, and his authority enhanced the perceived validity of previous sightings and caused investigations at the Loch to be taken seriously by the media and the scientific world. He died in 1989.

See also Nessiteras rhombopteryx.

Scott, R.J. Claimed sightings on 12 and 14 July 1934. The first sighting, made at about 300 yards, was of an animal he believed was about 18-24 feet long with three humps that protruded about 2 feet out of the water. It was light brown in colour and darker towards the water and had some form of mane where the neck met the body. The creature, to all intents and purposes, appeared to be swimming on its side, as he could see part of its underside.

His second sighting, rather less dramatic, was of a stationary black object which protruded about 8 inches out of the water before it submerged.

Incredibly, Scott reported a third sighting on 30 July 1934, when he saw a 14-foot hump, with three portions showing, moving slowly in the water. This submerged, reappeared and submerged again. This sighting, according to **Mackal** (*The Monster of Loch Ness*) seems also to have been witnessed by Mr Evan Strang.

seal   That sightings of the Loch Ness Monster might in fact simply be of seals is an explanation suggested by **Sir Edward Mountain** in *The Field* (22 September 1934). 'The grey seal ... grows to a much larger size than the seals often seen around the coasts of the British Isles, and in a body of water as comparatively calm as Loch Ness would be capable of making a disturbance which would lead people to believe it much larger than it probably is in actuality.' **Marmaduke Wetherell** also claimed to see what everyone believed was the creature on 15 January 1934. He confirmed that his sighting was that of a seal.

Searle, Frank E.   Ex-soldier and London greengrocer, whose obsession with the monster caused him to change his way of life. He arrived at the Loch in June 1969, living in a tent at Ballacladaish Farm, near **Dores**, later moving to a field below Boleskine House, and finally to Lower Foyers, where he procured a caravan which bore the official-sounding title 'Loch Ness Information Centre'. Searle claimed to have spent more than 20,000 hours systematically watching the Loch's waters, and there can be no doubting his intense knowledge of the Loch and the legends accompanying it. However, much of his work should not be taken as serious research. Searle somehow lost his way, and became preoccupied with his own importance as a self-proclaimed 'expert'.

In October 1972 he produced photographic 'evidence' of the animal and subsequently claimed to possess over 20 independent shots of it. Despite their use by the media, though, none of these illustrations can be remotely classed as authentic. Between April 1977 and December 1983 he produced a quarterly newsletter from his caravan, but this was subjective and tended to dismiss more serious research at the Loch. It contained very little positive data and rather more self-publicizing propaganda.

By 1985 Searle, who had become something of a nuisance to other investigators, moved to pastures new, leaving a legacy of hoax which many people still discuss to this day. Searle did make a contribution to Loch Ness investigation, though, because the publicity his photographs and stories attracted drew the world's media to the Loch. He was even successful (albeit for a short time) in fooling science into believing that he was an authentic source.

See also Nessie: Seven years in Search of the Monster.

Seddon-Smith, Mr and Mrs *See under* **Lowrie R.H.; MacLeod, Torquil.**

Senior, Guy *See under* **Lichtervelde, Count Emmanuel de.**

shark In correspondence to the *Inverness Courier* (20 October 1933), Mr D. Murray Rose suggested that the Loch Ness creature might be nothing more than a shark. It seems that Rose believed that 'throughout the ages sharks might well have got into Loch Ness'. Rose failed to confirm how sharks could survive in the Loch's fresh waters.

Shaw, Alexander and Alistair The Shaws reported a sighting of 'something different' on the Loch on 11 May 1933: it appeared to be a single 8-foot-long 'log-type' hump moving faster than a rowing boat and creating a terrific wake. It seemed to sink gradually beneath the surface and disappeared.

Shaw, J. One of five people who made a surface sighting from the driveway of Foyers Hotel on 27 July 1973. Shaw saw a dark-coloured shape appear on the Loch's surface, but was unable to distinguish precisely what it was – although was later quoted as saying, 'Seeing is believing, and we are now of the opinion that something exists in the Loch.'

See also **Moran, E.J.R.**

Sheals, Dr John   The Keeper of Zoology at the **British Museum of Natural History**, in October 1972 Sheals was one of a team of five scientists, who examined **Dr Rine**'s underwater photographs of what was claimd to be the monster. The results of the examination were hardly what the Rines team, or monster hunters, expected to hear. In a June 1976 BBC television documentary Sheals was quoted as saying:

> I don't believe these photographs prove a thing. There's no evidence whatsoever to support the view that the objects in the photographs are large living animals. The earlier **'flipper' photograph** is, of course, quite intriguing, but there's the problem of scale. I feel Dr Rines has insufficient evidence to make his assertion that this object is 6-8 feet in length. Now, if it was smaller – and some photographic experts have said that it could be very much smaller – then obviously one would be very inclined to think in terms of fish fins, although there are of course other possibilities. It seems to me that in this situation some control runs might be useful. That is to say, it would be useful if the investigators photographed the fins of familiar fishes in turbid water with a strobe light and then subjected the results to the computer-enhancement process. This might help solve the mystery.

In the same programme, Shiels notably referred to the unknown creature in the Loch as 'this wretched monster'. Dr Alan Charig, also of the Museum, claimed that different scientists at the Museum held different opinions on the phenomenon, implying that no individual comment should be interpreted as being an official statement.

Sheldon, R.W.   In 1972, Sheldon, of the Fisheries Research Board of Canada, claimed in an article in *Limnology and Oceanography* that, taking theoretical figures for the standing stock of the fish population, 'it seems likely that Loch Ness must contain a small number of large monsters, weighing as much as 1,500 kg, with a population of 10 to 20'.

Shield, Ian   Ian Shield was a member of the **Loch Ness Investigation Bureau** who, along with **Gerry Baker**, filmed a strange wake moving through the Loch on 16 September 1969. The footage was studied by various experts such as Dr Maurice Burton, and subsequently claimed as being 'a genuine misinterpretation of natural phenomena: the wakes were apparently caused by birds swimming in the Loch. Despite this, a number of people who saw the film believed the theory to be incorrect.

See also **Baker, Gerry; film footage.**

Shields, David, and family   Sighting at 3.00 p.m. on 6 February 1997. The Shields family were returning to their hotel at **Foyers**, on the south shore of the Loch, when a dark-coloured and apparently moving object suddenly appeared on the Loch surface. It submerged again after about two minutes.

Shiels, Anthony Nicol (Doc)   A professional psychic who allegedly saw the animal from the foot of the tower of **Urquhart Castle** on 21 May 1977. He claims to have taken two photographs of it. Shiels described the creature as having a smooth and glossy skin, with powerful neck muscles. The animal surfaced for about 4-6 seconds, with about 1.5 metres of neck and head being clearly visible. Other people who were in the area at the time of this sighting and who were looking in the same direction saw nothing.

Shiels believed that he conjured the animal to surface to appear by use of ancient magic as – with the assistance of witches and a worldwide group of psychics – he had done with Morgawr, the Cornish Sea Serpent. The main Shiels photograph of the two frames taken has been examined by a number of photographic experts, and there is great debate about its authenticity. The negative was examined and declared to be free of any touching up, yet enlarged prints, when examined, have flaws. One of the main objections raised is that, given the distance and angle from which the shot was allegedly taken, it should include part of the Loch's shoreline, but it does not do so. There is a strong belief among students of the mystery that the photograph is yet another hoax, and that it was set up in another piece of water. Shiels vehemently denies such allegations.

Shine, Adrian   A self-taught naturalist and leader of most of the main expeditions into the biological characteristics of Loch Ness since 1980. Shine has become renowned as one of the top experts on the ecology of the Loch. Before his Loch Ness research, he led expeditions to **Loch Morar**, and designed and built his own one-man submersible: a globe-like fibreglass object, just 3'6" in diameter, this was affectionately known as 'Machan' (now on display at the Official Loch Ness Exhibition at **Drumnadrochit**).

Adrian Shine was one of the main inspirations behind **Operation Deepscan**, a massive echo-sounding expedition in 1987, **Project Urquhart** in 1992 and, more recently, **Project Rosetta**. His research is not into the existence or non-existence of any monster, but into the ecology of the Loch.

See also **bathymetrical survey.**

Shulman, Mrs N. On 28 September 1966, at 3.30 p.m., Mrs Shulman saw a single black object surface on the Loch. It remained stationary for a few moments before submerging, creating a large water disturbance as it did so.

Sigel, Gordon Skipper of the Loch Ness pleasure boat *Scott I*, who made a sighting on 7 July 1975. From the bridge of the boat, Sigel, engineer James Dunn and mate Donald Patience saw a black object swimming across the Loch. Sigel estimated its size as 12-15 feet long overall.

Silcock, Comdr. and Mrs R.K. Surface sighting of a 6-8-foot-long hump at 3.30 p.m. on 19 September 1968. The couple described the hump as being dark in colour, and it was apparently cruising through the water at a reasonable speed. They watched it submerge and surface on three different occasions, each time leaving a V-shaped wake behind it.

Simpson, Mr and Mrs J. Surface sighting on 27 May 1933. Mr and Mrs Simpson saw what appeared to be two large humps appear on the Loch surface; they described these as being similar to 'an upturned boat'. The object then made a great splash, began moving, and disappeared from sight. Mrs Simpson claimed to have had a number of separate sightings of the creature: on 22 October 1933 she announced her fifth such observation, when she believed she saw a 2-foot neck, and the splashing action of two flippers beneath the surface.

size   Research into witness sightings reveals that the creature's size differs according to the individuals' perceptions and their viewing position and distance from object. Estimating distance and size with the naked eye is no easy task and is more difficult still when looking over a moving body of water. From assessment of witness testimony, it is reasonable to believe that the creature could average anywhere between 30-40 feet in total length.

Skeldon, Jean   While travelling towards Inverness on the A82, at 6.30 p.m. on 24 August 1983, Jean Skeldon witnessed something strange in the Loch. From the **Abriachan** turning she was watching a trawler as it drew level with Tor Point, when she saw what appeared to be 'two piles of asphalt' in the water close to the road. Looking closely, she saw that the 'asphalt' was actually two distinct black humps, one of which was about 7-8 feet long and projected almost 2 feet out of the water; the second hump appeared to be about half the size. The texture of both looked rough and knobbly. The humps then sank.

Skelton, Alison   An enthusiastic member of the **Loch Ness Investigation Bureau**, Alison Skelton was on a surface watch at **Achnahannet** on 23 June 1969. At around 10.00 a.m. she noticed a V-shaped wake moving across the Loch, past **Inverfarigaig**. She filmed it, and examination of the film later revealed that the wake was 'probably' caused by a bird, though this was never confirmed.
   See also **film footage**.

Skelton, Clem Lister   A **Loch Ness Investigation Bureau** technician who saw a large body porpoising through the water on 26 September 1966. Skelton claimed eight separate sightings of a mysterious object in the Loch during his time with the Bureau. On 5 October 1967, at 3.00 p.m., he filmed two light-coloured objects moving slowly in the **Foyers** area of the Loch; two minutes of film was used. According to **Mackal**, these creatures are most probably 'large gulls'.

Smith, Andrew   *See under* **Considine, Anthony**.

Smith, Gwen and Peter   Alleged sighting and film of a strange animal in the Loch at about 5.05 p.m. on 22 August 1977 which coincided with the sighting of **Christopher Idle** and **John Coulton**. While standing on the shore near **Urquhart Castle** in poor weather conditions, Peter and Gwen Smith saw something rise vertically out of the water about 160 metres to their left. Through binoculars Peter Smith saw a strangely thick periscope-type object, which he judged to be around 30cm thick, with a thick rectangular head. The object was a leathery brown colour and about the height of a man. As it began to sink Gwen filmed it with a 8mm Printz T3 Zoom camera. The image taken on this footage shows a dark pole-like object projecting from the water. No features can be defined. It surfaced three more times, during which it appeared to move its head from side to side, reflecting the sunlight. It finally disappeared from view at 5.15 p.m.

See also **Coulton, John; film footage; Idle, Christopher.**

Smith, Mr and Mrs Maurice   Sighting of a single hump at around 3.30 p.m. on 26 July 1969. The hump, which was estimated as about 6 feet long and 3 feet tall, moved through the water at around 6-7 m.p.h. When it submerged it created a large wake.

See also **Clayton, Mr and Mrs D.**

Smith, Nellie   Employee at Fort Augustus Abbey who claimed to have a sighting on 5 August 1933, at about 2.00 p.m. On a sunny afternoon Miss Smith saw a large dark hump appear on the water. It was the size of a rowing boat and moved in large circles: 'It seemed to have huge legs, which could be seen working quite distinctly.' Miss Smith watched the creature for a full ten minutes before it submerged.

See also **Keyes, Prudence; Meiklem, Comdr. and Mrs R.A.R.**

sonar   Sonar (SOund Navigation and Ranging) was first developed by French physics teacher Paul Langevin in 1918. (It was then called 'echo sounding'). It operates by way of a transducer, which coverts electrical pulses into sound and returns sound waves back into electrical signals. In effect, it emits a sound pulse, then receives echoes which are subsequently interpreted via computer. It is mainly used for underwater location and has been used to find shipwrecks on the seabed, submarines, icebergs and (most commonly) shoals of fish.

At Loch Ness such equipment has been used to trace large moving objects deep below the surface. A number of moving traces have been identified over the years, although none has provided conclusive evidence of the monster's existence. Sonar equipment can be affected by idiosyncracies of the marine environment, and many earlier readings have been classified as possible false echoes.

Spear, Michael   Searchlight operator in October 1962 for **Loch Ness Investigation Bureau**. Two war-surplus searchlights were played across the Loch surface every night, in the hope of attracting the animal. On the night of 19 October 1962 Spear observed a finger-like object standing 6-8 feet out of the water; it submerged almost immediately, before Spear could gain any clear impression.

Spicer, Mr and Mrs George F.T.   Land sighting on 22 July 1933, between 3.30 and 4.30 p.m. Spicer, a London-based company director, and his wife were travelling south from John O'Groats via the road on the east shore between **Dores** and **Foyers**. As they approached a rise in the road, some 200 yards ahead of them appeared, without warning, what they both later described as a 'prehistoric animal'. It crossed the road in front of them. Spicer described what he saw in a letter to the *Inverness Courier*: 'A long neck, which moved up and down in the manner of a scenic railway. The body was fairly big with a high back.' The couple both believed that the creature carried something in its mouth, possibly a small lamb.

The size of the creature was estimated at about 25 feet, the neck being 6-8 feet long. The body was a greyish colour, and where the neck joined the body, they saw something flapping up and down. They both believed this to have been the tail, which was bent round. It has subsequently, and incorrectly, been claimed that this land sighting was the first of its kind. Research shows that there had been at least twelve previous alleged land encounters.

Spring-Rice, Lady   Surface sighting in company with **Lady Maud Baillie** and family, on the afternoon of 19 April 1950. What initially appeared to be a large rock in the water, in the region of **Urquhart Castle**, suddenly began to move in a northerly direction, leaving a terrific wash behind it. Lady Spring-Rice described two big dark humps, and a wash big enough to have been made by a powerful speedboat.
See also **Baillie, Lady Maud**.

Sprout, Chief Engineer   *See under Arrow.*

Spurling, Christian   Just before his death in March 1994, photographer Christian Spurling reportedly told a close friend that the 'surgeon's photograph' was in fact a hoax, concocted by himself in order to trick the world into believing that the monster existed. Taking a toy submarine, he fitted a model neck and head on top of the craft and sent it out into the Loch where he photographed it, providing the world with a monster hoax.
See also **Wilson, Lt.-Col. R.K.**

Stalker, Philip   Scottish journalist and naval reservist, who arrived at the Loch in October 1933 on behalf of the *Scotsman* 'to carry out a full investigation into the tales of the so-called monster'. This investigation lasted just two days, his main interviewees being **Alex Campbell** and **Commander Meiklem**, both of them great 'believers' in the creature's existence. The results of the investigation were published in the *Scotsman* later that month, but were little more than rephrasings of material already recorded in the *Inverness Courier*. The appearance of Stalker's reports did, however, prompt the national press into action, and it was not long before a number of the national daily papers were at the scene.

Later that month Stalker was invited to talk about the mystery on BBC national radio, and much of what he said appeared in the *Listener* of 8 November 1933.

> Of course, you say, it's impossible. But nothing is impossible until experience has proved it to be so, and no scientist on earth would say that the sea cannot contain the legendary sea serpent, however remote the possibility, or that such a creature, if in existence could not possibly find its way, perhaps before full growth, up the River Ness, which is separate from the **Caledonian Canal**, and into the Loch.

Stewart, David   Land sighting in March 1933. While out walking near **Alltsaigh**, Stewart came across a 'grey-coloured creature' which lunged out of the bushes close to the Loch and dived straight into the water. Shocked, all he could recall of the incident was the fact that the creature possessed a long neck, thicker and more extended than a giraffe's.

Stewart, Molly   Sighting reported in the *Belfast Telegraph* of 24 August 1935. The report stated that six days earlier, both witnesses, who were maids at Knockie Lodge, Whitebridge, had 30-minute surface sighting of a monster from a hillside overlooking the Loch.
See also **Grant, Ray.**

Stone, R.   Sighting on 5 September 1935, reported in the *Scotsman* of 9 September 1935. Mr Stone, who was a chauffeur at Killin shooting lodge, Stratherrick, along with Mrs Bird, who was employed there as a cook, and a friend were motoring to Inverness along the **Dores** road, when they saw a large dark object travelling at speed up the Loch. The creature moved in a lurching motion, one end being considerably higher out of the water – this they took to be the head. The sighting lasted 3-5 minutes.

Strone   Situated on north-west side of the Loch above **Urquhart Castle.** Sighting made here by **Kirk Wolfinger** (June 1997).

Stuart, Lachlan   A Forestry Commission woodsman who allegedly photographed a sighting of the monster when with **Taylor Hay.** Stuart lived in a croft at **Whitefield**, about five miles south of **Dores.** At 6.30 a.m. on 14 July 1951 he claimed to have witnessed three humps surface separately on the Loch; grabbing his camera, he ran down to the Loch side and photographed them. The result was dramatic to say the least. The developed photograph – which was first published in the *Sunday Express* of 15 July 1951, just one day after the sighting – clearly shows three clear hump-like objects in the water. The authenticity of the print has been questioned ever since, and one does have to wonder at the haste with which such shots are sold on to national newspapers.
The humps have a definite square look to them, and the middle one appears to be closer to the camera than the other two. Recently the whole thing has been revealed as a hoax – the so-called monster being little more than three partially submerged and tarpaulin-covered bales of hay.
See also **Hay, Taylor; MacPherson, John.**

sturgeon   Some people believe that the creature which has caused so much controversy over the years is nothing more than a large fish. This theory gained greater credibility when on 5 November 1987 an 11-foot-long sturgeon, weighing in at 900 lb, was caught in Lake Washington, Seattle, USA. This creature, which was believed to be over 80 years old, was immediately linked to tales of a duck-eating monster which had been circulating in the area for many years.

Some writers claim that in 1661 a giant sturgeon, some 12 feet long, was caught at Kirkhill, near Inverness, and that this confirms the possibility that the Loch Ness creature could in fact be a sturgeon. According to a sturgeon specialist, Gail Kreitman, 'the breed can live to be 100, and grow more than 20 feet long; some specimens have weighed in at over a ton'.

Realistically, reported sightings of the Loch Ness monster do not correspond with a sturgeon. A sturgeon possesses a row of spinal fins, and, as monster-hunter **Steve Feltham** positively states, 'no known sighting of the Loch Ness monster has yet indicated the presence of such fins.'

Submarine, Loch Ness   A former Royal Navy mini-submarine, *Taurus*, originally used for deep-sea rescue, was brought to Loch Ness by **Alan Whitfield** initially for tourist trips, but it also assisted with occasional underwater searches. The vessel, which was sponsored by Swatch, a Swiss watch company, was about 34 feet long and 13 feet wide, and would submerge to depths of around 750 feet in the Loch. The submarine remained at the Loch for just over two years, before moving to the Lake District.
See also **Whitfield, Alan.**

'surgeon's photograph'   On 1 April 1934, **Lt.-Col. R.K. Wilson** photographed what was claimed to be 'the most conclusive evidence yet that a prehistoric monster lives in Loch Ness'. Wilson never actually declared it to be so, preferring to refer to it as a 'mysterious object'. It is now known to be a hoax.

Alastair Boyd, along with David Martin, was influential in dismissing the authenticity of the photograph, recreating an exact replica of the model created by Wilson and **Spurling** to perpetrate their hoax. It is now claimed that the subject of the 'surgeon's photograph' was nothing more than a model 'monster head and neck' attached to a tin toy submarine. The precise location of the hoax has not been accurately determined, but it is believed that the only two possible locations would be at either Invermoriston Bay, or Inchnacardoch Bay.

See also **Boyd, Alastair and Sue; Spurling, Christian.**

Sutherland, Margaret   *See under* **Chisholm, Hugh.**

Sutherland, Mrs   Claimed sighting on about 25-6 August 1933 at approximately 9.00 a.m. Both Sutherland and **Mrs McDonnell** saw an undulating hump moving in the water around 300 yards from them. It was a warm, sunny day on a calm Loch, and the sighting lasted for two minutes. The women believed the hump to be a brown-black colour, and some distance behind it there appeared to be some form of water disturbance which Mrs Sutherland felt might have been the splashing of the creature's tail in the water.

Synge, Dr Richard   Synge, who was awarded the Nobel Prize for Chemistry in 1952, was without doubt a very difficult man to fool. He reported sighting the animal in the summer of 1938, while staying with his parents in **Fort Augustus**. At around 8.00 a.m. he saw a dark-coloured hump-like object in the Loch. It began to move northwards close to the west bank, Synge managed to follow it by car for about 3 miles, travelling at a fair speed and leaving a wake behind it until it suddenly stopped and submerged.

T

Tait, Mrs Jessie   Made a surface sighting and took photographs of something on the Loch on 16 August 1969. Mrs Tait was out with her friend Pheomie Ross and her sister Joan, and they stopped their car at the Loch side near **Foyers**. Joan Ross, who was gazing out across the Loch, exclaimed, 'There's the monster!' (she later believed that she had seen six humps, each about 10 feet long). Jessie Tait grabbed the camera from the glove compartment of the car and began taking photographs.

The **Loch Ness Investigation Bureau** claimed this sighting was of nothing more than a boat wake, **David James** later publicly criticized the press for publishing the photographs without first consulting the LNIB team. However, the Ross sisters told reporters that they hailed from a seafaring family and that there was no sailing vessel or anything similar anywhere near the scene of the sighting. All three women claimed to be able to recognize a boat wake, and were adamant that this was nothing of the sort.

Tait, Joan   *See under* Tait, Mrs Jessie.

Taylor, A.G.   *See under* Pyman, Col. D.

Taylor, Dan   A former US Navy submariner, Dan Taylor was the designer and builder of the *Viperfish*, a miniature submarine with on-board sonar which was brought to the Loch by the **Loch Ness Investigation Bureau** in 1969.

Although Taylor made no clear sightings of anything unusual, he reported a strange occurrence whilst he was surveying the depths of the Loch in late October. The *Glasgow Herald* of 20 October 1969 quoted him under the sub-heading 'Nessie Hunter to return with new Submarine':

I was about 130 feet down when I suddenly found that the bottom had been stirred up. I thought at first it must have been my own prop wash and I stayed there for a few minutes. Then I found I was facing up the slope and not down. An ordinary fish could not have turned a two-ton submarine right round, and there are no currents. Something might have been sitting there and left in a hurry when it heard me coming. Unfortunately I did not have my forward sonar search going at the time.

Taylor was not given to making ambiguous statements, and he had no doubt in his mind that some anonymous creature did exist in the Loch. 'It's pretty well established,' he said. 'Not just one – probably between twenty and fifty'.

See also underwater searches; *Viperfish*.

Taylor, Doreen   Land sighting in February 1934, in the region of Foyers. Mrs Taylor believed she saw a large creature with a long neck, a heavy body and short thick legs with webbed feet moving close to the water. Unfortunately, no further details are known of this sighting.

Taylor, G.E.   Holidaymaker from South Africa, who saw an object in the water at 12 noon on 29 May 1938. Standing opposite **Foyers**, he saw what appeared to be a large dark shape about 200 yards from the opposite shore. It was a rounded shape, tapering down to the neck, which was moving up and down. The neck, Taylor thought, was about a foot to eighteen inches long.

Taylor filmed the creature, shooting about three minutes of film. It seems that he actually took a break in between filming, for he left the scene and told a Scottish lady of his incredible sighting. The lady insisted on viewing the scene for herself, so Taylor returned with his witness, and when he returned the creature was still clearly visible, although it had moved to within 150 yards of the opposite shore.

Dr Maurice Burton viewed the film, and stated that the object in question *looked* like an animal, but nonetheless dismissed the possibility because its movements were unlike those of any animal known to mankind.

Tea Rose   Fraserburgh trawler whose on-board sonar detected a large object rising diagonally through the water at about 7 knots at a depth of about 600 feet, in April 1970. No one has been able to determine what the object was.

See also **Duthy, Charles.**

temperature   According to **Carruth** (*Loch Ness and Its Monster*), the water in Loch Ness never freezes, because the water at the bottom of the Loch never grows colder than about 5.5°C. The surface water gets cooled by contact with cold air but as a result becomes heavier and sinks and the warmer water rises from below to replace it. This makes it virtually impossible for ice to form on the main body of the Loch.

Dr Samuel Johnson (1709-84) the lexicographer, believed that the Loch never froze because it was sheltered by its surrounding mountains. Air which did manage to penetrate simply agitated the water, which again prevented ice from forming. Despite this theory, however, he confessed that he was still at a loss to understand fully how this phenomenon failed to occur on such a vast expanse of water.

Temple Pier   Situated on the north-west side of the Loch in **Urquhart Bay**, Temple Pier has long been used as a base for scientific study into the mystery, most notably in 1968, with the visit of **Birmingham University**, and in 1972, when the **Academy of Applied Science** based underwater sonar devices there. It was here that the infamous **'flipper' photograph** was recorded on 8 August 1972.

See also **Birmingham, University of; 'flipper' photograph; Rines, Dr Robert.**

Thompson, John   On 19 August 1964, along with three others, Thompson saw a single hump, end-on. This was estimated to measure 4 feet long and 4 feet high, and was thought to be dark in colour. It was stationary at first, but moved off at great speed before finally disappearing.

Tor Point   In **Dores** Bay on the south-east side of the Loch. Scene of sighting in July 1963, when **Dan McIntosh** and **James Cameron** were fishing from a boat about 200 yards from Tor Point. Suddenly the head and neck of an animal surfaced about 20–30 yards from them, and behind it a small hump came into sight. The creature sank from view almost immediately, causing a commotion in the water. The two men then noticed how the water in the immediate area was devoid of any fish.

Tucker, Dr Denys W.   Principal Scientific Officer at the **British Museum of Natural History** and a worldwide expert on eels. Tucker organized a team of 30 graduates and undergraduates from both Oxford and Cambridge Universities for a one-month investigation from 27 June 1960 to assess the ecological capability of the Loch to support a colony of large animals. Their findings proved that it was so capable. Unfortunately, Tucker was dismissed from his position with the Museum earlier in June 1960, and so could not lead the expedition. He blamed his dismissal partially upon his outspoken belief that a large creature, possibly a plesiosaur, did exist in Loch Ness. He later published articles upon the phenomenon in the *New Scientist* (London) of 27 October 1960 and 17 November 1960.

See also **Baker, Peter; Cambridge University.**

Tucker, Prof. D.G.   Led expeditions from Birmingham University in April 1968, in August of the same year and in September 1969. The findings of the sonar searches, carried out from a base off **Temple Pier**, were published in the *New Scientist* (19 December 1968).

A cross-section of the Loch was kept under continuous sonar observation for a total of 19,960 minutes. It was during this period, on 28 August 1968, that thirteen minutes of madness occurred. The sonar equipment based at Temple Pier transmitted a sonar pulse across the Loch every 10 seconds, and a camera was aligned to photograph any readings on the oscilloscope screen. At 4.30 p.m. that day a large object was detected rising from the Loch floor at a vertical velocity of 100 feet per minute, before descending and then rising again. Simultaneously, another object was believed to have travelled horizontally, and then dived down at somewhere in the region of 450 feet per minute. The results of this expedition were publicly belittled by other scientific authorities, and it was asserted that Tucker had no right to claim that he had found the monster (a claim that he had never made). Further visits to the Loch by Tucker and his team have remained private

and the expedition has refused to publish any further results.
See also **Braithwaite, Dr Hugh.**

Turl, Wallace V. An English schoolmaster who had a sighting on 18 April 1968. Driving along the Loch side near **Drumnadrochit** he suddenly saw three humps surface in the water. They were black, semi-eliptical, and looked like stationary small islands or rocks in the water. The humps then moved forward and appeared to be rising and falling together, as though propelled. Mr Turl claimed that when the animal submerged it left an oily sheen on the surface.

Twelves, Eric *See under* **Field, David.**

Tyrrel, Mr and Mrs John Sighted an unknown animal in the Loch on 18 July 1970, in **Urquhart Bay**. Through his binoculars Mr Tyrrel, a university lecturer from Nairobi, Kenya, observed several distinct wakes as something moved in the water. He could see a narrow, sleekish neck which tapered towards the end. 'It seemed to move in two or three surges'.
See also **Cary, Wg.-Comdr and Mrs Basil.**

U

Ullrich, Prof. James   Consultant to the Smithsonian Institute, who led the **Black and White Scotch Expedition** to the Loch in 1970. Before arriving at Loch Ness, Ullrich took out a £5,000 insurance policy with Lloyds against being bitten or maimed by the creature – clearly taking its presence very seriously.

See also **Black and White Scotch Expedition.**

underside view   On 20 June 1975, at 11.45 a.m., using underwater camera equipment attached to sonar sensors at a position southeast of **Temple Pier**, the **Academy of Applied Science** team managed to shoot film of some strange creature beneath the Loch surface. The two frames of importance were those which seemed to show a mysterious creature's head **(gargoyle head)** and a second which gives the appearance of and underside view of some large anomalous creature, including an extended neck, estimated at being around 17 feet in length. The clarity of the underside view frame is poor, due to the density of peat particles within the water. This has allowed the sceptics to question the authenticity of what appears to be a straightforward shot of a prehistoric-type creature in the water, many claiming it to be a sunken tree trunk or a miscued camera angle of the Loch's bottom. Irrespective of such opinions, the underside view is an impressive photograph and should not be subjectively dismissed.

See also **Academy of Applied Science**; **'gargoyle' head**; **Rines, Dr Robert.**

underwater searches   The two most notable underwater searches carried out at the Loch occurred in 1969 using mini-submarines. The first was *Viperfish*, used by the **Loch Ness Investigation Bureau**, which brought in **Dan Taylor** from the USA, with his purpose-built one-man craft, which was a distinctive yellow colour. *Viperfish* had a built-in sonar, which was operated by American electronics expert **Robert Love** from the chartered vessel *Rangitea* on the surface of the Loch. Unfortunately, due to the murky conditions at the lower regions of the Loch, no substantial evidence was gathered.

Pisces, a six-man submarine owned by Vickers Ltd, was also fitted with sonar. It was brought to the Loch to help in the shooting of the film *The Private Life of Sherlock Holmes*. Its main task was to tow a five-ton dummy of the Loch Ness Monster around the **Urquhart Castle** area, although early on in the filming the towing cable connecting *Pisces* and the dummy snapped, and the dummy drifted free and then sank.

Undeterred, *Pisces*' crew volunteered to explore the depths of the Loch and produced some exciting results. On one occasion they tracked an object about 600 feet from the submarine and about 50 feet from the Loch bottom. As *Pisces* closed in about 400 feet, the object moved away and was lost. This encounter occurred in 520 feet of water, 300 yards north-east of Urquhart Castle.

During its 250 hours of underwater searching *Pisces* made some other notable discoveries. What has been described as a sunken Zulu-type fishing vessel, built sometime in the 1870s, was found in the **Temple Pier** area, and numerous ancient weapons were located in the silt of **Urquhart Bay**, believed to have been dumped there after the defeat of Bonnie Prince Charlie's uprising of 1745.

See also Pisces; **Taylor, Dan**; *Viperfish*.

Underwood, Kathleen   Surface sighting on 15 June 1968. Kathleen saw a large disturbance in the water at **Drumnadrochit**.

As though something very large and very powerful was moving just beneath the surface. I watched it for about two minutes, before a pole-like object rose into the air at the front of the disturbance. This must have been three feet long. As it re-entered the water it curved and disappeared from view. It was spectacular, like nothing I had ever before seen. My first impression was that it must have been a giant eel, yet the water disturbance was far too great for it to be something so slender as an eel. There must have been something large behind what I saw, since its wash made a terrific crash upon the shore a few minutes later. I return to the Loch every couple of years in the hope of catching another glimpse, but have never again been fortunate enough to see anything.

Urquhart Bay   On the north-west side of the Loch, this is one of the most frequent locations and sightings anywhere on the Loch. The bay is very deep and has an array of channels and undulating mounds. The River Enrich flows into the bay, and some experts hold that, because fish congregate here, the Loch Ness animal swims through the channels to feast on them – which is why there have been so many sightings in this part of the Loch.

Urquhart Castle   Situated on southern-most tip of **Urquhart Bay** overlooking the Loch. Notable sightings to occur near here include: **Young, John** (June 1934); **Zendal, Unwal** (October 1997). Also the positive sonar traces of **Anderson, John** (1958); **Anderson, Peter** (1954) occurred close to the castle.

V

Veitch, Angela   Surface sighting at 6.00 p.m. on 29 September 1966. Angela Veitch saw a 20-foot black object rise out of the water, causing a great deal of disturbance around it, and then sink almost immediately.

Veron, Michael   Saw some strange creature surface on the Loch off **Fort Augustus** on 26 November 1979. Veron was a member of a coach party that was visiting the Loch for the day. He was sitting at the Loch side eating his sandwiches at around 1.30 p.m. when he noticed a commotion in the water in front of him.

> It was about one hundred yards out, something briefly rose to the surface and dived again. I thought it was one of those huge trac-tor tyres. It was very black and had a high arched appearance. I cannot say it was the monster. However, I will say that the best description I can give is that it must have been the size of a small whale, since it was bigger than any seal or salmon I have ever seen. There were people behind me, but all they could say was 'what was that?' since they never saw it but heard and noted the water disturbance.

Vincent, Paul   On 28 September 1944, when aged 8, Vincent was staying with his uncle Reg Murray in Scotland.

> Reg was something of a cynic. He would not believe anything anyone told him unless he had seen it himself. As we watched the Loch from somewhere near Dores (I cannot recall the precise location) he suddenly stopped and began to stare at something way offshore. He lifted me into his arms and told me to look, he said something like 'It's the bloody monster.' I could not see anything, but Reg was very excited.

We returned home, where he could hardly wait to tell the rest of the family what he had seen. No one believed him. Reg drew a sketch of what he saw; I kept that sketch for years. I made an entry in my diary about what happened – though I was never allowed to forget it, as Reg would always remind me when I saw him. The sketch gives the appearance of a huge hump, with a pole-like object pointing upwards at an angle to the front. It looks like a head at the foremost tip of this.

Viperfish Bright yellow one-man submarine, owned by an American, **Dan Taylor**, which was used by the **Loch Ness Investigation Bureau** to scour the depths of the Loch in 1969. It had on-board sonar, which it was hoped would locate and trace anonymous objects. Sadly, it failed to discover any new evidence about the monster.
See also **underwater searches.**

visibility above surface   There is a popular belief among those who have never been to Loch Ness that the roads which run round it are littered with people armed with binoculars and cameras, intent on seeing the animal. This, thankfully, is not the case; visibility from the roads which run on the north-west and south-east sides is hardly conducive to observations. Trees and bushes often block the view from the road and allow only the occasional glimpse of water between them. There are few good vantage points on the road, and the only way to find a good viewing position is to park the car and venture forth on foot to find one. In addition, weather and atmospheric conditions have a great effect on visibility. Mist, rain, low cloud and even bright sunshine all create their own problems for Loch-watchers – something which must be borne in mind when assessing reports of sightings.

visibility under water   Due to the fact that the lower area of Loch Ness is filled with floating peat particles that enter through the rivers and streams feeding the Loch, visibility below a depth of about thirty feet is extremely difficult. This has proved something of a problem in the underwater searches for the creature. The peat particles also create a barrier, preventing sunlight from penetrating beneath top surface water, which further exacerbates the problem of visibility.

The **Japanese expedition** of 1973 were horrified by the 'blackness' beneath the Loch's surface, and had not been prepared for this, some members of their diving team refusing to continue with the expedition due to the Loch's fearful appearance below a depth of about thirty feet. The diver who searched for the body of **Mrs Durand Hambro** in August 1932 was thwarted by the density of the peat particles, which made his task virtually impossible without the use of powerful lights which could penetrate the gloom.

See also 'gargoyle' head; Hambro, Mrs Durand; Japanese expedition; Rines, Dr Robert; underside view.

W

Wallis, Wg.-Comdr K. Wallis, a designer and builder of autogiros from Norfolk, was employed by the **Loch Ness Investigation Bureau** to fly his *Wallis 117* autogiro over the Loch for a month in 1970, but the flights revealed no new evidence. Using much the same surveillance technique, Wallis flew for a further week over **Loch Morar**, to search for that Loch's unknown creature, but again his search was unsuccessful.

See also **autogiro.**

Ward, Robin An 18-year-old who was climbing **Meallfuarvonie** with **Gordon Lowe** in April 1955. From a height of about 1,500 feet, they both saw two dark-coloured humps moving at great speed out of Foyers Bay and causing a commotion on the water surface. The sighting was intermittent, due to the obstruction of trees. The creature reappeared and moved towards **Fort Augustus**, and this time the two observers had the impression that there was a third, smaller, hump behind the first two.

The humps gave the impression of being part of something very large and looked to be about 20 feet long. A definite V-shaped wash spread from the front of the first hump, where there also appeared to be something which was 'snow-white' in colour. The object moved in a straight line before disappearing from view.

See also **Lowe, Gordon.**

Warr, Angus and Jonathan *See under* **Baillie, Lady Maud.**

Warren, Mr and Mrs Kenneth On 27 May 1968 the couple were surveying the Loch through binoculars when, about half a mile away, they saw two separate double-humped objects just below the surface. The humps, which appeared to be moving away from the Warrens' position, changed direction before sinking from view. The Warrens thought that they had seen two individual creatures.

water-bull   Term used to describe an unknown, almost mythical, creature of the water. There are many tales surrounding such creatures living in Scottish Lochs. Depending upon the tale, the creature could take the form of a bull, a horse, a kelpie, or even a human. The creature is supposed to have made a pact with the devil, but has also been blessed by saints.

See also **Columba, Saint; Kelpie, Water.**

water horse   *See under* **Kelpie, Water.**

Water Kelpie   Also referred to as the **water-bull,** water horse or Each Uisge. According to Scottish legend, the Water Kelpie is an associate of the devil. As is the case with most unknown phenomena, descriptions of the Water Kelpie differ vastly. It is generally depicted as a dark-coloured beast, a cross between a bull and a horse, with two prominent sharp horns on its head.

When seeking prey, the Kelpie can change form. It can be a fine, tame horse – bearing exquisite saddlery and calmly grazing beside a Loch or river, which, when mounted turns into a wild stallion and gallops into the water, where it drowns its rider and devours his flesh. It is also said to take the appearance of a dashing young man, who entices maidens to their watery grave (though a maiden can identify such a Kelpie, by the fact that its hair is always wet, and matted with waterweed and sand; the one weakness which it cannot disguise).

The Loch Ness Monster is often referred to as a 'Water Kelpie'. In view of the legendary description of the beast and its actions, the monster which may reside in Loch Ness is clearly not a typical Kelpie.

See also **Adamnan, St; water-bull.**

Wathen, David   Had a clear sighting of a strange animal in the Loch one evening in March 1967. A dark brown-grey animal appeared about 150-200 yards away. It bore a resemblance to a large worm, or perhaps a seal; no eyes were seen. It stood about 15-20 inches tall and was around 6 inches in circumference. It swam through the water in a curving course and at one point appeared to fall over sideways as it disappeared beneath the surface.

Watson, Barry In 1966 Barry Watson from Bingley, West Yorkshire, made an attempt to swim the length of Loch Ness. To ensure his safety in the water, he was shadowed by two sailing vessels armed with harpoon guns, 'just in case the animal in the Loch decided to alter its habits and to attack a human being'. Watson ultimately failed in his attempt to swim the Loch's entire length.

Watson, Prof. D.M. From London University, Watson expressed the opinion that, 'if there was such a creature as the Loch Ness monster, it was simply a large piece of waterlogged peat floating round Loch Ness at the mercy of wind and currents.'

Watt, Mr and Mrs George, and Joyce Surface sighting in September 1935. Mr George, a former Sheriff of Inverness, was travelling in a car with his wife and daughter. Mr Watt was driving the car on the A82 when his wife noticed something break the surface of the Loch, about one mile east of **Temple Pier**. According to Mrs Watt, 'several humps appeared – five in total – with a great deal of water disturbance'. Joyce Watt, however, claimed to have counted 'six or seven humps'. Unfortunately, George Watt was unable to get a clear look at the creature, because he had to drive some distance before he could bring the car to a halt, by which time it had gone.

waves It has been suggested that many monster sightings can be dismissed as different types of natural waves occurring in the waters of the Loch. Campbell (*The Loch Ness Monster – The Evidence*, 1986) discusses this in some detail. A wave is described in *Webster's Comprehensive Dictionary* as being: 'a ridge or undulation moving on the surface of a liquid'. Many eye-witness reports indicate undulating movement and ridges, and the wave effect present on all expanses of water provides an alternative solution for sceptics.

West, Ralph A London-based scientist who was driving along the Loch side on 23 may 1963 when he saw a terrific disturbance in the water. A huge bow wave was followed by a black body that was about 20 feet long and projected 2-3 feet above the water.

Wetherell, Marmaduke A. A self-proclaimed big-game hunter whose attempts to prove the existence of a monster in the Loch greatly undermined the real efforts of those carrying out scientific research. Wetherell managed to get the backing of the *Daily Mail* to mount an expedition to the Loch in December 1933. According to one source, then employed at the *Daily Mail* office:

> Wetherell promised us results before he had even left for Scotland. We took it all as a bit of a joke; I don't think anyone involved with the press of that era really understood the seriousness of the situation. People went Nessie-crazy. We received dozens of letters complaining about Wetherell – not him personally, but the 'big game hunter bit'. Our readers actually thought that he was going to track it down, kill it and drag it back to Fleet Street. It was a great shame that things turned out as they did. I am sure the big-game hunter was only living up to his title: playing a big game.

Within days of arriving at the Loch, Marmaduke Wetherell claimed to have located evidence of a monster's footprint on the shoreline. A cast of this was made and later identified as the footprint of a **hippopotamus,** planted by some prankster. Wetherell also managed to get himself involved in the **Arthur Grant** land sighting of 5 January 1934 when he returned to the scene with Grant and began examining footprints, flattened shrubbery and the carcass of a dead goat, recklessly claiming that these were all connected with the monster. The statements he made were later disproved by **H.F. Hay**.

On 15 January 1934 Wetherell claimed to have sighted one of the animals himself, while on the deck of the *Penguin*, a motor-cruiser used by the expedition, though no other soul on board the vessel saw it. He was convinced that the creature he saw was nothing more than a large grey seal. The *Daily Mail* was satisfied with this assumption and concluded that Wetherell had 'determined the source of the enigma'.

It is unfortunate that Wetherell has been, correctly or incorrectly, associated with some of the major hoax discoveries at the Loch. Innocent or not, his evidence will never be given a great deal of credibility by those who carry out serious research into the phenomenon.

See also **Grant, Arthur; Hay, H.F.**

White, Richard When travelling down the south side of the Loch on 22 March 1997 Richard White saw a number of black humps moving through the water some 200 metres from the shore.

Whitefield Village situated on the south-west side of the Loch, virtually opposite **Urquhart Bay**. A notable sighting to occur here was that of **Lachlan Stuart** (July 1951).

See also **Hay, Taylor; Stuart, Lachlan.**

Whitefield, A.S. Alleged sighting on 11 May 1933, when he saw a wake appear on the Loch. This was followed by the appearance of an 8-foot-long hump which created considerable water disturbance behind it. The object then submerged.

Whitfield, Alan Pilot of the mini-submarine *Taurus*, which at one time took tourists into the depths of the Loch and was also used for an ecological survey of the Loch basin. Whitfield, an experienced underwater pilot, reported hearing strange noises during one dive. He claimed that these noises were unknown to him and he could not determine what they were – the implication being that they could have emanated from the monster.

See also **submarine.**

Whyte, Constance E., MB, BS Author of *More Than A Legend: The Story of the Loch Ness Monster* (1957). Constance Whyte was a staunch supporter of the monster theory and did a great deal to argue the case for its existence. Her research into witness testimony has always appeared exemplary, although recently it has begun to seem as if her bias in favour of such a creature's existence may have clouded her judgment. Constance Whyte lived at Clachnaharry, near Inverness, for twenty years and used the diaries of the late **Dom Cyril Dieckhoff** of **Fort Augustus** Abbey for some of the evidence in her book.

Wilkins, Alan Schoolteacher from Annan, Dumfriesshire, alleged to have had four separate sightings of some unknown animal in the

Loch on 18 July 1975, whilst on holiday there. At about 7.20 a.m. he and his son Ian saw a long dark line appear in mid-Loch; this sank and resurfaced several times, and Wilkins photographed the latter part of this sighting. He described what he saw as being of a great size with water swirling at its base, suggesting that a bulky body lay below the surface.

In his second sighting he presumed that what he was watching was a black inflatable boat, gyrating rapidly as though it had a powerful motor on board. A short time later he saw a dark line, very similar to his initial sighting, and he finally saw the creature making its way across the Loch at what is described as a 'leisurely pace'. Wilkins told fellow holiday-makers at the Rubha Ban caravan site, near **Invermoriston**, of his sightings. This resulted in others watching the Loch for much of the day, and other strange sightings of objects on the water were made that day – most notably by Roger Selwyn, and his girlfriend Sylvia Williams, who were in the next caravan to the Wilkins family and saw a dark, unidentifiable object moving in the water in the middle of the Loch.

Williams, Alexander Student who was fishing on the Loch in September 1981 when he saw an object on the water around 150-200 metres away and photographed it. The Loch was flat calm with poor visibility, due to low-lying mist. The photograph was too poor in quality to be able to define anything clearly, thus it remains invalid as serious evidence.

Williams, Dennis *See under* **France, Sid; Marshall, Mr and Mrs Bruce.**

Williamson, John Ernest According to Nigel Blundell (*The World's Greatest Mysteries*, 1980). Williamson was a leading American expert in underwater photography. He visited Loch Ness in the summer of 1934, with sophisticated photographic equipment, the main item of which he termed a photosphere – a globe-shaped submersible with windows, providing excellent all-round vision. Williamson intended to sit in the globe beneath the water taking photographs of what he hoped would be the monster. What he did not realize was that the Loch's dark, peaty waters were most unsuitable for such a task. On discovering this, he apparently packed his photosphere and returned home.

Williamson-Hurley, Carol   Reported sighting the creature in the Loch on 23 June 1971. About two-thirds of a mile from **Urquhart Bay** a 20-foot-long hump emerged on the surface and moved through the water; it then gradually submerged, but left a considerable wake on the surface. No distinctive features could be discerned. There have been subsequent claims from Loch-watchers that the 'hump' seen by Miss Williamson-Hurley was no more than a boat wake.

See also **Cary, Wg.-Comdr Basil.**

Wilson, Lt.-Col. R.K., MA, MB, Ch.B.Camb., FRCS   In April 1934 Wilson allegedly took two photographs which have been portrayed for over sixty years as authentic pictures of the Loch Ness monster. At the time of the incident Wilson was a gynaecologist with a practice off Harley Street, London. He claimed that he had never before heard of the Loch Ness Monster.

Whilst visiting the Loch on 1 April 1934, he and a friend, Maurice Chambers, happened upon the animal two miles north of **Invermoriston.** The creature was about 200-300 yards out when Wilson managed to photograph it, taking four shots, of which only two showed positive. The first depicts a long neck and small head, the second a similar shape, which has slightly submerged. The creature was in sight for about one minute before it gradually sank. This infamous photograph (the third of the four taken) that has since been tagged the **'surgeon's photograph'** was first published in the *Daily Mail* of 21 May 1934. Today it is known to be a fake (perhaps the date of the sighting – April Fools' Day – provides a clue to Wilson's motives). It had been suggested that the object in the main photograph shows a model submarine with a model monster head and neck placed on top, and this was confirmed by the confession of the late **Christian Spurling.** Shortly before his death in 1994, Spurling, a professional photographer, told a close friend that he had set up the 'surgeon's photograph' using a toy self-propelled submarine with a model monster neck and head attached to it. It has further been suggested that, along with Wilson, big-game hunter **Marmaduke Wetherell** was involved in the hoax, in an effort to substantiate claims of the monster's existence.

More recently it has become known that Wilson confessed to a friend that his photographs were indeed forgeries and had been intended to be little more than a practical joke. (The reason Wilson shunned publicity was fear of being found a fraud, rather than embarrassment at being an object of curiosity). More damaging still is the fact that Wilson's youngest son also allegedly revealed the photographs as fraudulent.

Despite the Spurling confession, the work carried out in 1993 by the Discovery Channel seems to prove beyond all doubt the photograph was a hoax. Photographic experts examining the same image believed that the object was being pulled along by some unnatural force. Experts claim a white spot on the water surface in front of the supposed head and neck has ripples emanating from it, indicating that the contraption was being pulled along. This is contrary to the Spurling confession, but provides further evidence of the hoax. **Alistair Boyd** carried out much research in proving that the photograph was a fake, and claims that Spurling's confession was legitimate. He built a replica model to prove the point. Thus, this infamous, almost legendary photograph can no longer be considered as credible evidence.

Wiseman, David   A member of the expedition from the **Academy of Applied Science**. Wiseman was present on board *Narwhal* when the sonar identified a large moving object close to an underwater camera in the Loch. This led to the taking of the 1972 **'flipper' photograph**.

Witchell, Nicholas   BBC television newsman, whose many years of research into the phenomenon resulted in the publication of *The Loch Ness Story* in 1974. Witchell spent a number of years at the Loch side and spoke to a great many witnesses who claimed to have had first-hand sightings or knowledge of the animal. In 1972, in collaboration with the **Loch Ness Investigation Bureau**, he carried out a one-man observation of the Loch at **Urquhart Bay**, using shore-based photography. At one time he believed that the 1972 and 1975 underwater photographs produced by the **Academy of Applied Science** were positive proof of the creature's existence, but since their authenticity has been queried he has taken a more reserved line on whether the monster exists or not. Witchell is a respected expert on the subject who has practical, in-depth knowledge of the area and speaks sensibly on the matter.

Wolfinger, Kirk   While filming a documentary for an American company at Strone Point at 9.00 a.m. on 21 June 1997, Wolfinger and his team saw a dark object moving swiftly across the Loch about a mile south of **Urquhart Castle**. The team were at a vantage point above the Castle when they made their sighting. Despite having camera equipment with them, they failed to capture the object's movements, and it disappeared before any film could be shot.

Wotherspoon, Mr and Mrs Robert   Alleged sighting in the summer of 1938 at a distance of just 20 yards. Three humps were seen to surface, one of which was larger than the other two; as the animal moved the humps evened out, and the object was seen to form one long back. A salmon was thought to have jumped out of the water ahead of the creature, which began to move at a fair speed, as though pursuing it.

Wright, William   Reported a sighting of the animal at 3.00 a.m. on 17 June 1978. Wright was a process worker for Falkirk who regularly fished the Loch. While he was fishing off **Urquhart Castle** in **Urquhart Bay**, suddenly a large, black, arch-shaped body, not unlike a rowing boat, rose out of the water. This was followed seconds later by a round brown head and long neck. Mr Wright estimated that the head was the size of a football and the neck about 12 feet long.

Y

Young, John A 70-year-old grave-digger from Lewiston who made a sighting in June 1934. While he was walking past **Urquhart Castle** the animal rose out of the water. It had a long neck and a small head and was, he later stated, 'very big'.

Young, Stephen Sighting of a strange creature in the water close to Cherry Island on 25 November 1998. Young, a draughtsman from Birmingham, was visiting relatives in Inverness and decided to take a journey around the Loch:

> It was about 1.00 p.m. I had laughed about the question of whether or not Nessie existed with my family. I was always very dubious about the sighting reports, I have been to Loch Ness countless times and never once seen anything. As I was looking up the Loch from a position on the north-wet side (slightly north of **Fort Augustus**) I saw a large black shape emerge on the surface. At first it was unidentifiable, like a black mound, then it seemed to stretch out and I saw an elongated appendage rise from the main body to an almost vertical position – this must have been about 3 feet tall. I believe it was probably a neck or something. It remained in a vertical position for about 10 seconds before it slowly dropped back into the water. A few seconds later the black mound submerged. I really wouldn't like to say what it was. I could say it looked like a dinosaur but that just isn't possible. I'm certain there must be a reasonable explanation, but will never understand what it was I saw.

Younger, Andrew Brief sighting of hump-backed object in the water off **Foyers** on 21 September 1995. Younger was walking close to the Loch side with his wife Heather. He looked out across the Loch with his binoculars:

About 150 yards from where we stood, a large hump appeared in the water. It must have been 4-5 feet in the air at its highest point. It is difficult to approximate its length, but 10 feet would be a fair estimate. This was no boat wake or freak wave; I watched this thing for a good ten minutes, and it hardly moved – perhaps a few feet at the most. It was dark in colour and gave me the distinct impression of having a spine, since it had 'knobbly' bits running over the uppermost part of the curvature. I am at a total loss as to what it was, but it was like nothing I have ever seen before. My belief is that it was a living creature. It sank quite slowly, in what I would think was a forward-moving direction.

Z

Zendal, Unwal   South African tourist, had a surface sighting on 24 October 1997. At around 9.30 a.m. a log-like object rose out of the water off **Urquhart Castle**, and jokingly, Unwal remarked to his partner Samantha, 'Look! There's Nessie.' The pair peered at what initially seemed like a horizontal floating piece of debris (it had assumed this position after originally rising vertically). To their surprise, the object began to move with a wriggling motion. Neither of them could appreciate what they were seeing, and believed that it was some kind of natural illusion. Without warning though, the front portion of the object rose vertically into the air – it had a definite curve at its uppermost tip.

It was now clear to both observers that what they were watching was in fact a living creature. For a few seconds what they identified as a head and neck seemed to look round, before slowly sinking, only to rise again, a few feet ahead of their previous location. It then appeared to dive, and a huge portion of a broad body rose to the surface when the head and neck plunged beneath the water.

Zendal described the animal as:

Very dark in colour – brown/black. Its neck must have been some four feet in the air; it had a very small head. As the body rose and dived, this seemed to be very wide – wider than any normal water dweller (other than a whale) that I know of. Its entire body [width] was not displayed, but I estimate it must have been at least 4 feet wide. It was almost certainly propelled beneath the water by some form of front flipper, since something that size could not dive so swiftly.

Zendal is philosophical about the sighting.

I knew of all the tales surrounding the 'monster', I was always the first to dismiss such a phenomenon, but I know what I saw. I was not imagining it – otherwise, how could Samantha witness the very same event? People will laugh it off as 'one of those things'. The experts will try to persuade me that it was a tree trunk or a log, or perhaps a seal or an otter. There is no way that the animal I saw was any of these things. It was massive, and very awe-inspiring. Something strange does exist in the Loch. I know – I saw it. I can think of no worse horror than to have to travel on that stretch of water in a small boat. But good luck to it anyway. I hope it continues to elude correct discovery.

Zug, Prof. G.R. Curator of the Division of Reptiles and Amphibians at the Smithsonian Institute, who examined the **'flipper' photograph** supplied by the **Robert Rines** expedition of 1972. Professor Zug stated, 'It has the shape of a palmate newt.'
See also **Parliament.**

Postscript

The Loch Ness Monster Research Society

This independent organization was formed to act as a centralized location for the collation of sighting reports and all research matters pertaining to the phenomenon of the Loch Ness Monster. It has a world-wide membership and has proved successful as a data source, providing news and historical information to both the media and the public.

The aims of the Society are to maintain correct and proper historical records of the phenomenon, for educational and promotional purposes. Many members are committed to carrying out regular research into previously recorded data in order to confirm or deny alleged facts. Up-to-date sightings and incidents are also committed to the database.

A regular newsletter sent out to all members, includes up-to-date news, research requests and a unique 'For Sale' page advertising rare books and ephemera concerning the Loch Ness Monster. To supplement this, there is a 'Wanted' feature.

Lectures and educational talks have been delivered by Society members internationally, and have been welcomed by educationalists as most successful and much needed. Special project kits for schools are available, as well as lectures and talks.

Anyone requiring further information about membership or other matters relating to the Society should contact:

The Membership Secretary
Loch Ness Monster Research Society
PO Box 5560
Market Harborough
Leicestershire LE16 7YQ
England.

Other Useful Addresses

The Official Loch Ness Monster Fan Club
9 Burnbrae Place
Inverness IV1 2TA
Scotland.

The Ness Information Service
7 Huntshieldford
St John's Chapel
Bishop Auckland
County Durham DL13 1RQ
England.

Bibliography

Books about the Loch Ness Monster

Bauer, Henry, H: *The Enigma of Loch Ness* (University of Illinois, 1986)

Baumann, Elwood, D: *The Loch Ness Monster* (Franklin Watts, 1972)

Binns, Ronald: *The Loch Ness Mystery Solved* (Open Books, 1983)

Burton, Maurice: *The Elusive Monster – An Analysis of the Evidence from Loch Ness* (Rupert Hart-Davis, 1961)

Campbell, Steuart: *The Evidence about the Loch Ness Monster* (Aquarian Press, 1986)

Carruth, J.A: *Loch Ness and Its Monster* (Abbey Press, 1971)

Costello, Peter: *In Search of Lake Monsters* (Berkley Publishing, 1974)

Dinsdale, Tim: *Loch Ness Monster* (Routledge and Kegan Paul, 1961)

——: *The Story of the Loch Ness Monster* (Alan Wingate, 1973)

——: *Project Water Horse* (Routledge and Kegan Paul, 1975)

Dunkling, Leslie: *The Mystery of the Loch Ness Monster* (Longmans, 1979)

Gould, Rupert T: *The Loch Ness Monster and Others* (Geoffrey Bles, 1934)

Grimshaw, Roger, and Lester, Paul: *The Meaning of the Loch Ness Monster* (Centre for Contemporary Cultural Studies, University of Birmingham, 1976)

Harmsworth, Anthony, G: *The Mysterious Monsters of Loch Ness* (Photo Precision, 1980)

Hastain, Ronald, and Witchell, Nicholas: *Loch Ness and the Monster* (J. Arthur Dixon, 1971)

Holiday, F.W: *The Great Orm of Loch Ness* (Faber and Faber, 1968)

Mackal, Roy P: *The Monsters of Loch Ness* (Swallow, 1976)

Meredith, Dennis: *The Search at Loch Ness* (Quadrangle, 1977)

Munro, Captain D.J: *The Loch Ness Mystery* (Privately published, 1937)

Owen, William: *The Loch Ness Monster* (Jarrold, 1987)

Picknett, Lynn: *The Loch Ness Monster* (Pitkin Guides, 1993, 1997)

Searle, Frank: *Nessie, Seven Years in Search of the Monster* (Coronet, 1976)

Smith, Warren: *Strange Secrets of the Loch Ness Monster* (Zebra Books, 1976)

Snyder, Gerald S: *Is There a Loch Ness Monster?* (New York: Julian Messner, 1977)

Steffens, Bradley: *The Loch Ness Monster* (Lucent Books, 1995)

Whyte, Constane E: *More Than a Legend* (Hamish Hamilton, 1957)

Witchell,Nicholas: *The Loch Ness Story* (Terence Dalton, 1974; Penguin, 1975)

Further information on selected Books about the Loch Ness Monster

The Enigma of Loch Ness   Book by Henry H. Bauer. The most rational and objective study yet published. Bauer neither dismisses nor admits to the presence of a monster, but reviews and discusses with some degree of common sense virtually everything that has appeared in print, ranging from sightings to illustrations and film evidence.

The Evidence about the Loch Ness Monster   Book by Steuart Campbell. Case study of the sightings, photographs and film records. Campbell subjectively dismisses all evidence of the creature's existence, and in every instance he offers reasons justifying doubt and disbelief. Republished in 1991 by Aberdeen University Press as *Loch Ness: The Evidence*.

Loch Ness Monster   Records the major events at the Loch, incorporating Dinsdale's own theories and interpretations of events.

The Loch Ness Monster   Booklet by William Owen. Contains a foreword penned by David James. A fairly reliable case hist ry up to the 1980s, and a worthwhile companion guide.

The Loch Ness Monster   Booklet by Lynn Picknett. Very basic in concept, yet a very thorough and informative guide. Few modern booklets can match it.

The Loch Ness Monster   Book by Bradley Steffens. Briefly discusses the major issues of the phenomena since 1933, it is directed at a young audience and is illustrated.

Loch Ness and Its Monster   A small and popular paperback booklet by J.A. Carruth, published virtually annually by the Abbey Press, Fort Augustus. Briefly records the basic case history and local folklore.

The Loch Ness Monster and Others   Book by Rupert T. Gould. A reliable discussion of the case facts as then known. Gould is objective in his opinions and provides a good deal of accurate information; some 42 sightings between May 1923 and May 1933 are detailed.

The Loch Ness Mystery   Book by Capt. D.J. Munro, RN. Another basic retelling of the facts as then known; compared with Rupert Gould's *The Loch Ness Monster and Others*, contains very little new information. Now a collectors' item, and fairly difficult to obtain.

The Loch Ness Mystery Solved   Book by Ronald Binns. Binns investigates all known facts about the phenomenon and cautiously discusses possible misinterpretation of sightings and the rationality of such incidents. The book is sensibly researched, and provides evidence supporting the author's supposition that the creature is a known animal rather than a monster.

The Loch Ness Story   Book by Nicholas Witchell. The author is persuasive in his argument for the presence of plesiosaur-type creatures living in the Loch. Witchell, an undoubted expert on the subject, has spent a great deal of time studying the case, assisting the Loch Ness Investigation Bureau as a teenager and carrying out his own studies since. The book has been reprinted and updated several times.

More Than a Legend Book by Constance E. Whyte. Constance Whyte was a qualified doctor and the wife of Frank Whyte, Manager and Engineer of the Caledonian Canal. She moved to Inverness in 1937, and lived there for 23 years. In 1949 she wrote a brief article on the 'monster' for a local magazine, after which her fascination for the subject led her on to the research eventually published in her book. The book details over 60 eyewitness sightings and is now regarded as a 'classic' by students of the case.

The Mystery of the Loch Ness Monster Booklet by Leslie Dunkling. Informative non-fiction children's book with detailed information relating to the basic known facts of the phenomena.

Other Books

AA Illustrated Guide to Britain (Drive Publications, 1971)

Adamnan: *The Life of St Columba* (Routledge, 1908)

Alexander, Marc: *Enchanted Britain* (Book Club Associates, 1981)

——: *To Anger the Devil: An Account of the Work of Exorcist Extraordinary – The Reverend, Dr Donald Omand* (Spearman, 1978)

Barber, Dulan: *The Horrific World of Monsters* (Marshall Cavendish, 1974)

Basset, F.S.: *Legends and Superstitions of Sailors and the Sea* (Chicago, 1885)

Bergier, Jacques: *Mysteries of the Earth* (Sidgwick and Jackson, 1974)

Berlitz, Charles: *World of Strange Phenomena: Vol 3 – The Odd and the Awesome* (Sphere Books, 1991)

Blashford Snell, Col. J.: *Mysteries – Encounters with the Unexplained* (Bodley Head, 1983)

Blundell, Nigel: *The World's Greatest Mistakes* (Octopus Books, 1980)

——: *Mysterious Britain* (Paladin/Grafton, 1974)

——: *The Secret Country* (Elek Books, 1976)

——: *Alien Animals* (Granada, 1980)

——: *Sacred Waters: Holy Wells and Water Lore in Britain and Ireland* (Granada, 1985)

——: Bord, Janet and Colin: *Ancient Mysteries of Britain* (Paladin/Grafton, 1987)

——: *Modern Mysteries of Britain: 100 Years of Strange Events* (Grafton Books, 1987)

——: *Atlas of Magical Britain* (Sidgwick & Jackson, 1990)

——: *The Enchanted Land* (Thorsons, 1995)

Bright, Charles: *Sea Serpents* (Bowling Green State University Popular Press, 1991)

Border, Rosemary: *The Loch Ness Monsters and Other Mysteries* (MacDonald, 1980)

Buehr, Walter: *Sea Monsters* (Norton, 1974)

Cameron, A.D.: *The Caledonian Canal* (Terence Dalton, 1972)

Campbell, Elizabeth: *The Search for Morag* (New York; Walker, 1973)

Campbell, Alexander: *Popular Tales of the West Highlands* (4 vols) (Alexander Gardner, 1893)

Campbell, Lord Archibald: *Waifs and Strays of Celtic Tradition* (5 vols) (David Nutt, 1892)

——: *A Year Book of Legends* (Mowbray, 1958)

Chaundler, Christine: *A Year Book of Folklore* (Mowbray, 1959)

Childe, V. Gordon: *The Pre-History of Scotland* (Kegan Paul, Trench, Trubner, 1935)

Cohen, Daniel: *A Modern Look at Monsters* (Tower, 1970)

Darling, F. Fraser, and J. Morton Boyd: *The Highlands and Islands* (Fontana, 1974)

Darwin, Charles: *The Origin of Species* (Watts, 1929)

Dictionary of Animal Life (Claremont Books, 1995)

Dictionary of Prehistoric Life (Claremont Books, 1995)

Finlay, Ian: *The Highlands* (Batsford, 1963)

Folklore, Myth and Legends of Britain (Reader's Digest Association, 1973)

Fort Augustus Abbey (Photo Precisions, 1972)

Forte, Charles: *The Book of the Damned* (Holt, Rinehart and Winston, 1941)

Glen Albyn Tales and Truths of the Highlands (Abbey Press, 1909)

Gould, Rupert T.: *Oddities: A Book of Unexplained Facts* (P. Allen, 1928)

——: *Enigmas: Another book of Unexplained Facts* (P. Allen, 1929)

——: *The Case for the Sea Serpent* (P. Allen, 1930)

Grant, John: *Monster Mysteries* (Grange Books, 1995)

Henderson, George: *Survival in Belief Among the Celts* (James Maclehose, 1911)

Henderson, I.: *The Picts* (Thames and Hudson, 1967)

Heuvelmans, B.: *On the Track of Unknown Animals* (Rupert Hart Davis, 1958)

——: *In the Wake of the Sea-Serpents* (Rupert Hart Davis, 1968)

Hippisley Cox, A.D.: *Haunted Britain* (Hutchinson, 1973)

Hoare, Bob: *More True Mysteries* (Carousel, 1974)

Holiday, F.W.: *The Dragon and the Disc* (Sidgwick and Jackson, 1973)

Hough, Peter: *Supernatural Britain* (Piatkus, 1995)

Hull, Eleanor: *Folklore of the British Isles* (Methuen, 1928)

Jack, Mary, and John L. Blair: *Chambers Guide To Scotland* (Chambers, 1957)

Landsburg, Alan: *In Search of Myths and Monsters* (Bantam, 1977)

Leach, Maria, (ed.): *Funk and Wagnalls Standard Dictionary of Folklore, Mythology, and Legend* (2 vols) (Funk and Wagnalls, 1949-50)

Lochhead, Marion: *Scottish Tales of Magic and Mystery* (Cassell, 1978)

Macdonald, Rev. K.: *Social and Religious Life in the Highlands* (Edinburgh, 1902)

Mackenzie, Donald A.: *Scottish Folk-Lore and Folk Life* (Blackie, 1935)

Mackenzie, Osgood: *A Hundred Years in the Highlands* (Geoffrey Bles, 1956)

McCallum, Neil: *It's an Old Scottish Custom* (Denis Dobson, 1952)

McCulloch, J. Herries: *The Charm of Scotland* (Oldbourne, 1960)

McEwan, Graham, J.: *Sea Serpents, Sailors and Sceptics* (Routledge and Kegan Paul, 1978)

McKay, W.: *Urquhart and Glen Moriston* (Northern Counties, 1914)

McKinley, J.M.: *Folklore of Scottish Loch and Springs* (W. Hodge, 1893)

McPherson, J.M.: *Primitive Beliefs in the North East of Scotland* (Longmans, Green, 1929)

Michell, John and Robert Rickard: *Phenomena – A Book of Wonders* (Thames Hudson, 1977)

Oudemans, A.C.: *The Great Sea Serpent: An Historical and Critical Treatise* (London, 1892)

Out of This World (Macdonald, 1989)

Parker, Derek and Julia: *Atlas of the Supernatural* (Guild, 1990)

Proujan, Carl: *Secrets of the Sea* (Reader's Digest, 1979)

Quinn, Daniel: *Land and Sea Monsters* (Hubbard Press, 1971)

Randi, James: *The Supernatural A-Z* (Headline, 1995)

Room, Adrian: *Dictionary of Britain: An A-Z of the British Way of Life* (Oxford University Press, 1986)

Ross, Anne: *Everyday Life of the Pagan Celts* (Batsford, 1970)

——: *The Folklore of the Scottish Highlands* (Batsford, 1976)

Sisman, Adam, (ed.): *The World's Most Incredible Stories: The Best of Fortean Times – The True Life X-files* (Warner Books, 1996)

Spence, Lewis: *The Mysteries of Britain* (Rider, 1928)

Stone, Reuben: *Encyclopedia of the Unexplained* (Blitz, 1993)

Sweeney, J.B.: *A Pictorial History of Sea Monsters and Other Dangerous Marine Life* (Crown, 1972)

Swinton, W.E.: *Dinosaurs* (British Museum of Natural History, 1973)

Swinton, W.E.: *Fossil Amphibians and Reptiles* (British Museum of Natural History, 1973)

Swire, Otto, F.: *The Highlands and their Legends* (Oliver and Boyd, 1963)

Sykes, Egerton: *Everyman's Dictionary of Non-Classical Mythology* (Dent, 1974)

Taylor, Michael, and John G. Martin: *Big Mouths and Long Necks* (Leicestershire Museums, 1990)

Tutt, Keith: *Sci-Fi Channel True Life Encounters – Unexplained Natural Phenomena* (Orion, 1997)

The Unexplained Files (Orbis, 1996)

Wainwright, F.T. (ed.): *The Problem of the Picts* (Nelson, 1955)

Walker, Charles: *The Atlas of Occult Britain* (Hamlyn, 1987)

——: *Strange Britain* (Brian Trodd, 1989)

Welfare, Simon, and John Fairley: *Arthur C Clarke's Mysterious World* (Book Club Associates, 1981)

Westwood, Jennifer: *Albion: A Guide to Legendary Britain* (Granada, 1985)

Williams, Guy A: *Guide to Magical Places of England, Wales and Scotland* (Constable, 1987)

Wilson, Colin and Damon: *Unsolved Mysteries* (Headline, 1993)
Wilson, Damon: *The Giant Book of the Unexplained* (Magpie Books, 1997)

Archives, newspapers and journals

British Museum of Natural History:
  Official files held in library section.
Home Office Files (held at the Scottish Records Office, Edinburgh):
  Nos HH1/588, HH55/1395, AF62/4398, AF62/4939.
Loch Ness Investigation Bureau:
  Reports on film taken by Tim Dinsdale. Annual Reports for 1966, 1967, 1969.
Ministry of Defence, London:
  Joint Air Reconnaissance Intelligence Centre (U.K.) photographic report no. 6611.
Official Loch Ness Monster Fan Club:
  Nesspapers and newsletters/sighting updates.
Aberdeen Evening Express:
  1973: 18 September.
Aberdeen Press and Journal:
  1934: 6 January. *1958*: 22 May. *1979*: 1, 18 September.
Animals:
  1962: 30 July.
Belfast Telegraph:
  1935: 24 August.
British Journal of Photography:
  1984: 20 April.
Commonwealth:
  1934: 20 April.
Daily Express:
  1933: 12 August; 22, 29 December. *1957*: 25 July; 8 October. *1989*: 1 April; 24 May; 17 September. *1990*: 27 April; 18, 28 May; 29 July; 19 August; 30 September; 5, 6, 26 October; 29, 30 November. *1991*: 7, 10, 15 January; 27 March; 28 April; 2, 23 June; 15, 19 July; 11 August; 10 September. *1992*: 14, 17, 24 July; 1, 3, August; 2 September; 29 October; 7 November. *1993*: 23 March. *1994*: 14, 30 March; 1 April; 26, 30 October. *1995*: 29 April; 29 July. *1997*: 11, 25 January; 20 February; 11 June.

Daily Herald (Glasgow)
　1934: 3 March. *1954*: 6, 7, 18 December. *1969*: 20 October.
Daily Mail:
　1933: 6, 21, 31 December. *1934*: 3, 4, 5, 8 January; 21, 23 May.
　1952: 26 August. *1953*: 16 December. *1969*: 15, 24, 27
　September. *1975*: 25 November. *1983*: 25 March. *1998*: 1
　January.
Daily Mirror:
　1933: 30 December. *1970*: 27 July. *1975*: 11 December.
Daily Record:
　1933: 6 December. *1975*: 25 November. *1982*: 16 July.
Daily Telegraph:
　1913: 19 August. *1922*: 9 March. *1933*: 6 December. *1972*: 1
　April. *1998*: 1 January.
Distant Shores
　1998: pp. 22-5.
Evening Sentinel:
　1983: 2 September.
Evening Standard:
　1971: 2 September.
Field:
　1933: 4 November. *1934*: 27 January; 22 September; 6 October.
　1961: 23 November. *1975*: 27 November; 4 December.
Fishing Times:
　1934: 20 January.
Fortean Times:
　Nos 24, 33, 34, 46, 50, 58.
Glasgow Herald:
　1934: 3 March. *1936*: 26 September.
Harpers Magazine:
　1956: February.
Highland Herald:
　1958: 7 August.
Illustrated London News:
　1933: 11 November. *1934*: 6, 13 January; 28 April; 5 May; 18
　August. *1951*: 8 December. *1960*: 20 February, 24 June; 11, 23,
　30 July.
International Society of Cryptozoology Journals:
　1982-1996: vols 1-12.

International Society of Cryptozoology Newsletter:
  1982-96: vols 1-12.
Inverness Courier:
  1926: 6 November. *1933*: 2 June; 8, 11 August; 6, 14, 15, 26
  September; 10, 24, 27, 31 October; 8, 14, 15, 20, 22, 26, 29
  December. *1934*: 5, 9, 12, 16 January; 2, 11, 13, 27 February; 6,
  30 March; 3, 17, 20 April; 8, 18, 25 May; 1, 5, 12, 26 June; 3,
  13, 17, 27, 31 July; 3, 7, 14, 24, 28 August; 11 September; 2, 9,
  16 October. *1935*: 22 January; 8 February; 23 April; 24 May; 21,
  25 June; 6, 20 August; 10 September. *1936*: 24, 31 March; 23
  June; 15, 22 September; 24 November. *1937*: 12 February; 2, 16
  March; 20 April; 27 July; 3, 17 August; 24, 28 September; 9
  November. *1938*: 28 January; 1 March; 14 June; 12 July; 19, 26
  August; 2 September. *1939*: 18 January; 7 April; 26 May; 23
  June; 4 July; 8, 15, 18 August. *1946*: 30 July. *1947*: 8 April; 27
  July; 1 August. *1948*: 16 January; 15 June. *1951*: 27 February;
  29 June. *1952*: 29 February; 22 August; 12 September. *1954*: 13
  July; 10, 13, 17 August; 10, 17 September; 11, 17 October.
  1955: 29 July. *1957*: 18 June. *1959*: 10 July. *1960*: 6 November.
  1963: 2, 23, 27 August. *1964*: 11 September. *1976*: 16 April; 24
  August; 15 October. *1994*: 25 March. *1995*: 4 August. *1997*: 21
  February; 16 May; 5 August.
Irish Independent:
  1963: 23 May.
Irish Times:
  1967: 2 March.
Levende Natuur:
  1934: 10 August.
Limnology and Oceanography:
  1972.
Mayfair:
  1973: vol. 8, no. 6.
National Geographic:
  1961: April. *1976*: January. *1977*: June.
Nature:
  1933:16 December. *1934*: 13 January; 18 August; 17 November.
  1968: 28 December. *1969*: 11 January. *1970*: 18 July; 19
  September; 28 November. *1975*: 11 December. *1976*: 15
  January. *1981*: 29 January.

Nessletter:
Complete collection.
New Scientist:
1960: 22 September; 27 October; 17 November. *1968*: 19 December. *1969*: 23 January. *1976*: 12 February. *1982*: 24 June; 1, 8 July; 5 August. *1983*: 17 February.
New York Times Magazine
1976: 1 August.
New York Times
1965: 13 June. *1969*: 27 January; 13 July.
Nineteenth Century:
1934: February.
Northern Chronicle:
1930: 3, 10 September. *1933*: 3 May; 7, 21 June; 12, 26 July; 9, 12 August. *1934*: 31 January; 1, 7 March; 4 April; 9, 23 May; 6, 13, 27 June; 25 July; 1, 8, 15 August; 5 September; 3 October; 21 November; 12 December. *1935*: 2 January; 20 February; 12, 19 June; 10 July; 21 August. *1936*: 13 May; 24 June; 16, 23, 30 September; 25 November. *1937*: 30 June; 11 September. *1938*: 3, 10, 17 August. *1939*: 31 May. *1960*: 16 June.
Observer
1933: 29 October. *1962*: 3 June; 19, 26 August; *1964*: 19 May. *1969*: 1 July.
Oui:
1974: May.
Photographic Journal:
1986: November.
Saturday Evening Post (Philadelphia):
1947: 8 March.
Science:
1979: 13 July.
Science Digest (New York):
1967: January.
Scientist:
1968: 19 December.
Scots Magazine:
1962: May. *1980*: January.
Scotsman:
1933: 23 January; 6, 17, 18, 20, 23 October; 29 December. *1934*: 22 January; 27 February; 12, 26 June; 7 July. *1935*: 9 September.

1938: 31 August. *1956*: 16 June. *1959*: 5 December. *1960*: 12, 14, 17 September. *1966*: 22 August. *1978*: 1 September.

Skeptical Inquirer:

1982/83 (winter). *1984/85* (winter).

Spectator:

1933: 22 December.

Star:

1933: 12 December.

Strange Magazine:

No 2.

Sun:

1975: 27 November. *1997*: 22 September.

Sunday Express:

1937: 27 June. *1951*: 15, 22 July. *1959*: 3 August. *1969*: 7 September. *1975*: 5 October. *1990*: 7 October.

Sunday Mail:

1976: 15 August.

Sunday People:

1972: 20 February.

Sunday Post:

1952: 27 July. *1964*: 31 May. *1979*: 12 August. *1981*: 12 April; 6 September.

Sunday Times:

1960: 14, 21 August. *1972*: 2 April.

Technology Review:

1976: March/April; December.

The Listener:

1933: 8 November. 1937: 10 March, 7 April.

Time:

1942: 29 June.

The Times:

1856: 6 March. *1922*: 20 April. *1933*: 9, 11, 13, 14, 15, 18, 21, 27, 29 December. *1934*: 1, 4, January; 18 June; 16 July; 28 September. *1938*: 9 May; 7, 14 June.

TV Times:

1969: 31 July.

Underwater Nature:

1970: no. 6.

Underwater Science:

1977.

The Unexplained:
  1980: vol. 2, nos. 13, 14.
The Universe:
  1934: 10 February.
Weekly Scotsman:
  1960: 16 June.